Early Golf

Royal Myths and Ancient Histories

Neil S. Millar

EDINBURGH
University Press

Edinburgh University Press is one of the leading university presses in the UK. We publish academic books and journals in our selected subject areas across the humanities and social sciences, combining cutting-edge scholarship with high editorial and production values to produce academic works of lasting importance. For more information visit our website: edinburghuniversitypress.com

Edinburgh University Press Ltd
The Tun – Holyrood Road
12 (2f) Jackson's Entry
Edinburgh EH8 8PJ

Typeset in 11/14 Bembo by
IDSUK (DataConnection) Ltd, and
printed and bound in Great Britain

A CIP record for this book is available from the British Library

ISBN 978 1 3995 0381 5 (hardback)
ISBN 978 1 3995 0383 9 (webready PDF)
ISBN 978 1 3995 0384 6 (epub)

Published with the support of the University of Edinburgh Scholarly Publishing Initiatives Fund.

Contents

Part II A Thematic History of Early Golf

Figures

Abbreviations of Archives Consulted

ACA	Aberdeen City and Aberdeenshire Archives, Aberdeen
AYA	Ayrshire Archives, Ayr
BL	The British Library, London
BLO	Bodleian Library, Oxford
BNdF	*Bibliothèque Nationale de France*, Paris
CUL	Cambridge University Library, Cambridge
ECA	Edinburgh City Archives, Edinburgh
ELA	East Lothian Council Archives, Haddington
GCA	Glasgow City Archives, Glasgow
GUL	Glasgow University Library Special Collections, Glasgow
HL	Huntington Library, San Marino, CA, USA
LBA	Lloyds Banking Group Archives, London
LMA	London Metropolitan Archives, London
NA	The National Archives, London
NLS	The National Library of Scotland, Edinburgh
NRS	The National Records of Scotland, Edinburgh
NYA	New York State Archives, Albany, NY, USA
RNA	Royal and Ancient Golf Club of St Andrews Archives, St Andrews
RPS	Records of the Parliaments of Scotland to 1707 (www.rps.ac.uk)
SCA	Stirling Council Archives, Stirling
UCO	University College, Oxford
UEC	University of Edinburgh Centre for Research Collections, Edinburgh
UStA	University of St Andrews Special Collections, St Andrews
WAL	Westminster Abbey Library and Muniment Room, London

Acknowledgements

I would like to express my gratitude to the large number of people who have provided assistance in a variety of ways during the writing of this book. The help provided by the following people is greatly appreciated:

Dr Jackson Armstrong, Phil Astley, Diane Baptie, Robin Bargmann, Kevin Barker, Stephen Barnard, Dr Blyth Bell, Gavin Bottrell, James Bracken, Dr Thomas Brochard, Dr Philip Burnett, Dr Robert (Bobby) Burt, John Bushell, Ian Cairns, Dr Donald Cameron, Professor Craig Clunas, Chris Cooper, Dr Wade Cormack, Peter Crabtree, Dr Markus Cruse, Jeffery Ellis, Richard Fisher, Alec Fitzgerald O'Connor, Hannah Fleming, Catriona Foote, Iain Forrester, Peter Fry, Olive Geddes, William (Bill) Gibson, Dr Jane Gilbert, Professor Heiner Gillmeister, Bob Gowland, Dr Marco Grilli, Dr David Hamilton, John Hanna, Jennifer Hogg, Dr Ulrike Hogg, Angela Howe, Professor Michael Hunter, Arnout Janmaat, Rand Jerris, Simon Johnson, Alastair Johnston, Professor Naguib Kanawati, Jean-Bernard Kazmierczak, Sara Kieboom-Nijs, Georg Kittel, Czeslaw Kruk, Neil Laird, Peter Lewis, Alastair Loudon, John Lovell, Marion Lynch, Professor Hector MacQueen, Professor Gesine Manuwald, Professor Sally Mapstone, Rob Maxtone-Graham, Kevin McGimpsey, Roger McStravick, Karen Millar, Sylvia Millar, John Moffett, Dr Michael Morrison, Sarah Moxley, Professor Richard Oram, Amanda Noble, Nigel Notley, Mungo Park, John Pearson, Rebecca Phillips, Professor David Purdie, Dr Alasdair Raffe, Neil Scaife, Dr Michael Sheret, Adam Sherman, Ted Shields, Richard Simmons, Danielle Spittle, Dr Colin Strachan, Nancy Stulack, Pehr Thermaenius, Ashleigh Thompson, Philip Truett, Tara Valente, Fred Vuich, Robin Welford, Richard Williams, Nicholas Winton, Frances Woodrow, David Wright and Dr William Zachs.

I would also like to acknowledge assistance that has been provided by the following organisations:

Aberdeen City and Aberdeenshire Archives, Ayrshire Archives, Bodleian Library, British Library, *Bibliothèque Nationale de France*, Edinburgh City Archives, East Lothian Council Archives, Glasgow

City Archives, Glasgow University Library Special Collections, Gloucester Cathedral Archives, Lloyds Banking Group Archives, *Museé Condé Chantilly*, National Archaeological Museum of Athens, National Archives, National Galleries Scotland, National Library of Scotland, National Records of Scotland, Royal and Ancient Golf Club of St Andrews, R&A World Golf Museum, Royal Collection Trust, Royal College of Physicians of Edinburgh, Royal College of Surgeons of Edinburgh, Stirling Council Archives, University College Oxford, United States Golf Association, USGA Library, University of St Andrews Special Collections, University of Edinburgh Centre for Research Collections and Westminster Abbey Library and Muniment Room.

In addition, I would like to thank Edinburgh University Press and all of those who have been involved in the commissioning, editing and production of this book, including Ian Brooke, Eddie Clark, Ersev Ersoy and Louise Hutton.

Some of the material included in this book is based on a series of articles that were published previously in *Through the Green*, the quarterly magazine of the British Golf Collectors' Society (see Bibliography: Millar, 2013–20; Millar and Hamilton 2012, 2015; Millar et al. 2013). I am grateful to the editors of *Through the Green* for permission to reproduce material from these articles.

To Karen, Kate and Beth.
And to my parents, David and Sylvia.

Introduction: Royal Myths and Ancient Histories

Numerous myths and misconceptions have become entrenched in the popular history of golf. Frequently these appear to have arisen as a consequence of golf historians having made speculative claims, often with a degree of hesitancy. However, such claims can subsequently take on a life of their own by being repeated uncritically, thereby acquiring the status of established historical facts and entering into the folklore of golf history. One of the primary motivations in writing this book has been to re-examine and reassess some of the claims that have been made by previous golf historians but it is also an opportunity to present new findings, based on seemingly overlooked early documentary sources.

The subtitle of this book ('Royal Myths and Ancient Histories') was suggested to me by a friend. The intention was to reflect the book's focus on myths, together with its re-examination of the evidence underpinning the early history of golf. Of course, it is also an allusion to the frequent claim that golf is 'The Royal and Ancient Game'. Some, however, have pointed out that 'not all the myths are *royal*' and that 'the history isn't really *ancient*'. Nevertheless, I hope such concerns will be overlooked.

Fact-checking the early history of a sport such as golf can be a laborious process but it can also reveal fascinating and sometimes unexpected new information. It appears that some important early documentary sources have been overlooked by earlier golf historians. Other sources are better known but, occasionally, their re-examination and reassessment can reveal the mistakes that were alluded to earlier (the myths and misconceptions). For example, the often-quoted role of Catherine of Aragon in the history of golf is based on an error in transcribing a sixteenth-century manuscript. Many of the numerous stories relating to the perceived importance of Mary Queen of Scots in the early history of golf are exaggerations that are based on a single historical document of questionable reliability. It would appear that no evidence exists to support the often-repeated claim that golf was played at Blackheath shortly after King James VI of Scotland transferred his court from Edinburgh to London in 1603. Similarly, there is no contemporary documentary evidence to support the frequent assertion that James, Duke of York participated in what has been described as 'the first international golf match' in 1682. These and many other topics are addressed in this book.

Of course, there have been some very good written accounts of the early history of golf. However, with the advances in the digitisation of historical texts and handwritten documents, it has become less of a challenge to undertake evidence-based historical research and, as a consequence, it is considerably easier to fact-check historical claims. In turn, this makes it easier to arrive at a clearer and more accurate assessment of early golf than was possible when earlier histories of golf were written. In undertaking the research for this book several important documents have been uncovered that may have previously been overlooked. Therefore, this book also presents new historical findings and discusses their possible significance to early golf history. On occasion, when it is clear that a frequently repeated story is unsupported by documentary evidence, an alternative hypothesis has been proposed. Of course, this can be potentially dangerous, since hypotheses can evolve into myths. For that reason, I have always aimed to make it clear when what I have written is based on speculation and that any such conclusions are tentative. As further research is conducted, it is inevitable that yet further primary sources will be identified and these will hopefully help to provide further clarity into the early history of golf.

The aim of this book is to provide a broad overview of important and, in some cases, overlooked aspects of the origins and evolution of the game of golf. To a large extent the story is presented chronologically but, on occasion, it deviates from a rigid chronological approach for stylistic or thematic reasons. Knowing where to start can be a challenge when retelling history. A common format of several books dealing with the history of golf is to begin by speculating, for example, about a hypothetical Scottish shepherd absent-mindedly hitting a pebble into a rabbit hole. While there is nothing wrong with speculating (as long as it's clear that it *is* speculation), starting at a point in the unrecorded past presents a challenge to a writer who wishes to rely upon documentary evidence. The earliest written reference to golf can be found in a Scottish Act of Parliament from 6 March 1457/8 and, for that reason, this history of early golf begins in the fifteenth century. However, golf's less well-documented 'prehistory' will be considered in the final chapter. The early documented history of golf coincides with the Stewart/Stuart period of Scottish and British history. Indeed, the reigns of Scottish monarchs, and latterly (following the Union of the Crowns in 1603) British monarchs, provide a convenient means of subdividing golf's early history and this is an approach that has been adopted in Part I of this book:

King James II	(b.1430, d.1460)	Chapter 1
King James III	(b.1452, d.1488)	Chapter 2
King James IV	(b.1472/3, d.1513)	Chapter 3
Catherine of Aragon	(b.1485, d.1535/6)	Chapter 4
King James V	(b.1512, d.1542)	Chapter 5
Mary Queen of Scots	(b.1542, d.1586/7)	Chapter 6
King James VI/I	(b.1566, d.1625)	Chapters 7 and 8
King Charles I	(b.1600, d.1648/9)	Chapter 9
King Charles II	(b.1630, d.1684/5)	Chapter 10
King James VII/II	(b.1633, d.1701)	Chapter 11

This book does not attempt an exhaustive retelling of all aspects of the history of golf. Typically, each chapter in Part I focuses on a historical figure or event and uses this as a starting point to review what is known about various periods in golf's early history. Chapters in Part II deal with broader thematic topics that span a more extensive period in the history of golf (such as early golf balls, golf clubs and golf societies). While one of the central aims of this book is to illustrate how historical errors can arise and how easily they can be perpetuated, a greater hope is that, by reference to contemporary documentary evidence, it will be possible to tell a reliable history of a sport that has existed for more than five hundred years and which is now estimated to be played by more than 60 million people worldwide.

A Note Concerning Dates

In Scotland prior to 1600 and in England prior to 1752, the start of the year was 25 March (the Feast of the Annunciation, also known as Lady Day), rather than 1 January. As a consequence, dates corresponding to events such as the earliest written reference to golf (in a Scottish Act of Parliament) have been cited using either the 'old-style' (6 March 1457) or the 'new-style' (6 March 1458). Here, in an attempt to avoid confusion, whenever there may be ambiguity about a date, the 'dual-dating' system will be used to denote the year (for example, 1457/8).

Part I

A Chronological History of Early Golf

Chapter 1

King James II, a Scottish Act of Parliament and some Fifteenth-century Golf Myths

An appropriate place to start a history of golf might be Scotland in the mid-fifteenth century or, more specifically, in Edinburgh on 6 March 1457/8. This is the date and the location at which the Scottish Parliament of King James II issued an Act containing the earliest known written reference to golf, a handwritten document that survives to the present day in the National Records of Scotland[1] (Figure 1.1).

The early history of golf is a notoriously contentious topic and, as may become apparent in subsequent chapters, much of what has been written on the subject has been based on speculation, rather than upon documentary evidence. While there seems little

Figure 1.1 King James II of Scotland and the earliest written reference to golf. The first appearance of the word 'golf' is in a Scottish Act of Parliament (6 March 1457/8) that was issued in the reign of King James II of Scotland (r.1437–60). Left image: © National Records of Scotland, PA5/6, f.43v. Right image: © National Galleries of Scotland, PG 683.

doubt that the Act of Parliament issued on 6 March 1457/8 is the earliest surviving document containing the word 'golf', some have questioned the extent to which the game referred to in that Act resembled the modern-day game (a topic that will be returned to later). Others have argued that there were stick-and-ball games played in other countries at an earlier date that should be considered as being precursors to the Scottish game of golf. Questions such as this, concerning the 'origin' of golf, have been debated extensively but they could also be seen as belonging to the ill-defined 'pre-history' of stick-and-ball games. This is a subject that will be revisited in the final chapter of this book.

Whatever the merits of arguments concerning golf's pre-historic origins, there is abundant documentary evidence demonstrating that a game referred to as 'golf' flourished in Scotland in the sixteenth century and that the Scots were largely responsible for the spread of golf to other parts of the world in the seventeenth and eighteenth centuries. The evidence supporting this conclusion will be presented in the penultimate chapter. It is also clear that, while golf flourished in Scotland and elsewhere, games that have been claimed as being precursors of golf (whether they be the ancient Chinese game of *chui wan* or the Dutch game of *colf*) largely disappeared before the modern game of golf took hold.

The 1457/8 Act of Parliament

One of the purposes of the 1457/8 Act of Parliament, entitled 'Concerning wappenschaws',[2] was to ban recreations such as football and golf. So, perhaps the first question to address is why such activities might have been banned in the mid-fifteenth century. This was a time of constant feuding between rival Scottish clans but, more importantly, Scotland was wary of the threat posed by its English neighbour. The two countries had been engaged in conflicts for centuries[3] and it was probably the need to prepare for the possibility of war that led King James II of Scotland to decree in an Act of Parliament that archery practice should be made compulsory and, at the same time, that football and golf should be banned. The rationale appears to have been that, by discouraging time-consuming recreational pastimes, the Scots would have more time to practise archery in readiness for battle. The relevant passage in the Act states 'futbawe ande the golf be utirly criyt doune and nocht wsyt' [football and golf be utterly cried down and not used].[4]

When similar Scottish Acts of Parliament were passed in 1471[5] and 1491[6] (in the reigns of James III and James IV), the content of the Acts with respect to golf was broadly similar. However, in 1491 the punishment for playing football, golf or other 'unprofitable' sports was specified as being a fine of forty shillings. Whereas these three Scottish Acts of Parliament contain the earliest known written references to golf, an earlier Scottish Act had been introduced in 1424 (during the reign of King James I) that had banned football but which did not mention golf.[7] The significance of golf having not been mentioned in the Act of 1424 is unclear but it has been argued that this may indicate that golf was insufficiently popular in 1424 to necessitate a ban.[8] It has also been suggested that the absence of golf in the Scottish Act of 1424 may have been an inadvertent omission,[9] perhaps resulting from the Scottish Act having been based on an English Act of Parliament from 1363 that had banned football but didn't mention golf.[10] Whatever the relative merits of these explanations, it is unlikely that we will ever know for certain why golf was mentioned in a Scottish Act of 1457/8 but wasn't included some thirty years earlier in 1424. What we can conclude is that a game called 'golf' was sufficiently popular in Scotland in the middle of the fifteenth century to warrant it being banned by three Acts of Parliament.

The Origins and the Meaning of 'Golf'

It should be noted that there has been some debate about how the word 'golf' should be interpreted in early written documents such as the Scottish Acts of Parliament. This has focused, in particular, upon whether the word refers exclusively to a game similar to the modern-day game of golf. For example, there are good reasons for thinking that the word 'golf' may have been used, particularly in the fifteenth and sixteenth centuries, to describe two related but distinct Scottish games. It seems probable that, in addition to what has been described as a 'skilled long game',[11] similar to the modern-day game of golf, there was also a 'short game' played in more enclosed spaces.[12] The primary reason for thinking that a short form of golf existed in Scotland are several references in the sixteenth and seventeenth centuries to golf being played in churchyards.[13] An argument has been made that the early 'long game', which used expensive clubs and balls, was played primarily by wealthy members of Scottish society, whereas the short form may have been a more accessible game that could be played by those who were less affluent.[14] More specifically, it is sometimes argued that what was banned in the Scottish Acts of Parliament was the 'short game' of golf. It has also been suggested that, since football is a team game, it is more likely that the game referred to as 'golf' in the three Acts of Parliament was also a team game, perhaps resembling hockey or the Scottish game of shinty.[15] However, all we can be certain of is that a game called golf was banned in Scotland in the second half of the fifteenth century.

How the word 'golf' should be interpreted in early documents has become contentious for another reason. It is seen as having relevance to the question of which stick-and-ball game should be viewed as having the greatest antiquity. This issue is frequently associated with the perennial question of whether the Scottish game of golf has ancestral links to other stick-and-ball games, such as *colf* that was popular in the Low Countries,[16] a question that will be revisited in the final chapter.

Romanticism and Myths in Early Golf History

There is a tendency for the early history of golf to be romanticised and it is perhaps a consequence of this that so many myths have emerged and why such stories have remained so popular. As will be discussed in Chapter 6, this is a phenomenon that could be seen as reaching a peak with stories concerning Mary Queen of Scots. To an extent, this romanticism is perhaps also reflected in the frequency with which the phrase 'The Royal and Ancient Game' appears in the title of so many published histories of golf.[17] While there is clear documentary evidence that several Stewart/Stuart kings of Scotland and Britain played golf (for example, James IV, James VI/I, Charles I, Charles II and James VII/II), there is often an assumption that all Stewart/Stuart monarchs did so. For example, while King James II of Scotland issued the Act of Parliament containing the first written reference to 'golf' there is no evidence to suggest that he played the game himself. However, despite this absence of documentary evidence, it is not uncommon to see claims such as King James II of Scotland (as opposed to the later King James II of Britain) 'played golf on the Links of Leith'.[18] Similarly, the implication that James II of Scotland played golf can be found in a suggestion that, despite him having prohibited the game, 'there is no evidence that James II [. . .] stopped playing golf'.[19] In addition to unsubstantiated claims that King James II played golf, it has also been suggested that his father, King James I, was a golfer. For example, inexplicably, one writer has claimed (without citing any evidence) that 'between 1427 and 1437 records show that King James I of Scotland was spending a considerable amount of money on golf equipment'.[20]

There has been a considerable amount of speculation about when golf was first played in Scotland and, although the earliest identified written reference to golf occurs in 1457/8, dates that are frequently mentioned in histories of golf and which are said to have relevance to the origins of Scottish golf include 1413, 1420/1, 1448, 1452 and 1456 (Figures 1.2 and 1.3). These claims are discussed below.

The 1452 Golf Ball Myth

One of the central themes of this book is a re-examination of some of the more implausible stories that have become embedded within the history of early golf. Because one of the topics discussed in this opening chapter concerns the earliest known reference to the word 'golf', this may also be an appropriate opportunity to re-examine an anecdote that has been retold frequently in golf histories. This may also provide a useful illustration of how what appears to be a simple and inadvertent error can result in prolonged confusion and misinformation. It concerns the purchase of a golf ball in 1452 and it is a story that, if supported by evidence, would represent the earliest known written reference to the game of golf, being five years earlier than the 1457/8 Act of Parliament.

The earliest occurrence of this story that I have come across is in *The Curious History of the Golf Ball* (1968), written by the American sports writer John Martin. In his book, Martin states, 'The first recorded sale of a golf ball was in 1452; the price ten shillings.'[21] However, although the claim is both detailed and specific, no documentary evidence was cited by the author in 1968. Following the publication of Martin's book, the story has been repeated almost verbatim on numerous occasions, although on none of

University of
St Andrews
FOUNDED
1413
1421
LA BATAILLE
DU VIEIL-BAUGÉ
1452
First record of a "goiff" ball for sale. It costs 10 Scottish shillings—around $5 today—and is made of down-filled leather (a "featherie" like the one above) or possibly wood.
EST^D 1456

Figure 1.2 Four dates associated with fifteenth-century golf myths. Several dates in the fifteenth century (for example, 1413, 1420/1, 1452 and 1456) have been mentioned in connection with the early history of golf but none of these appear to be supported by documentary evidence.

these occasions has any contemporary documentary evidence been cited. The story has been mentioned in several books devoted to the history of golf and it is notable that when these books have been reviewed in the press the reviewers have often highlighted this story as being of particular interest. For example, this was commented upon by the *Santa Cruz Sentinel* when reviewing *The Curious History of the Golf Ball*[22] and also by *Golf Magazine* when reviewing *The Story of the Golf Ball* (2004).[23] A further example is that when reviewing *The Golf Ball Book* (2000), the *San Francisco Chronicle* drew attention to the 'fascinating revelation' that the first recorded sale of a golf ball was in 1452.[24] More recently, *Golfweek* magazine reviewed *From Sticks and Stones* (2011) and commented

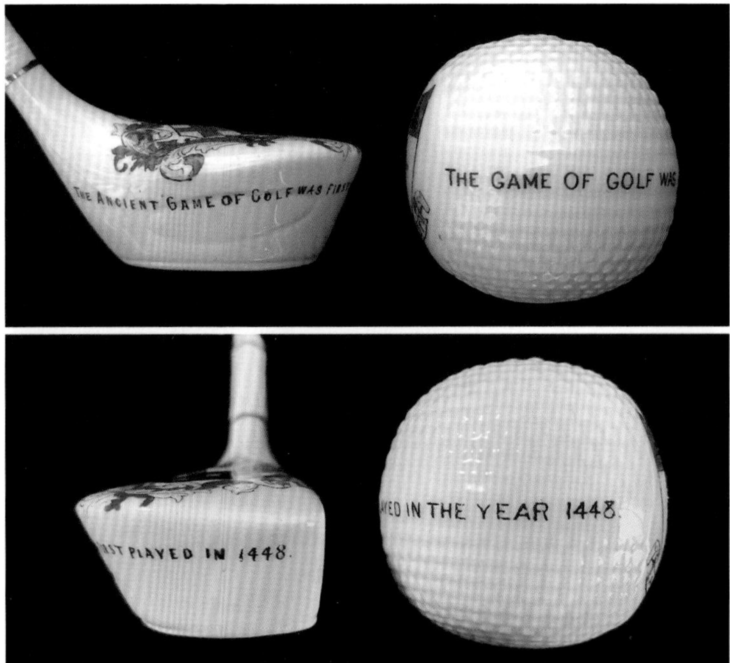

Figure 1.3 Golf-related crested china and an unreliable date (1448). It is common for items of crested china produced in the early twentieth century to state that golf was first played in 1448 but this is a date that is not supported by documentary evidence.

that the book provided information that 'starts in 1452 with the first recorded sale of a golf ball for 10 shillings'.[25] The story has also been repeated in publications as diverse as the newsletter of the American Singles Golf Association,[26] a leaflet accompanying a set of replica golf balls that was sold by the Worthington Ball Company[27] and a university MSc thesis.[28]

Almost inevitably, the story has evolved somewhat over the past fifty years. For example, authors have made claims about the type of golf ball that was bought for ten shillings in 1452. It has been described as being a wooden ball,[29] a 'feathery'[30] and, more specifically, a 'well-made featherie'[31] (a feathery/featherie being a feather-filled leather ball). It is not uncommon for writers to imply that documentary evidence exists concerning the purchase of a golf ball in 1542. For example, it has been claimed that the information concerning the purchase of a golf ball was derived from 'documents from the archives of 1452' (though none were cited).[32] In addition, a magazine article that took as its theme the importance of 'factual documentation' in golf history stated that 'documentation is the golf historian's bible and the earliest references to the game date to 1452 when a golf ball sold for ten Scottish shillings'[33] but, once again, no documentary source was cited.

Of course, if golf was sufficiently popular to be banned in 1457/8 it is almost certain that golf balls were, indeed, being purchased in 1452. Consequently, it is not inconceivable that an elusive document exists that describes the purchase of golf balls for ten shillings in 1452. However, a more plausible explanation for the origin of this story may be that the author of *The Curious History of the Golf Ball* in 1968 was incorrectly recalling evidence of a well-documented incident that occurred in the 1600s. The handwritten account books of the Earl of Montrose, dating from his time as a student in St Andrews (1627–9), were subsequently transcribed and provide evidence of golf balls having been bought for ten shillings.[34] It seems possible that the author of *The Curious History of the Golf Ball* was recalling this event from the seventeenth century but inadvertently provided an incorrect date (inexplicably, 1452). If so, it is an error that has been repeated frequently during the last fifty years and one that has developed into an increasingly popular and enduring golf myth.

Although there is unambiguous evidence that an Act of Parliament banning golf was enacted by James II in 1457/8, it is now increasingly common to see the date of this Act of Parliament being reported as 1452. It seems likely that this error has arisen as a consequence of a confused attempt to reconcile two competing claims: on the one hand the claim that the earliest reference to golf dates from 1457/8 (the Act of Parliament) and, on the other hand, the unsubstantiated claim that a golf ball was bought for ten shillings in 1452. Evidence that this may have been a source of confusion can be found in an archived version of a *Wikipedia* page concerning the history of golf. An early version of the *Wikipedia* entry 'History of Golf' contained the statement 'golf was first mentioned in writing in 1457 on a Scottish statute on forbidden games as gouf'. However, this was subsequently modified (and contradicted) in 2007 by the addition of the following supplementary comment: 'But there is an even earlier reference to the game of golf and it is believed to have happened in 1452 when King James II banned the game.'[35] Statements claiming that the Act banning golf dates from 1452 have appeared with increasing regularity in recent years. This has included numerous online articles,[36] as well as printed publications.[37] A notable example is a lavishly prepared 'infographic' depicting the timeline of golf history (from the fifteenth century to the twenty-first century) that was published online and begins with 1452 being identified as the date when James II banned golf.[38]

A further development of the story has been a claim that 1452 is the date of the first recorded golf match and the date that the game of golf originated. For example, a press release issued in 2008 described the city of Edinburgh as being 'where the first recorded game of golf was played in 1452'.[39] An even bolder claim has been made on the website of a golf resort in Kazakhstan. It describes several theories concerning the possible origins of the game of golf but concludes, 'perhaps the most truthful and generally accepted version of golf's origin is a version according to which golf appeared in Scotland in 1452'.[40] If nothing else, this illustrates the extent to which an unsubstantiated claim that appears to have arisen due to an inadvertent and understandable error can result in considerable confusion and misunderstanding.

The 1413 St Andrews Golf Myth

Another claim that has been made in several histories of golf is that there is evidence of the game having been played in St Andrews as early as 1413. Once again, it is a claim that, if true, would provide evidence of golf that pre-dates the 1457/8 Scottish Act of Parliament. It is possible that the story originated in 1910, when the American sports writer Walter Camp wrote, 'There is plenty of proof that when the University of St Andrews was founded in 1413, golf was even then a popular pastime in Scotland.'[41] Camp did not cite his 'proof' and neither did subsequent authors who have described the story as being based on 'some evidence'[42] or upon 'reliable evidence'.[43] The claim of golf being played in St Andrews when the university was founded in 1413 has been repeated on numerous occasions, including by the great American golfer Bobby Jones in 1939.[44] Similarly, another writer stated (in 1969) that 'Golf was invented in Scotland soon after the foundation of the University of St Andrews' and continued, 'This momentous fact has not hitherto been fully appreciated.' It has also been claimed that 'golf was already popular at St Andrews when its university was founded'[45] and that 'St Andrews University had its own [golf] course in 1413'.[46] These claims, linking the origin of golf to the founding of the University of St Andrews, presumably explain why some sources have suggested that golf originated in 1413 but without indicating explicitly any connection to the founding of the university. For example, it has been suggested, without explanation, that golf's origins 'can be traced to 1413'.[47] A similar claim resurfaced in 2008 in a book that described golf as 'a game that began as far back as AD 1413 at St Andrews'.[48] It is notable that, while the story is still being retold a hundred years after Walter Camp's magazine article, as far as I am aware no evidence has been cited by any of those who have repeated the story in the intervening century. Speculation about the date 1413 may also explain why it is often stated that golf has been played at St Andrews for '600 years',[49] a claim that has even featured as a 'Guinness World Record'.[50] Although it is not inconceivable that golf was played in St Andrews as early as 1413, it is a claim that does not appear to be supported by any documentary evidence.

The 1420/1 Battle of Baugé Golf Myth

Robert Browning, who had been the editor of the British magazine *Golfing* for forty-five years before publishing *A History of Golf* in 1955,[51] deserves considerable credit for having written one of the most readable and popular early histories of golf. Browning will, however, feature quite prominently in subsequent chapters of this book, a book that aims to examine the origins of popular golf myths.

Robert Browning was probably the first golf writer to include a chronological list of early events in golf's history,[52] a concept that has been repeated frequently. One event that Browning included in his 'Chronological Table' was the Battle of Baugé (6 March 1420/1), a conflict involving Scottish soldiers fighting in France that formed part of the Hundred Years War. Browning mentions that, during the battle, the Scots were 'playing at ball'[53] and he suggests that this was likely to have been the French stick-and-ball game of *chole*.[54] His theory was that the Scottish soldiers may have taken their knowledge of the game of *chole* back to Scotland, where it became a forerunner of Scottish golf. Browning was conscious that golf in Scotland had first been mentioned in the 1457/8 Act but that it had not been mentioned in the earlier 1424 Act banning football.[55] He was clearly interested in exploring possible links between golf and stick-and-ball games played in continental Europe. In connection with this he commented, 'It would be pleasing to imagine that golf may have been an offshoot of *chole*',[56] a game that Browning describes as being played in Belgium and Northern France that was a 'half-way stage between hockey and golf'.[57] Browning mentions that evidence indicating Scottish soldiers may have encountered the game of *chole* in France could be found in *Liber Pluscardensis*,[58] a Latin history of Scotland written during the reign of King James II. However, Browning's conclusions were based on an English translation of the original Latin text that described the Scottish soldiers as 'playing ball and amusing themselves with other pleasant or devout occupations'.[59] Browning explains at some length why he feels that it is unlikely that the Scots were playing games such as football, shinty or golf and then concludes:

> Some form of cross-country ball game, however, it must have been, and I think the best guess is that the Scots had taken up the game of *chole*. If they learned it in this campaign, brought it back to Scotland, and transformed it into golf, the dates would fit. The *chole* of 1421 might easily have developed into golf in time to become widely popular by 1457.[60]

However, while Browning claims that *Liber Pluscardensis* describes the Scots 'playing ball', examination of the original Latin version of the text indicates that this is incorrect. The phrase used was '*Scotis ad palmam ludentibus*' which, as will be discussed, suggests that the Scots were 'playing' but does not mention a ball.[61] This is a golf myth that was originally uncovered by Fred Hawtree, the prominent golf course architect, and it may be the only golf myth to have been rebutted by being the subject of an entire book: Hawtree's *Triple Baugé*.[62] It appears that, on the basis of Browning's conclusions concerning the Battle of Baugé, Hawtree had undertaken extensive research into the history of the battle and had also visited the site where it occurred in Anjou, France. It was only after Hawtree had invested considerable efforts into his research that he discovered there was no evidence in *Liber Pluscardensis* to suggest that the game played by Scottish soldiers was *chole*. In *Triple Baugé* (1996) Hawtree describes his realisation that *Liber Pluscardensis* does not mention 'playing ball' and comments, perhaps a little wryly, that the Scottish soldiers 'could have been hand-wrestling or tossing the caber'.[63] Hawtree eventually arrived at the conclusion that '*palmam*' was a reference to the game of *jeu de paume*,[64] an early form of tennis in which a ball was hit with the palm of the hand. He came to this conclusion despite having consulted an 'Oxford don' and having been advised that the Latin expression *Scotis ad palmam ludentibus* was an 'ablative absolute' and, therefore, a more accurate translation was that the Scots were simply 'playing for a prize'.[65] Robert Browning's source for the phrase 'playing ball' was an English translation of *Liber Pluscardensis* published in *Scottish Pageant* (1949)[66] and Hawtree's source for the Latin version appears to have been a printed edition of *Liber Pluscardensis* published in 1877.[67] Having examined two fifteenth-century manuscript versions of *Liber Pluscardensis*[68] and having taken advice from an expert in medieval Latin, it seems the safest translation would be something along the lines of 'Scots playing for a prize/victory' (as was suggested by Hawtree's 'Oxford don').[69] More to the point, there appears to be no reason, at least on the basis of *Liber Pluscardensis*, for concluding that golf originated from the French game of *chole* in 1420/1. However, as might be expected given the influence of Browning's *A History of Golf*, the events of the Battle of Baugé continue to be reported as being a plausible explanation for the origin of golf in Scotland. For example, a recent publication stated confidently that the game of *chole* 'was brought to Scotland when the Scottish helped the French fight the English at the Siege of Baugé in 1421'.[70] It has also been claimed that, following the Battle of Baugé, the Scots 'brought *chole* back to Scotland, where the game eventually evolved into modern golf'.[71] Another author has suggested that *chole* is 'the most likely ancestor' of golf and then goes on to explain that 'golf was born' when 'the Scots took *chole* and made a few subtle changes to improve it, most importantly by adding a hole for the ball to be aimed at'.[72]

The 1448 Crested China Myth

Items of 'crested china' became popular in Britain in the early 1900s and were, typically, small items of pottery containing a crest, for example of a city or town, that were sold to tourists as inexpensive souvenirs. They included items in the shape of golf balls and golf clubheads containing phrases such as 'The ancient game of golf was first played in 1448' or 'The game of golf was first played in the year 1448' (Figure 1.3). Before producing these items in such large quantities, it might be expected that a date would have been selected that was supported by evidence. However, what seems more likely is that a pottery designer was incorrectly recalling the date of the Scottish Act of Parliament of 1457/8 (1448 differing by only one digit from 1458). It is not unreasonable that the owners of such items of pottery might assume that the claim concerning '1448' was reliable and, indeed, there is evidence that this is the case. For example, one golf writer who had described in 1993 his collection of golf-related crested china[73] subsequently wrote an article about Irish golf history in which he stated that golf had been played in Scotland 'as early as 1448'.[74] Another golf writer, when discussing such an item of crested china containing a reference to '1448', commented, 'I believe the date on my small china golf ball must be about right.'[75] However, while it is true that the date may be 'about right', the precise date of 1448 does not appear to be based on any reliable evidence.

The 1456 Golf Tavern Myth

A final example of a claim concerning a date in the reign of King James II is one that has been made in connection with an Edinburgh public house, 'Ye Olde Golf Tavern' at Bruntsfield Links. It is claimed that the pub was 'founded in 1456' and that, as a consequence, it is 'the oldest golf pub in the world'. This bold claim, which is mentioned on its website[76] and on its social media page,[77] is ostensibly supported by the phrase 'Est^{D}. 1456', which appears in large letters on the building's stone facade. While some authorities have suggested that this is a 'doubtfully long pedigree',[78] the claimed foundation date has been frequently repeated uncritically.[79] However, the history of the building has been examined in some detail and it appears to have been built in the early nineteenth century (probably in the 1830s).[80] There is evidence that it was used as a clubhouse by the Bruntsfield

Links Golfing Society from 1852 until the society relocated to Musselburgh in 1876.[81] Significantly, in 1893, following the departure of the Bruntsfield Links Golfing Society, the building was renovated by a brewery company (James Muir and Co.), in what could be seen as an early example of a brewery creating a themed pub. During the renovation in 1898 it was rebranded 'Ye Olde Golf Tavern', 'Ye Olde' being an expression that gained popularity in the late nineteenth century as a clichéd way of denoting bogus antiquity. It would appear that the pub's new name and the phrase 'Est^{D}. 1456' were added to the building's façade at the time of the refurbishment in 1898, a conclusion that is supported by an image showing the same building prior to its renovation that lacks these embellishments.[82]

An obvious question might be, if a bogus foundation date were to be adopted for a renovated golf-themed public house in 1898, why was the date 1456 selected? The most plausible argument I have seen proposed is that Robert Cameron, the architect who was employed by the brewery company in 1898, was aware of evidence that golf in Scotland had been banned by an Act of Parliament in 1457/8. A logical conclusion might be that, if golf had been banned in 1457/8, golf must have been played *prior* to that date (hence the selection of '1456', as a date that was prior to 1457/8).[83] This assumption would seem to be consistent with the contrived adoption of the pseudo-archaic phrase 'Ye Olde'.[84] It might also be consistent with the commercial objectives of a themed-pub makeover, rather than a reliance on reliable historical evidence. However, whether or not this is the correct explanation, there seems little doubt that the building dates from no earlier than the nineteenth century. It is, however, located close to an earlier property, 'Golfhall', that was built in 1717 and was used by golfers at Bruntsfield Links in the eighteenth century (but was demolished in the 1950s).[85]

The foundation date of a public house may seem a relatively peripheral issue in the history of golf but it is a topic that has attracted some attention. In 2016 the online golf magazine *Golf Punk* published an article entitled 'World's Oldest Golf Pub', in which it lamented the possible demise of the Musselburgh public house Mrs Forman's (which is said to have been built in 1822).[86] A few days later *Golf Punk* reported that it had been 'called out on Twitter' and its attention had been drawn to the fact that Ye Olde Golf Tavern at Bruntsfield Links had been 'founded in 1456'. The magazine concluded that Ye Olde Golf Tavern was, indeed, 'the world's oldest golf pub' and stated in conclusion, 'Well, we hope we've now got our facts right.'[87] In addition, it seems possible that the claimed foundation date of the Golf Tavern may have inspired one writer to conclude that 'the first recorded game of golf for which records survive was played at Bruntsfield Links, in Edinburgh, Scotland, in A.D. 1456'.[88]

Several lines of evidence would suggest that the earliest sites where golf was played were seaside locations (for example, at St Andrews in Fife and at Leith in Edinburgh), rather than at inland locations such as Bruntsfield Links. Although it has been claimed that there is evidence of golf having been played at Bruntsfield Links in 1579[89] (and even 'before 1450'),[90] no supporting documentary evidence has ever been cited. The earliest evidence of golf being played at Bruntsfield Links is an entry in the Edinburgh Town Council records dating from 1695,[91] which is more than two hundred years after the seemingly mythical foundation date that is claimed by Ye Olde Golf Tavern.

In Summary

There is no evidence to support the suggestion that golf was played in St Andrews in 1413 at the time the university was founded, or that golf was introduced to Scotland in 1420/1 by Scottish soldiers who had encountered the game of *chole* in France. Similarly, there is no evidence of golf balls having been purchased for ten shillings in 1452 or that golf was first played in 1448, as is stated on several items of crested china. There is also no evidence that a golf tavern at Bruntsfield Links was instituted in 1456. In contrast, there is clear and unambiguous documentary evidence of 'golf' having been mentioned in a Scottish Act of Parliament in 1457/8. This is the first recorded use of the word 'golf' and, as such, provides a convenient starting point for the documented history of golf.

Chapter 2

King James III and Two Poetic Fifteenth-century Golf Myths

King James III of Scotland (Figure 2.1), who reigned from 1460 to 1488, is rarely mentioned in histories of golf, other than to point out that the second of three Acts of Parliament banning golf was enacted during his reign.[92] This Act, which was passed by the Scottish Parliament in 1471, reaffirmed a ban on golf that had originally been imposed by an earlier Act (of 1457/8) from the reign of James II (see Chapter 1). No documentary evidence has been identified to indicate that King James III played golf

Figure 2.1 King James III of Scotland. James III (r.1460–88) was the second Scottish king to issue an Act of Parliament banning golf. © National Galleries Scotland, PG 684.

but nevertheless claims that he did so have emerged in recent years. For example, it has been suggested, seemingly without any evidence, that James III 'became a golf lover',[93] while another account mentions, without any explanation, that King James III was encouraged to take up golf by his wife.[94]

Possible References to Golf in Early Scottish Poems

Other than the well-documented references to golf in three fifteenth-century Scottish Acts of Parliament (see Chapter 1 and Table 15.1), it has been suggested that additional written references to golf from this period are to be found in Scottish poems by William Dunbar (c. 1460–c. 1513) and Gilbert Hay (c. 1397–c. 1466). In the case of Dunbar's poem, the claim is undoubtedly incorrect and in the case of Hay's poem it is highly questionable.

William Dunbar and 'The Makar's Complaint'

In 1909 the golf writer William Dalrymple wrote a letter to *Golf Illustrated* entitled 'The Earliest Poem on Golf', in which he drew attention to a poem that he described as having been written by 'our Scottish Poet Laureate, William Dunbar'. Dalrymple quotes the following stanza:

> But when they a' begin to bowff
> Till misery haunts the muse's howff
>   Better I left the paper white
> An' took to poaching, or to gowff
>   Than write an' kenna what to write[95]

William Dunbar was closely associated with the Scottish court[96] and has been described as 'the best Scottish poet prior to the Reformation'.[97] It may have been the poet's close proximity to the court that led Dalrymple to speculate that the poetic association between golf and an illegal activity such as poaching might have been influenced by the Scottish Acts of Parliament that had banned golf in the fifteenth century. However, this reference to 'gowff' that Dalrymple had come across turns out to be from a book of poems that was published in 1895 and which was written by Hugh Haliburton (a *nom de plume* for James Logie Robertson, 1846–1922).

Dalrymple's confusion may have arisen as a consequence of Haliburton's poems being a deliberate pastiche of the poetry of William Dunbar. Significantly, the title of Haliburton's book of poems is *Dunbar: Being a Selection from the Poems of an Old Makar, Adapted for Modern Readers*. Haliburton's poem that mentions 'gowff' is entitled 'The Makar's Complaint' and is a modern interpretation of Dunbar's much earlier poem 'Faine wald I, with all diligence', a poem that makes no reference to golf.[98] It is notable that, when Haliburton's book of poems was reviewed in 1895, the reviewer commented, 'Haliburton should not have taken such liberties with a Scottish classic as are to be found inside the covers of this book'.[99] Dalrymple's claim about this being 'the earliest poem on golf' has been repeated by a number of subsequent golf writers who have also assumed incorrectly that this late nineteenth-century poem by Haliburton is one of the very earliest written references to golf.[100]

Gilbert Hay's Fifteenth-century Poem

It has also been suggested that golf is mentioned in *The Buik of King Alexander the Conquerour* (Figure 2.2), a Scottish narrative poem by Sir Gilbert Hay (c. 1460).[101] It is a claim that has had a significant impact on how aspects of early golf history have been assessed and it contributed to the *Encyclopædia Britannica* concluding (in 2010) that the claim of golf originating in Scotland is 'a popular fallacy'.[102] However, it seems likely that an error was made when the poem was transcribed in the sixteenth century and this may have misled golf historians.

In 2002 the German golf historian Heiner Gillmeister suggested that claims of golf having originated in Scotland were 'unsubstantiated', a conclusion he based on what he described as 'new source material which proves the continental origins of Scotland's national game'.[103] A central plank of Gillmeister's argument relied upon his interpretation of *The Buik of King Alexander the Conquerour*. Indeed, when rewriting the entry for 'golf' in the *Encyclopædia Britannica* (2010), Gillmeister stated that it was an analysis of this poem that provided 'proof' that the Scottish word 'golf' had 'exactly the same meaning as its Flemish counterpart *kolve*', which he describes as 'a hockey stick'.[104] It is an apparent reference in this fifteenth-century poem to a 'golf-staff' that played a significant part in leading Gillmeister to his conclusions about the origins of golf.

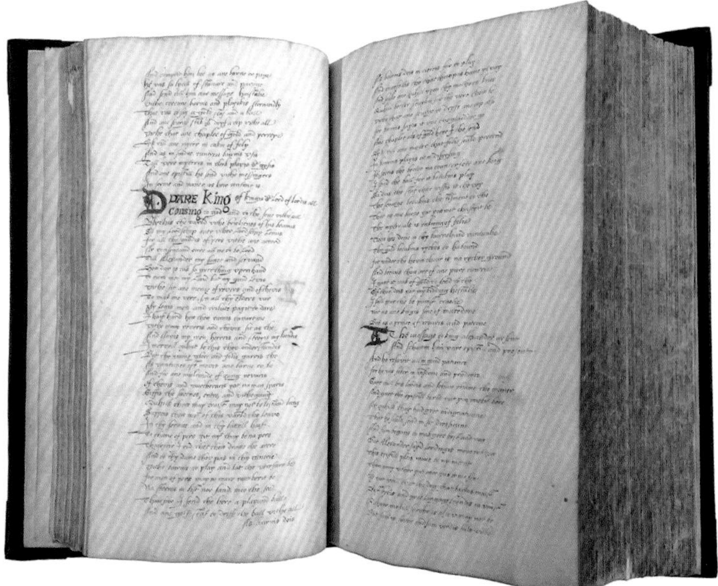

Figure 2.2 *The Buik of King Alexander the Conquerour.* This is one of two sixteenth-century copies of the Scottish narrative poem *The Buik of King Alexander the Conquerour.* It contains a reference to a 'golf staff', the meaning of which has been the focus of some debate. It seems likely, however, that the original version of the poem (c. 1460) contained a reference to a 'gold staff' and that this was incorrectly transcribed as 'golf staff' in the sixteenth century. National Records of Scotland, GD112/71/9.

While Gilbert Hay's original fifteenth-century manuscript has not survived, there are two sixteenth-century manuscript copies, one of which is thought to have been produced around 1530[105] and another thought to date from 1580–90.[106] Having consulted the two surviving manuscript copies of Hay's poem, I will argue that the poem's relevance to golf has been interpreted incorrectly.

The Buik of King Alexander the Conquerour

The Buik of King Alexander the Conquerour is a poem of epic proportions, containing approximately twenty thousand lines of verse and some one hundred and fifty thousand words. The poem describes the life of King Alexander the Conqueror (356–323 BC) and the passage that is of interest to golf historians deals with the siege of the Tyre (332 BC), a Phoenician city on the Mediterranean coast that Alexander's Macedonian army overran and destroyed during his conquest of Persia. The conflict between Alexander and Darius III, the king of Persia, is a popular story in medieval literature and forms a genre that is often referred to as the Alexander Romances. The poem describes an insulting letter sent by Darius to his adversary Alexander. Darius implies that Alexander is no more than an inexperienced child and that he should return home to play with his toys, rather than risking death in Persia. For example, Hay describes in his poem how Darius suggests that Alexander should return to his mother, Olympias of Epirus, and suckle on her knee.[107] However, the couplet that has attracted the attention of golf historians occurs four lines earlier:

> Tharefore I send the here a playing ball,
> And ane golf-staff to driff the ball withall.

> [Therefore, I send thee here a playing ball,
> and a golf staff to drive the ball withal.][108]

When commenting upon the significance of this reference to a 'golf-staff' it appears that golf historians have relied upon John Cartwright's twentieth-century transcription of the poem (as quoted here), rather than upon either of the two surviving manuscripts. As a consequence, what may have been overlooked is that a few lines earlier in the manuscript versions is a reference to a 'gold staff'. When a transcription of Hay's poem was published by Albert Herrmann in 1898, Herrmann retained the original wording that is used in the two manuscripts ('gold' in the first instance and 'golf' in the second).[109] However, when a new analysis was published by John Cartwright (in 1986), he assumed that, because they were both references to the same object and occurred in a similar context (both are 'staffs' used to hit a ball), one or other must have been an error that was perhaps introduced when the manuscripts were copied from an earlier source by a sixteenth-century scribe. Cartwright appears to have come to the conclusion that it was the reference to 'gold' that was erroneous and therefore he corrected this to 'golf' in his published transcription.[110] As John Cartwright concluded, it is clear from the context of the poem that on the two occasions on which a 'staff' is mentioned[111] it is referring to the same object (a staff used to hit a ball) and, consequently, on both occasions it should be either 'gold staff' or 'golf staff'. Significantly, there is evidence to indicate that the scribes who copied the sixteenth-century manuscripts were prone to making errors.[112] Because Hay's original manuscript of 1460 has not survived, it is impossible to know with certainty what the author's intended meaning was. However, evidence is available by examining earlier texts upon which Hay's poem was based.

The Alexander Romance Genre

The Alexander Romance stories are considered to have originated during the second or third centuries. The original text is believed to have been written in Greek but, prior to the seventeenth century, the story had been translated in either prose or verse into some thirty other languages.[113] A seemingly constant feature of all versions of the story is a description of Darius sending Alexander a mocking letter, together with a variety of gifts. While the items that Darius sends differ in the varying accounts, they invariably include a ball, a whip and an item of gold. These accounts also contain an explanation by Darius of the metaphorical significance of the items that he is sending. For example, the earliest surviving Greek text describes Darius telling Alexander to go home and 'cuddle in the arms of your mother' and states that Darius is sending Alexander 'a whip and a ball and gold'.[114] An early Syriac version describes 'a whip and a ball and a box full of gold',[115] while an Armenian version mentions 'a leather thong, a ball and a chest of gold'.[116] The source for many of the later 'Western' versions of the Alexander Romance was a Latin text, *Historia de Preliis*, that mentions 'a ball, a whip for you to play with, and a chest of gold'.[117] There is strong evidence, however, that Gilbert Hay's primary source for his version was a French version of the Alexander Romance known as *Roman d'Alexandre* (Figure 2.3).[118] Several fourteenth- and fifteenth-century manuscript copies of *Roman d'Alexandre* survive that pre-date Hay's Scots version and these also include the anecdote concerning Darius sending items to Alexander. What is significant is that these French texts refer to '*une crosse d'or*',[119] a translation of which is 'a gold club/stick'. It seems that Hay was simply continuing the literary and poetic tradition of copying and modifying earlier texts when writing his

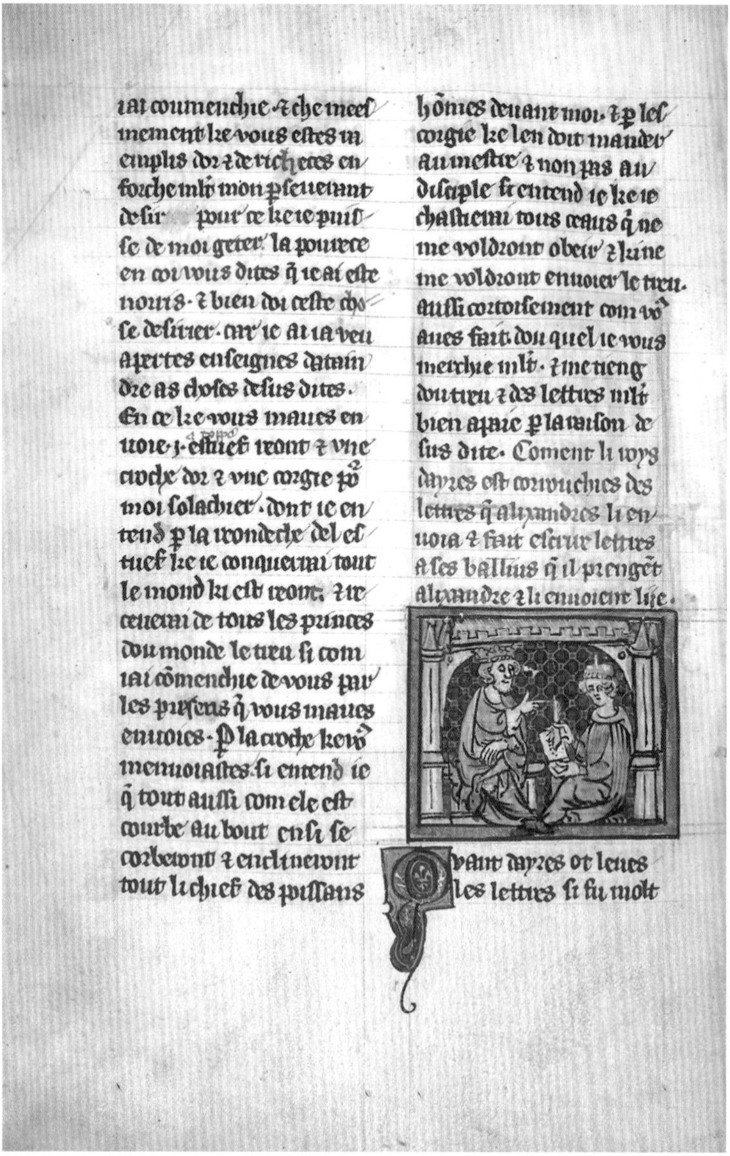

Figure 2.3 *Roman d'Alexandre* (c. 1290–1300). A French prose version of the *Roman d'Alexandre*, containing the phrase '*estuef reont et une crosse d'or*' [a round ball and a gold staff]. This is likely to be the origin of the phrase 'a gold staff and a ball' that can be found in the Scots poem *The Buik of King Alexander the Conquerour* (c. 1460). © British Library; Harley 4969, f.30v.

Alexander Romance in 1460 and that he included 'a gold staff' as a literal translation of the French '*une crosse d'or*'. It seems likely that Hay's original manuscript (now lost) included two references to a gold staff and that one of these was erroneously transcribed as 'golf staff' by a scribe in the sixteenth century, and survives in the two extant sixteenth-century manuscripts. Of course, if this interpretation is correct, it would indicate that *The Buik of King Alexander the Conquerour*, at least the original version written by Sir Gilbert Hay in 1460, has no relevance to the history of the game of golf.

The Debate among Golf Historians

The reason why it is important to establish whether Hay is likely to have written 'gold' or 'golf' in the original version of the poem is because so much has been made by golf historians concerning the presumed use of 'golf-staff' as a translation of the French term *crosse* in Hay's mid-fifteenth-century text.[120] To a large extent, this debate has been part of the same set of arguments that have been advanced to suggest that references to 'golf' in three Acts of Parliament (1457/8, 1471 and 1491) might be references to a hockey-like game, rather than the long game of golf. For example, with reference to Hay's supposed use of 'golf' in the Scots poem of 1460, Gillmeister assumes that the reference to a 'golf-staff' is accurate but has claimed that it is 'completely out of the question that this text cites a fifteenth-century example of golf'. Instead he argues that Hay was using the word golf to describe a form of 'medieval hockey'.[121] Another golf historian has taken a broadly similar view but has argued that, in using the word golf, Hay is likely to have been referring to the French game of '*soule à la crosse*', which the author describes as being a 'confrontational team game'.[122] Other authors have taken an opposing view, suggesting that the game that would have been described in *Roman d'Alexandre* is '*jeu de crosse*' and that this is a 'golf-like game' and 'certainly not hockey'.[123] Of course, if Hay wrote 'gold' rather than 'golf' in *The Buik of King Alexander the Conquerour*, as appears to be the case, this debate about the intended meaning of the word 'golf' in 1460 is immaterial.

The issue of whether golf should be considered to have originated in Scotland will be discussed in more detail in Chapters 15 and 16. However, it may be worth pointing out that, among those who have argued that golf originated in continental Europe, one of the most vocal has been Heiner Gillmeister, who relied upon the apparent reference to a 'golf-staff' in *The Buik of King Alexander the Conquerour* as a central plank in his arguments. This is illustrated by a German article written by Gillmeister that begins with the subtitle '*Alexander de Grosse als Mythenkiller*' [Alexander the Great as a myth killer].[124] Gillmeister's argument appears to be that it is the story of Alexander the Great/Conqueror that will be responsible for doing away with the 'myth' that golf originated in Scotland ('*Mit dem schottischen Golfmythos räumt jetzt jemand auf*').[125] This seems somewhat ironic, given that this seemingly erroneous interpretation of *The Buik of King Alexander the Conquerour* has all the hallmarks of a story that is in the process of developing into a frequently repeated golf myth.

A legitimate question might be what was the intended meaning of the sixteenth-century scribe who appears to have incorrectly copied Hay's manuscript – in other words, was the scribe using 'golf' to describe a hockey-like game? However, this has no bearing on the antiquity of the modern game of golf in Scotland because by 1503/4 (prior to the date the manuscripts were copied) there is unambiguous evidence of King James IV playing golf against the Earl of Bothwell[126] (see Chapter 3). This 'golf' match in 1503/4 is universally accepted as being an example of the non-confrontational golf that we know today, rather than a violent hockey-like team game, and indicates that golf was being played in Scotland at the time that the sixteenth-century copies of *The Buik of King Alexander the Conquerour* were written (c. 1530 or later).

In Summary

It is clear that a poem mentioning 'gowff' that was commented upon by William Dalrymple in 1909 dates from the nineteenth century, rather than being a fifteenth- or sixteenth-century poem by William Dunbar, as had originally been assumed. In addition, it seems likely that Hay's fifteenth-century narrative poem has no relevance to the history of golf. Rather, it would appear that an error introduced by a sixteenth-century scribe has been perpetuated and used as the basis for an erroneous analysis of the poem, even to the extent that it has been included in printed and online editions of the influential *Encyclopædia Britannica*.[127]

Chapter 3

King James IV, the Earliest Recorded Golf Match and Early Sixteenth-century Golf

In addition to the references to golf in fifteenth-century Scottish Acts of Parliament (see Chapter 1 and Figure 1.1), golf is mentioned in five documents dating from the first decade of the sixteenth century (from 1503/4, 1506 and 1507). These five documents will be discussed in this chapter, as will a reference to the purchase of 'clubbes' in 1502 that has been widely assumed to be a reference to golf clubs, but the extent to which this assumption is reasonable will be examined.

King James IV, the Golfer

Following the lead of both his grandfather and father (James II and James III), King James IV of Scotland (Figure 3.1) was the third consecutive Scottish monarch to issue an Act of Parliament (in 1491) prohibiting football and golf. While there is no evidence to suggest that either of the two preceding Scottish kings played golf, there is clear evidence that James IV did. Indeed, he is the first golfer (along with his opponent, the Earl of Bothwell) who can be identified by name. It should also be pointed out that there are just four brief references indicating James IV's involvement in the game of golf, all of which are entries in the king's accounts. These concern him playing golf with the Earl of Bothwell in 1503/4;[128] a purchase of 'golf clubbes and balles' in 1503/4;[129] a purchase of 'golf ballis' in 1506;[130] and a purchase of 'golf clubbes' in 1506.[131] However, despite the relatively limited evidence of James IV's participation in the game of golf, a degree of hyperbole has been used in describing his enthusiasm for the sport. For example, he has been described as being 'hooked' on golf,[132] a 'golf fanatic'[133] and a 'golf addict'.[134] It has even been suggested that golf was his 'favourite pastime'.[135]

Figure 3.1 King James IV of Scotland. James IV was the third Scottish king to issue an Act of Parliament banning golf and is also the earliest golfer (along with his opponent the Earl of Bothwell) who can be identified by name. © National Galleries Scotland, PG 685.

The 'bowar of Sanct Johnestoun'

An entry in James IV's accounts records a payment of fourteen shillings to a bow-maker from Sanct Johnestoun (Perth) for an unspecified number of 'clubbes' on 21 September 1502.[136] It has been widely assumed by golf historians that the 'clubbes' were golf clubs. However, it is of interest that James Balfour Paul, who transcribed the accounts, was of the opinion that such references to unidentified types of 'clubbes' were likely to be clubs used for the sport of hawking.[137] Paul was undoubtedly one of the greatest authorities on the Scottish Treasury Accounts, having transcribed the handwritten accounts covering a period of sixty-six years (those from 1500 to 1566).[138] Elsewhere in the accounts there are specific references to 'halk clubs'[139] and Paul describes these as being clubs that were designed for beating down undergrowth that might otherwise provide cover for the live prey ('quarry') that was used to train the king's hawks.[140]

Interestingly, the two types of clubs cost similar amounts; two 'golf clubbes' were purchased in 1506 for two shillings[141] and two 'halk clubbes' in 1503 for two shillings and fourpence.[142] In addition to these purchases of 'golf clubbes' and 'halk clubbes', the accounts record several instances where the king bought what are described simply as either 'clubbes' or 'clubs' between 1502 and 1506.[143] Paul was firmly of the opinion that the king's frequent purchases of such unidentified 'clubbes/clubs' were likely to have been clubs used for hawking, as is clear from the following comment:

> The 'golf clubbes and balles that he playit with' cost 9s. It is, I think, the only place in these Accounts [those of 1500–4] where golf clubs are expressly named as such; the clubs [i.e. those not identified as *golf* clubs] of which there is frequent mention were, as has been remarked above, for use in hawking.[144]

What may lend support to the assumption that the unidentified 'clubbes' were not golf clubs is that there are only two references to the purchase of 'golf clubbes' in the entire accounts of James IV (in 1503/4 and 1506) and these occur at the same time as, or in relatively close proximity to, the purchases of 'golf ballis'.[145] Yet, despite the various other purchases of unidentified 'clubbes', there are no further purchases of golf balls.

There seems little doubt that hawking was one of James IV's primary recreational activities.[146] Indeed, Paul states that 'the principal out-door sport [of James IV] was undoubtedly hawking'.[147] James IV even had his portrait painted holding a falcon, used in the sport of hawking (Figure 3.2). It is clear that James IV travelled regularly between his palaces in Scotland and he is reported to have had five falconers who accompanied him, not just on hawking expeditions but on almost all of his journeys.[148] There are also records in the accounts of James IV purchasing numerous items relating to the sport of hawking and of him paying considerable amounts of money for prized hawks.[149] Indeed, there are several hundred entries in the king's accounts relating to hawking and falconry, in contrast to just four references to golf. This could be seen as indicating that the king may have had a more regular need for hawk clubs than golf clubs. At the very least there must be some uncertainty about whether the 'clubbes' James IV bought in 1502 were golf clubs.

Figure 3.2 Portrait of King James IV of Scotland with a falcon. There is extensive evidence that King James IV of Scotland participated frequently in the sport of hawking and falconry. It has been suggested that references in the king's accounts to unidentified types of 'clubbes' may be clubs used for the sport of hawking, rather than golf clubs. © National Galleries Scotland, UP J 58.

Claims concerning Early Golf in Perth

There are several purchases of unspecified 'clubbes' recorded in the king's accounts. However, the reason why the purchase of clubs from a Perth bow-maker in 1502 has been so widely assumed to be a reference to golf clubs is probably due to a comment that was made by Peter Baxter in *Golf in Perth and Perthshire* (1899). After providing the relevant extract from the king's accounts, Baxter commented, 'From the above it may be inferred that the "bowar of Sanct Johnestoun" was a maker of bows and arrows and golf clubs.'[150] Baxter continued by speculating that 'judging from the sum of money named, four clubs would have been forwarded – perhaps a driver, a spoon, a putter, and a track cleque'.[151] When Robert Browning picked up on this story some fifty years later, he wrote, in *A History of Golf* (1955), that 'James IV began playing golf at Perth [in 1502]'.[152] It is important to note that, even if the 'clubbes' that the king bought from the Perth bow-maker *were* golf clubs, the accounts do not reveal whether this purchase actually took place in Perth (the bow-maker may have travelled to the king, rather than the king travelling to the bow-maker). This is important because it is frequently assumed that James IV used these 'clubbes' to play golf in Perth at the time of the purchase. Indeed, this has been the basis for suggestions that Perth is the earliest identifiable site where golf was played. For example, it has been claimed that 'when James IV began playing golf in Perth [. . .] it was to the local bow-maker that he sent for clubs and balls'.[153] Similarly, it has been suggested that 'the first golf player known by name, King James IV, did not hit his first golf ball on a links but on parkland, the North Inch of Perth'.[154] Such claims require three separate assumptions: that the 'clubbes' the king bought were golf clubs; that the purchase took place in Perth; and that, after purchasing golf clubs, the king used them to play golf in Perth. While no other purchases were recorded in the king's accounts on the precise day that he bought the 'clubbes' in 1502 that would help to identify the king's location, an entry on the following day suggests that the king was at Falkland Palace in Fife, one of his principal residences. On that day, the king is recorded as having made a payment 'in Faulkland' to 'Quhissilgibboun' (Whistlegibbon), who was one of the king's entertainers.[155] Consequently, there is no clear evidence that the king was in Perth on 21 September 1502 when the purchase of 'clubbes' was made.[156]

It is not unreasonable for golf historians to point out that James IV's purchases of 'clubbes' might have been golf clubs and that the king might have used them to play golf in Perth. However, a note of caution would seem to be appropriate. It is understandable that golf writers may wish to believe the 'clubbes' to be golf clubs; indeed, it is frequently stated that what James IV purchased from a bow-maker in Perth were 'golf clubs'[157] (or, adopting archaic language, 'golf clubbes'[158] or 'gowf clubbes'[159]). A development of this theme has been a claim that what the king purchased in 1502 were 'clubs and balls'[160] (or 'golf clubbis and ballis'[161]). It is now very common to see the purchase of 'clubbes' from the Perth bow-maker as being 'the first recorded purchase of golf equipment'[162] and it is likely that such statements will continue to feature, as they have, in 'Timelines of Golf History',[163] despite there being no clear evidence that they were golf clubs.

The Earliest recorded Golf Match

That James IV played a golf match with the Earl of Bothwell on 3 February 1503/4 is recorded in the handwritten accounts of the Lord High Treasurer of Scotland (Figure 3.3).[164] The accounts record the event as follows:

> Item, the third day of Februar, to the King to play at the golf with the Erle of Bothuile, iij Franch crounis; summa . . . xlij s
>
> [Item, the third day of February, to the King to play golf with the Earl of Bothwell, 3 French crowns; total . . . forty-two shillings]

The reason why a golf match involving King James IV was mentioned in the Treasurer's accounts is presumably because the king had lost a wager on the match, thereby necessitating a payment to the Earl of Bothwell (Patrick Hepburn). That the payment was in French crowns is not particularly unusual. Several foreign gold coins were in circulation in Scotland at this time, of which the French crown (equivalent to fourteen Scottish shillings) was the most common.[165] In addition, the king's accounts record that three days later (on 6 March 1503/4) he paid nine shillings for 'golf clubbes and balles'.[166]

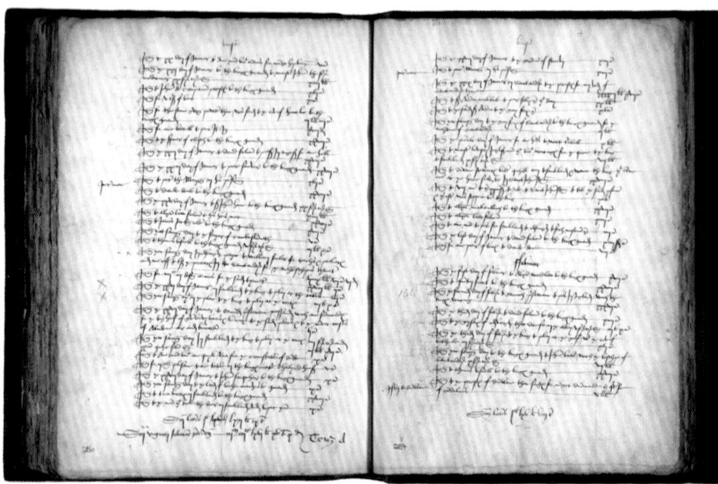

Figure 3.3 Accounts of the Lord High Treasurer of Scotland (1503/4). An entry from February 1503/4 provides the earliest evidence of a golf match played by identified individuals (King James IV and the Earl of Bothwell). © National Records of Scotland, E21/6, 286–7.

The entry in the king's accounts concerning the golf match is the earliest written record of golf being played by named individuals and, consequently, it has attracted a considerable amount of interest from golf historians. However, there is a lack of consensus about where this golf match took place. For example, it has been suggested that James IV's golf match with the Earl of Bothwell took place at Edinburgh,[167] Falkland,[168] Gosford,[169] Musselburgh,[170] Perth,[171] St Andrews[172] and Stirling.[173] In addition, it has been claimed that James IV played golf at Bruntsfield Links,[174] Holyroodhouse,[175] Leith[176] and Scone Palace.[177] On the basis of the surviving documentary evidence, it is hard to say with certainty where the golf match took place. However, as has been discussed in more detail elsewhere,[178] there are reasons for thinking that the golf match took place in St Andrews (Figure 3.4). For example, it has been established that the king was in St Andrews on 29 January 1503/4, just five days prior to the golf match (which took place on 3 February). The reason for the king's visit to St Andrews was to attend the funeral of his younger brother, James Stewart the Archbishop of St Andrews. The Treasurer's accounts provide extensive details of the king's travel arrangements prior to the funeral as well as the lavish preparations for the funeral in St Andrews.[179] In addition, on the day of the funeral the Treasurer's accounts reveal a substantial payment (£92 18 s) 'in Sanctandrois to the preistis, for my Lord of Sanctandrois tyrment [burial]'.[180] The king also made a payment of £3 on the same day to 'the Gray Freris [Greyfriars] of Sanctandrois'.[181]

The King's Purchase of 'golf clubbes and balles' in 1503/4

On 6 February 1503/4, just three days after the king's golf match with the Earl of Bothwell, he paid nine shillings for 'golf clubbes and balles',[182] as is confirmed in the original handwritten accounts.[183] Incidentally, one of the first golf historians to identify references to golf in the accounts of King James IV was Robert Clark (in 1875) but he states incorrectly that the two references to golf in 1503/4 both occurred on 3 February,[184] an assumption that has been repeated by several subsequent golf writers.[185] Given the scarcity of references to golf in the king's accounts, it seems likely that the king may have remained for several days at a golfing location (both where golf was played on 3 February and where clubs and balls were purchased on 6 February 1503/4). Of course,

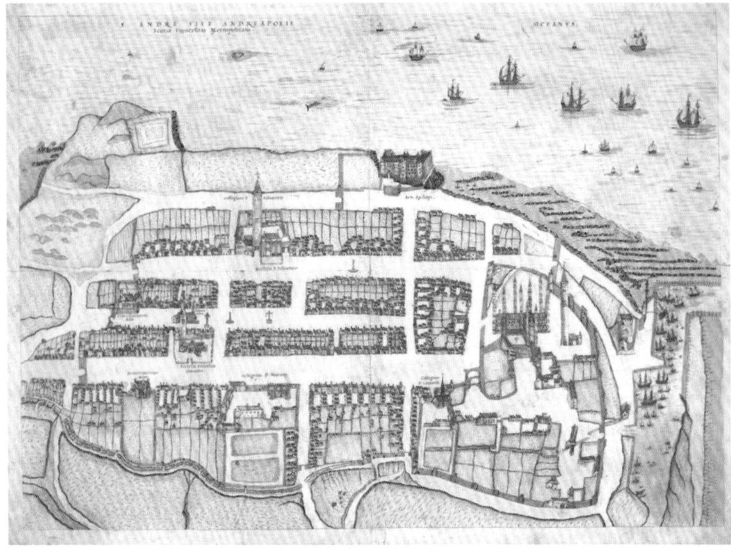

Figure 3.4 Plan of St Andrews (c. 1580). Showing the location of the golf links (top left) and the cathedral (centre right) where King James IV's brother the Archbishop of St Andrews was buried in 1503/4. Reproduced with the permission of the National Library of Scotland, MS.20996.

if both events occurred at St Andrews, it would also be possible that the king travelled back-and-forth between St Andrews and his palace at Falkland twenty miles away. However, it may be significant that the king's accounts indicate that he paid for lodgings on 6 February (the same day that he purchased 'golf clubbes and balles'). It was a payment of six French crowns to George Robison and is recorded as 'mail' [rent] when 'the King occupiit in his innys'.[186] Unfortunately, the location of the Inn is not mentioned. It has been argued that the king may have returned to Edinburgh after the funeral (and prior to the golf match), which has led to suggestions that the match took place in Edinburgh but the evidence supporting this conclusion is somewhat ambiguous.[187]

The King's Purchase of 'golf balles' and golf clubbes' in 1506

The final two entries in the accounts of James IV that mention 'golf' are purchases of twelve 'golf ballis' for four shillings on 29

March 1506 and two 'golf clubbes' for two shillings on 22 July 1506 (Figure 3.5).[188] The first golf historian to draw attention to these two entries in the king's accounts was probably Robert Clark in *Golf: a Royal and Ancient Game* (1875) but unfortunately the dates he provided were incorrect (22 February rather than 29 March and 18 July rather than 22 July)[189] and, once again, this is an error that has been repeated frequently by others.[190]

The consensus view appears to be that the clubs were bought in St Andrews,[191] whereas the balls may have been bought in Stirling.[192] Again, it is difficult to be certain as to the location but other entries in the Treasurer's accounts at the time of the two purchases provide some support for these conclusions.[193] It has also been argued that both purchases may have occurred in St Andrews (the balls as well as the clubs) and there is certainly evidence that the king was in St Andrews earlier in the month before he purchased the golf balls on 29 March 1506.[194] However, as is the case for the

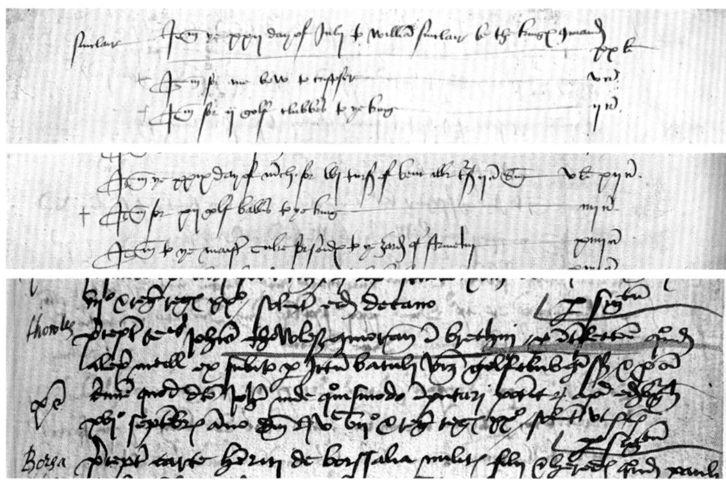

Figure 3.5 Three early written references to golf (1506 and 1507). Entries in the Treasury Accounts of King James IV record expenditure of four shillings for 'xii [twelve] golf ballis to ye king' (22 February 1506; top) and of two shillings for 'ii [two] golf clubbes to ye king' (22 July 1506; middle). Also illustrated is an entry in Latin from the Privy Seal Register, recording an assault that took place in Brechin involving a '*baculi, viz.* golf club' (16 September 1507; bottom). Top image: © National Records of Scotland, E21/7, f.129v. Middle image: © National Records of Scotland, E21/7, f.141v. Bottom image: © National Records of Scotland, PS1/3, f.160r.

two entries in the king's accounts from 1503/4, it is unlikely that it will be possible to identify the location definitively. Nevertheless, the king's purchase of golf balls in 1506 has been widely interpreted as indicating that he played golf at Stirling in 1506. However, even if James IV did play golf in Stirling in 1506, there is certainly no evidence of who his opponent may have been. Nevertheless, it is often stated that he played a match in Stirling in 1506 against the Earl of Bothwell. This is presumably due to the purchase of golf balls in 1506 having been confused with evidence of the king playing a match against Bothwell in 1503/4.[195] For example, this is how the event was described in *The Scotsman* newspaper in 2006:

> It was on 29 March 1506 that King James IV bought a dozen golf balls and rode out from his palace at Stirling Castle to play a match against the Earl of Bothwell. History does not record the result, but we do know the game was played on the Kings Park, then a royal hunting ground and now the home of Stirling Golf Club.[196]

Others have claimed that there is 'documented proof' of a golf match having taken place in Stirling that involved James IV and the Earl of Bothwell.[197] Indeed, the Stirling Smith Art Gallery and Museum organised a public exhibition in 2006 entitled '500 Years of Golf in Stirling'. This coincided with a series of events, including a costumed re-enactment of what was described as 'the second recorded golf game played in Scotland',[198] a claim that has been repeated in various forms and on a number of occasions.[199] The modern-day Stirling Golf Club was founded in 1869[200] and a painting by John Smart depicts golf being played in the fields below Stirling Castle shortly after the club's formation (Figure 3.6). Unsurprisingly, the club has drawn attention in its publications to the possibility that Stirling may have a lengthy golfing heritage by stating that 'James IV played golf [at Stirling] as early as 1506'.[201]

'Slaughter by the stroke of a golf-club' in 1507

The final documented reference to golf in the first decade of the sixteenth century (this time not involving James IV) concerns an assault with a golf club that took place in 1507 at Brechin (about eight miles west of Montrose) and, as a consequence of this event, it is common to see Brechin identified as being one of the earliest sites

Figure 3.6 Golf at Stirling. A view of golf at Stirling (1890) by John Smart. It is frequently claimed that golf was played in Stirling by King James IV in 1506. Reproduced with kind permission of the Royal and Ancient Golf Club of St Andrews, RNA 14 130.

at which golf was played. The account first came to the attention of golf historians when it was mentioned in *Ancient Criminal Trials in Scotland* (1833). The original source was an entry, written in Latin, in the Register of the Privy Seal and this was translated in 1833 as 'the Slaughter of Alexander Meill [. . .] by the stroke of a golf club'.[202] The original Latin text of the Register of the Privy Seal was transcribed in 1908 and refers to a '*baculi*' [stick/club] followed by the explanatory comment '*viz.*, golf club' ('*Alexandri Meill ex subito per ictum baculi, viz.,* golf club *commissa*').[203] This raises the question of whether the original handwritten Latin document referred only to a '*baculi*' (an unspecified type of club), with '*viz.*, golf club' having been appended by the transcriber in 1908. However, consultation of the original handwritten Privy Seal document confirms that it does indeed contain the phrase '*viz.*, golf club' (Figure 3.5).[204]

Golf Clubs used as Weapons

It would appear that the use of a golf club as an offensive weapon was popular in Scotland. In addition to the previous example from 1507, there are reported instances at Stirling in 1560/1[205] and 1613,[206] at

Leith in 1616[207] and at Falkirk in 1639.[208] The incident at Stirling in 1560/1 appears to have been a drunken assault in which Thomas Eduein attacked Thomas Kirkwood 'and straik at hym with ane goiff club'.[209] The report goes on to mention that the club missed Thomas Kirkwood and, instead, injured another man's wife. Following this, Eduein drew a knife and somehow injured his own wife. The court instructed Eduein to request forgiveness and to find a sponsor to provide a bond for his good behaviour. Perhaps because the incident sounds like a rather thuggish brawl, it has been suggested that the weapon may have been a club that was used for what is thought to have been a rougher 'shinty-like game', rather than golf.[210] Some fifty years later there is further evidence of a golf club being used as an offensive weapon in Stirling but, on this occasion, it involved local dignitaries. On 25 January 1613 'Johnne Scherar', the Dean of Guild, is reported to have struck Provost 'Duncane Patersone' with 'ane golf club'.[211] There seems no reason to think that the weapon used by Dean of Guild Shearer was anything other than what we would now understand as being a golf club.

In Summary

Five references to golf have been identified that date from the first decade of the sixteenth century. In addition to an incident at Brechin in 1507, these include references to King James IV playing golf in 1503/4 and buying 'golf clubbes and balles' in 1503/4, together with his purchase of 'golf ballis' and 'golf clubbis' in 1506. However, the frequent claims of golf being played in Perth in 1502 require the assumption that the king's purchase of 'clubbes' is a reference to golf clubs, which is uncertain. Although numerous different locations have been suggested as the site at which the earliest recorded golf match took place in 1503/4, it occurred just a few days after the king's visit to St Andrews for the funeral of his brother the Archbishop of St Andrews and it seems plausible, although not certain, that this may have been where the golf match took place.

Chapter 4

Catherine of Aragon and a Persistent Golf Myth

It is often stated that the earliest reference to golf being played in England, as opposed to Scotland, is contained within a letter written in 1513 by Queen Catherine of Aragon, the first wife of Henry VIII (Figure 4.1). It is a story that has become almost ubiquitous in published golf histories but a reassessment of the original document indicates it to be entirely apocryphal.

Figure 4.1 Queen Catherine of Aragon. A frequently repeated myth is that Catherine of Aragon (1485–1536), the first wife of King Henry VIII, played golf in 1513. Royal Collection Trust/© Her Majesty Queen Elizabeth, RCIN 404746.

The Origin of the Myth

As far as I am aware, the first person to have suggested that Catherine of Aragon wrote about golf was Elizabeth Benger, who in 1821 published a two-volume history entitled *Memoirs of the Life of Anne Boleyn, Queen of Henry VIII* (Figure 4.2). In compiling her history, Benger consulted original copies of Catherine's letters held in the British Museum (now part of the British Library collection).[212] One of these was a letter that Catherine of Aragon wrote on 13 August 1513 to Thomas Wolsey, who later became Cardinal Wolsey. Benger transcribed a passage from this letter as 'I shall not so often hear from the King. And all his subjects be very glad, I thank God, to be busy with the goff, for they take it for pass-time.'[213] In a footnote, the author wrote, 'this passage evidently alludes to the popular game of goffe'.[214] The significance of her discovery was highlighted in a book review that was published in *The London Literary Gazette* in 1821.[215] The reviewer of Benger's book commented:

> the first quarter of the volume is delightfully occupied with original documents from the British Museum [. . .] A letter from Queen Catherine to Wolsey of 13th August, 1513 (the period

Figure 4.2 Elizabeth Benger and the origin of a golf myth. Elizabeth Benger (c. 1775–1827) wrote in 1821 that Catherine of Aragon had mentioned golf in a letter written to Thomas Wolsey in 1513. It is a claim that has been repeated frequently and has been used to claim that golf was played in England (as opposed to Scotland) almost a hundred years earlier than might otherwise be assumed. However, a reassessment of the original letter reveals that Benger's transcription of the letter was incorrect.

> when Henry invaded France), is worthy of selection, were it only for its allusion to the game of Golf.

It seems likely that Elizabeth Benger's reference to golf caught the attention of golfers at the recently formed Manchester Golf Club. A transcription of Catherine of Aragon's letter, containing the reference to golf, appeared in a booklet entitled *Manchester Golf Club* (published c. 1821).[216] The text of Catherine's letter was also reproduced by John Kerr in *The Golf-Book of East Lothian* (1896)[217] and by Amy Pascoe in *World of Golf* (1898).[218] John Kerr gave his source as 'the old Manchester Club', whereas Amy Pascoe cited Kerr's book as her source. The story gained further prominence when it appeared in Hilton and Smith's influential *The Royal and Ancient Game of Golf* (1912).[219]

The story of Catherine of Aragon's letter became more widely disseminated in the 1950s, when it appeared in several popular golf history books. One of these, *A History of Golf in Britain* (1952), contained a chapter by Sir Guy Campbell entitled *The Early History of British Golf.*[220] Campbell's version of the text differs somewhat from earlier transcriptions, so it is possible that he may have rechecked the original source, Catherine's handwritten letter. His transcription of the letter begins 'Master Almoner', which is how Catherine of Aragon addressed Wolsey.

> Master Almoner from hence I have nothing to write you but that you be not so busy in this war as we be encumbered with it, I mean as touching my own concerns for going further when I shall not so often hear from the King. And all his subjects be very glad I thank God to be busy with the Golfe for they take it for a pastime; my heart is very good to it and I am horribly busy making standards, banners and baggets.

The story reappeared in Bernard Darwin's *Golf* (1954)[221] and also in Robert Browning's *A History of Golf* (1955).[222] Browning writes of Catherine's 'preference' for golf, rather than for games such as tennis, which may have been partly responsible for subsequent claims, made by other authors, that Catherine of Aragon was the first woman known to have played golf (see later). The story of Catherine of Aragon's letter, and of golf being played in England in 1513, has now become an established part of the game's history and, as will be discussed later, it has been repeated on numerous occasions in golf literature. Unfortunately, the story is incorrect.

The Alternative Interpretation

In 1513, Henry VIII was at war in France. In the king's absence, Catherine, the Queen Consort, had been appointed as Queen Regent and she kept in contact with Henry through letters written to Thomas Wolsey. With Henry away in France, it was the threat of war with the Scots that prompted Catherine to write to Wolsey on 13 August 1513. Catherine's letter was written just a month before the Battle of Flodden, at which James IV was killed in a decisive victory for the English. One of the earliest and more authoritative sources of information concerning Catherine of Aragon's letters is *Original Letters Illustrative of English History*, compiled in 1824 by Henry Ellis, Keeper of the Manuscripts in the British Museum.[223] Ellis was an expert at deciphering hand-written documents from this period, including letters written by Catherine of Aragon. His transcription of Catherine's letter makes it clear that she is referring to the 'Scots', rather than to golf. Retaining Catherine's original spelling, he transcribes the relevant passage as follows:

> I thanke God, to bee besy with the Scotts, for thay take it for passe tyme. My hert is veray good to it, and I am horrible besy w^{t} making standerds, banners, and bagies.

Ellis' transcription was rendered in more modern English in *The Modern History of England*, which was published a few years later (in 1826):

> all his subjects be very glad to be busy with the Scots; for they take it for pastime. My heart is very good to it; and I am horrible busy with making standards, banners, and badges.[224]

Similarly, *Lives of the Queens of England*, which was published in 1842, also provides a modern transcription of the text, although in this case retaining Ellis' original spelling of 'Scotts'.[225] Catherine's comment about 'standards, banners and badges' certainly makes more sense if these are seen as being items required in preparation for a battle. It is much harder to explain why 'standards, banners and badges' might be required for golf, an issue that some golf historians have commented on previously.[226]

The definitive collection of transcribed documents from the reign of Henry VIII is a twenty-one-volume series published between 1862 and 1932. This series contains edited versions of the original sixteenth-century texts and provides transcriptions in which the language has been modernised. In Volume I (published in 1862),[227] and also in an enlarged and corrected edition (published in 1920),[228] Catherine's letter is transcribed as 'busy with the Scots'. Although this alternative interpretation of Catherine's letter may be unfamiliar to many golf historians, it appears to be almost universally accepted by biographers of Catherine of Aragon and by historians of Henry VIII's reign, as is illustrated by the large number of books that have been published on this topic over a period of many years.[229]

Having examined the original handwritten letter that is held in the British Library (Figure 4.3), it seems certain that Catherine makes reference to 'the Scotts', rather than to 'the Golfe' (or any other spelling of golf). Although Catherine's upper-case 'S' might be misinterpreted as a 'G', an examination of how she typically wrote these two letters would appear to leave no doubt about her intended meaning. I suspect that the reason why the word 'Scotts' was misinterpreted as 'Golfe' (or 'goff' or 'golf') may, in part, be due to its proximity in Catherine's letter to the word 'pastime', which may simply indicate that Catherine was enjoying her role of Queen Regent and was referring to what she considered to be the entertaining 'pastime' of preparing for a war with the Scots.

The Myth Perpetuated

Many examples could be cited to illustrate the extent to which the myth of Catherine of Aragon's reference to golf has become entrenched in mainstream golf history. Instances range from internet websites[230] to a Vice-Chancellor's speech delivered during a university degree ceremony.[231] In fact, a glance through recently published golf histories indicates that the story of Catherine of Aragon's apparent reference to golf has become extremely widespread, having been mentioned in dozens of golf books in recent years.[232] It appears that, at times, golf historians have struggled to explain this apparent evidence for golf having been played in England at such

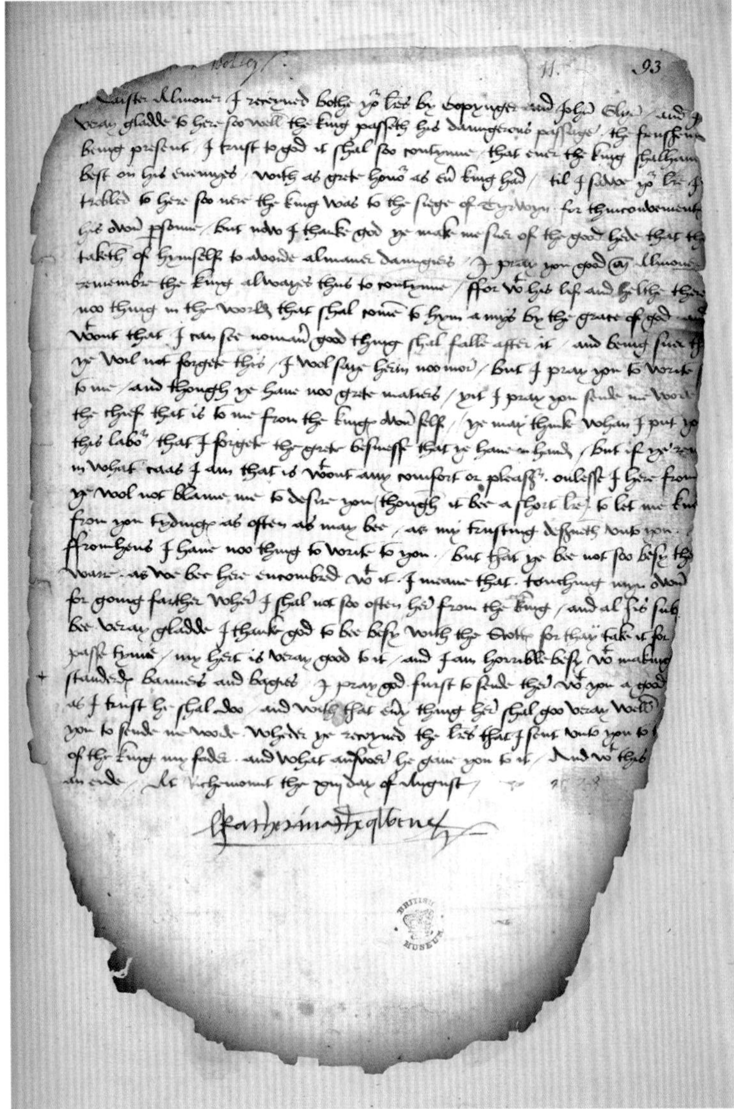

Figure 4.3 A letter sent by Catherine of Aragon to Thomas Wolsey (1513). This letter, written on 13 August 1513, has been frequently misinterpreted as providing evidence that golf was being played in England in 1513. © British Library, Cotton Caligula D VI, f.93.

an early date. Rather than examining the reliability of the evidence, some have speculated about possible explanations. For example, it has been suggested that 'English court officials became acquainted with the game during marriage negotiations [between James IV and the daughter of the English Henry VII]'.[233] Similarly, it has been suggested that this royal marriage 'brought the Scottish king's favourite sport into temporary fashion in England'.[234] Other writers have appeared more concerned that it was a woman playing golf in 1513. One such writer suggested in 1939 that this erroneous assumption was due to the claim 'being based on a curious misreading of the letter'. The writer goes on to explain that 'it perhaps needs a little care in reading [Catherine's letter to Wolsey] to make out that it was the [King's] subjects and not the Queen who were playing golf'.[235]

As will be discussed in Chapter 17, there has been a long-standing debate about the origins and antiquity of golf in Scotland and, in particular, whether it might have ancestral links to stick-and-ball games such as *colf* and *kolf* that were popular in the Low Countries. It is interesting to note that some of the arguments that have been put forward as part of this debate about the origins of the game have been based on the erroneous assumption that Catherine of Aragon's letter concerns a reference to golf. For example, one golf historian, writing in *Golf & Kolf* (1993), has suggested that the wording of Catherine's letter 'might confirm the fact that the success of golf in Scotland was a rather recent phenomenon',[236] while another author has written that Catherine of Aragon's letter 'certainly suggests that the vogue of the game was new'.[237] It has also been argued that the letter demonstrates 'the growing popularity of golf in England'.[238] In contrast, another writer has tried to explain the apparently isolated evidence of golf in England at such an early date by concluding, 'The English, however, appear to have gone off the game quickly, for no more is heard of it in England till after 1603, when James VI reintroduced it on inheriting the English throne.'[239]

Myths have a tendency to take on a life of their own and so it was perhaps inevitable that, over the years, the story would begin to be embellished. Catherine of Aragon has been described as golf's 'earliest recorded female advocate',[240] as 'one of the first female golfers'[241] and, even more emphatically, as 'the first known woman golfer'.[242] It has been suggested that 'aristocratic women likely dabbled in the sport, taking their cue from Catherine of

Aragon'.[243] It has also been claimed that, whereas 'Henry VIII played tennis', his wife Catherine 'preferred golf'.[244] Another author has commented that Catherine 'amused herself with golf while her husband was away on state business'[245] or that, while Henry was away, Catherine was 'finding comfort in golf'.[246] Additionally, in a recently published book, it was claimed that 'Henry VIII used to play golf with Catherine of Aragon'.[247] There has even been speculation that the site at which Catherine of Aragon played golf might have been Molesey Hurst, near Hampton Court.[248] What is abundantly clear is that an inadvertent error, made when transcribing a historical document in 1821, is still causing considerable confusion two hundred years later.

In Summary

Since Catherine of Aragon was not referring to golf in her letter of 13 August 1513, our assumptions about the spread of golf from Scotland to England must be reassessed. If we can no longer assume that golf was being played in England in the early 1500s, it would seem that the earliest evidence of golf being played 'south of the Tweed' occurred some one hundred years later, after the unification of the crowns of Scotland and England in 1603. It was in 1603 that King James VI of Scotland (now also James I of England) moved his court from Edinburgh to London. The appearance of golf in England in the seventeenth century is discussed in subsequent chapters but it seems clear that there is no reason to think that Catherine of Aragon ever played golf (or even wrote about it), so perhaps it is time to rewrite this aspect of golf history.

Chapter 5

King James V and the Gosford Golf Myth

King James V of Scotland

As is discussed elsewhere (Chapters 3 and 7), there is evidence that golf was played by at least two Scottish kings who reigned during the sixteenth century (James IV and James VI). Consequently, it may seem unimportant to question whether evidence exists to indicate that golf was played by the intervening Scottish king, James V (Figure 5.1). Nevertheless, because it is a claim that has been made on numerous occasions, it may be useful to examine the historical evidence.

Figure 5.1 King James V of Scotland. It is often claimed that James V (r.1513–42) played golf at Gosford in East Lothian but there is no evidence to support such a claim. Royal Collection Trust/© Her Majesty Queen Elizabeth, RCIN 402712.

A common theme in accounts describing James V playing golf is that he did so at Gosford in East Lothian. To paraphrase several published histories of golf (discussed later), the story is often presented along the following lines: *that James V played golf at Gosford, where he established his own private golf course and where he insisted that wooden-headed clubs were to be used, thereby avoiding damage to the turf.* It might be expected that this level of detail would be based on evidence derived from contemporary documents but it seems more likely that this story has a relatively recent origin and that it has been embellished in subsequent years.

The Origin of a Golf Myth

The origin of this story appears to be an article that was written in the late eighteenth century, some two hundred and fifty years after the death of James V. The story was published in 1792, in an article written by Reverend Dr Neil Roy entitled *Topographical Description of the Parish of Aberlady.*[249] Perhaps in an attempt to give some colour to his 'topographical description', the author describes frequent journeys that were made by James V to Gosford to visit 'three favourite ladies'. In doing so Roy states that

> King James V. is said to have been fond of Gosford, and that it was suspected by his contemporaries, that, in his frequent excursions to that part of the country, he had other purposes in view besides golfing and archery.

Rather than providing evidence that James V played golf, it seems that the author is simply indicating the sort of activities that a visitor to East Lothian might have been expected to participate in. Perhaps it is more a reflection of the fact that the author's readers in the late eighteenth century would have associated East Lothian with activities such as golf and archery. The story was repeated in several publications during the nineteenth century[250] but was given greater authority and prominence when it appeared in John Kerr's *The Golf-Book of East Lothian* (1896). John Kerr stated that 'there does not seem to be any doubt' that James V played golf at Gosford.[251] In the same year the *Pall Mall Gazette* published a review of Kerr's book and in doing so commented that 'King James V frequented Gosford with his golf-clubs under his arm'.[252]

The story reappears in *The Royal & Ancient Game of Golf* (1912)[253] and also in more recent golf histories. Indeed, variations of the story of James V playing golf at Gosford can be found in golf histories that have been published in every decade since the 1950s but in no case is a contemporary source cited. Sir Guy Campbell retold the story in *A History of Golf in Britain* (1952)[254] and, in doing so, added a fairly innocuous comment concerning the Earl of Wemyss that was factually correct but which describes events that occurred in the nineteenth century and, as such, appears to have been a source of considerable confusion to subsequent golf writers. It states:

> James V is recorded as having played at Gosford in East Lothian, where later the famous Earl of Wemyss had a private links on which he would allow only wooden clubs to be used.

The 'famous Earl of Wemyss' is a reference to Francis Richard Charteris, who was Lord Elcho from 1853 to 1883 and the 10th Earl of Wemyss from 1883 to 1914. In *The Golf-Book of East Lothian* (1896), John Kerr mentioned correctly that the Earl had built a private nine-hole course near Craigielaw, on his Gosford Estate.[255] The Earl of Wemyss is known to have spoken out against damage to golf courses that could be caused by iron golf clubs; indeed, he is reported to have invented a new type of golf club (c. 1895) that he argued would not damage the turf (Figure 5.2).[256] Rather whimsically, he called the club the 'Unionist', for reasons that were explained by Kerr in *The Golf-Book of East Lothian*.[257] He describes how the club that had been invented by the Earl of Wemyss was

> a club which resembles the old baffy, but has a brass sole, and which is used for approaching. It is called 'the Unionist,' because it does not 'wear the green,' the earl being very severe in his denunciations of Mr. Horace Hutchinson for actually recommending that in playing certain shots the turf should be cut by the club.

The reason that the club was called the 'Unionist' is an 'in-joke'. In addition to the club having been designed to not damage the turf, it needs to be recalled that this was a time when Irish nationalism was on the rise and when the second Irish Home Rule Bill had recently been defeated by unionist politicians at Westminster.

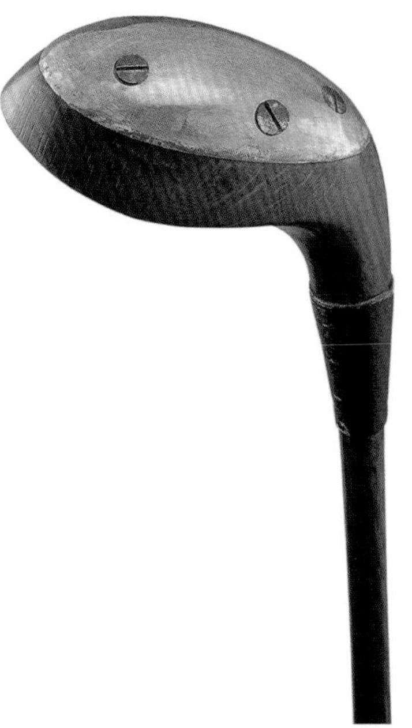

Figure 5.2 The Earl of Wemyss and the Unionist golf club. The Unionist golf club (c. 1895), so called because it 'doesn't wear the green', is believed to have been designed by Francis Charteris, 10th Earl of Wemyss (1818–1914; 'Lord Elcho' 1853–83). It has been suggested erroneously that this is a golf club that was favoured by King James V (r.1513–42). The image of Wemyss appeared in *Vanity Fair* (23 July 1870). For further details of the Unionist club, see Ellis (2007), 312. Image © Jeffery B. Ellis.

No self-respecting unionist would 'wear the green', the colour that is symbolic of Ireland.

The Gosford Story Evolves

Sir Guy Campbell's description in 1952 of the Earl of Wemyss objecting to the use of iron clubs on his private course at Gosford appears to have been misunderstood by a number of golf writers. For example, in 1966 the story of James V playing golf at Gosford was retold but it was claimed that it was James V himself who had established a private golf course at Gosford and who had favoured the use of wooden golf clubs.[258] The story presented in 1966 was that, while at Gosford:

> he [James V] set up a private links and spent many pleasant hours competing with his favorite golf companion the Earl of Wemyss. James V was so particular with his private course that he permitted only wooden-headed clubs to be used.

The story of James V establishing a private golf course at Gosford has been restated frequently and has gained momentum in several recent golf histories.[259] For example, it has been claimed that James V was concerned that iron-headed clubs 'would tear up the grass' of his private course at Gosford,[260] while another author has concluded that 'James V played many times at Gosford, in East Lothian, on a course privately owned by the Earl of Wemyss'.[261]

An Erroneous Link to Robert Burns

Somewhat unexpectedly, the story of James V playing golf at Gosford appears in several anthologies of the Scottish poet Robert Burns. The first appearance of the story in a Burns anthology was in 1808 and it was not until a hundred years later (in 1908) that it was identified as an error. *The Scots Musical Museum* is a collection of Scottish songs that was published in four volumes between 1787 and 1792. Shortly after its publication, Robert Burns made extensive annotations to several of the songs in handwritten comments on interleaved pages. For example, alongside *Highlander's Lament* Burns wrote, 'the chorus I pickt up from an old woman in Dunblane; the rest of the song is mine'. The annotated copy of *The Scots Musical Museum* is commonly referred to as the 'interleaved copy' and has been studied extensively by Burns scholars. In addition to the annotations made by Burns, the interleaved copy also contains additional handwritten comments by Robert Riddle, a friend and benefactor of Burns. Among the songs included in *The Scots Musical Museum* was *The Gaberlunzie-man*, an early ballad that has been attributed to James V.[262] The song is thought to describe the king's affections for a country girl and it seems that Robert Riddle identified a link between the song and the Gosford story that had recently been published by Neil Roy (in 1792). In an annotation to *The Gaberlunzie-man*, Riddle wrote that the song 'is supposed to commemorate an intrigue of James the

Vth'. Riddle then continued by appending part of Neil Roy's story concerning the king visiting Gosford for purposes other than 'golfing and archery'. Some years later, the Burns scholar Robert Cromek came across the interleaved copy of *The Scots Musical Museum* and mistakenly concluded that all of the hand-written annotations were the original writings of Robert Burns. As a consequence, Cromek included all of these annotations in *Reliques of Robert Burns*, an anthology published in 1808.[263] The passage concerning 'golfing and archery' was subsequently reprinted in anthologies compiled by other Burns scholars, for example in 1836, 1842 and 1844.[264] It was not until 1908 that James Dick re-examined the interleaved copy of *The Scots Musical Museum* and concluded that the annotations relating to *The Gaberlunzie-man* were in the hand of Robert Riddle, rather than having been written by Burns himself.[265]

The Gosford Story Retold

It seems that the earliest suggestion that James V might have been a golfer is the rather tentative comment concerning Gosford that was made by Neil Roy in 1792, some two hundred and fifty years after the king's death. Nevertheless, this has not prevented the story becoming widespread. For example, there are references to James V being 'very partial to the game',[266] 'a keen exponent of the game',[267] 'a regular on the links'[268] and being 'avidly devoted to the game'.[269] It is said that James V 'turned to the game of golf as a relaxation',[270] that he 'was taught golf from an early age at the insistence of his father'[271] and that he 'shared his father's enthusiasm' for golf.[272] It has been argued that golf in Scotland 'prospered at a greater rate than ever before, with the encouragement of James V'.[273] It has even been claimed that there is 'documented evidence' that James V played golf at Gosford, although no evidence was cited by the author.[274]

Early Golf at Barry Links

When discussing events in the reign of King James V, golf historians frequently refer to evidence that in 1527 golf was played at Barry Links on the east coast of Scotland, the approximate location of the current Open Championship course of Carnoustie. A reassessment of the evidence suggests that, although it is reasonable to conclude that golf was played at Barry Links in the sixteenth century, the frequently repeated date of 1527 is unreliable. The evidence of early golf at Barry was described in *Registrum de Panmure* (1874)[275] and was based on material that was originally compiled by The Honourable Harry Maule of Kelly in 1733. Maule, in turn, quotes a manuscript containing a history of the family of Panmure that was written in 1611 and which is preserved in the National Records of Scotland.[276] The relevant passage, describing golf being played by Robert Maule, is: 'he exerciset the gowf, and oftymes past to Barry lynkes, quhan the wadfie vos for drink' (he exercised at golf and oftentimes past to Barry Links, when the wager was for drink).[277]

This incident has been mentioned by golf historians such as John Kerr in *The Golf-Book of East Lothian* (1896)[278] but it seems likely that the date of 1527 was first attributed to this account of golf at Barry Links by Robert Browning in *A History of Golf* (1955).[279] Browning mentions that, 'apart from King James IV and the Earl of Bothwell, the first golfer we hear of by name is Sir Robert Maule'. This is a reasonable conclusion but Browning then continues with an unrelated quotation from *Registrum de Panmure*: 'This was the yeer of God 1527, or there abouts'. However, the relevant passages in the original handwritten document (dating from 1611) reveal that the statement concerning 'the year of God 1527' concerns an unrelated incident described several pages earlier in the manuscript. The events recounted in the document do not appear to be strictly chronological but the reference to golf is in much closer proximity in the manuscript to a description of events that occurred in the 1540s and is at a location in the text that is only shortly before the report of Robert Maule's death in 1560. So, if one were inclined to pick a date, somewhere in the 1540s might be a more logical choice than Browning's suggestion of 1527, but the safest conclusion might be that the account of golf at Barry Links took place no later than 1560.

It was perhaps inevitable that the questionable date of 1527 would be repeated after it was mentioned by Robert Browning and, indeed, this has happened in several golf histories[280] and also in 'chronologies' of golf.[281] In addition, given the proximity of Barry Links to the modern-day Open Championship course of

Carnoustie, it is not surprising that 1527 has been suggested as being the first recorded reference to Carnoustie.[282] One particularly imaginative account of Robert Maule playing golf at Barry Links has been described as follows:

> In 1527, Robert Maule played with the simplest of golf equipment. He probably only carried one club, a wooden stick that was handmade by either himself or a friend. The farthest he could hit the stone or the small wooden ball he played with was perhaps 70 or 80 yards. [. . .] Few, if any, golf rules existed in 1527, so Robert Maule and his golfing friends were free to make up their own.[283]

In Summary

There is certainly no historical basis to the claim, first made in 1966, that James V established a golf course at Gosford where he only played with wooden clubs. This is simply a misunderstanding by later authors of a comment concerning the Earl of Wemyss that was published in 1952. In addition, there appears to be no contemporary evidence to support the earlier claim, probably originating in 1792, that James V played golf at Gosford. It is of course quite possible that James V *did* play golf, particularly since there is evidence that both the preceding and the subsequent Scottish kings did so. In addition, while there is credible evidence that golf was played by Robert Maule at Barry Links during or shortly after the reign of James V, the frequently repeated date of 1527 appears to be unreliable.

Chapter 6

Mary Queen of Scots and the Romanticisation of Golf History

Mary Queen of Scots (Figure 6.1) has been the subject of considerable popular interest and historical study. In part, this is a consequence of her proximity to events such as the union of the Scottish and English crowns and the reformation of the church in these two countries. In addition, many have been fascinated by the struggle between Mary and her cousin, the English queen, Elizabeth I; it was their strained relationship that led to Mary's execution in England on 8 February 1586/7. However, one event during Mary's reign has attracted particular attention, the murder in February 1566/7 of Mary's second husband, Lord Darnley. It is the events surrounding Darnley's murder that brought Mary to the attention of golf historians.

Mary Queen of Scots has acquired a prominent place in the history of golf, with numerous claims having been made concerning her importance to the game. In this chapter, these claims are summarised and the evidence supporting them is examined. The main conclusion is that, despite the surprisingly diverse nature of the claims linking Mary to the game of golf, almost all of these lack any credible evidence. In fact, all of the claims appear to derive from a single source – a handwritten manuscript that is of rather doubtful reliability. As will be discussed in more detail, it is a document that was prepared by Mary's enemies with the aim of demonstrating her complicity in the murder of Lord Darnley. In this manuscript, Mary is accused of playing 'palmall and goif' at Seton Palace (about twelve miles from Edinburgh) shortly after Darnley's murder and at a time when she might have been expected to be mourning the death of her husband.

As far as I am aware, this is the only contemporary reference so far identified linking Mary Queen of Scots to the game of golf. However, despite this, numerous claims have been made concerning her supposed enthusiasm and aptitude for the game. She has been described as being an 'avid golfer',[284] a 'talented

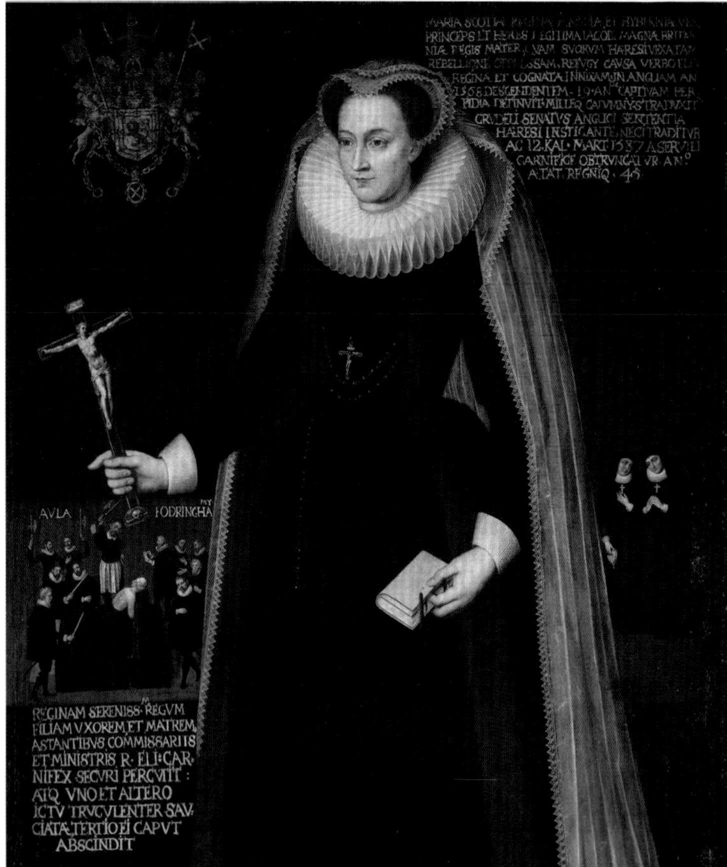

Figure 6.1 Mary Queen of Scots. A portrait of Mary Queen of Scots (b.1542–d.1587) in mourning dress, with a scene of her execution on the left. There have been numerous unsubstantiated claims linking Mary Queen of Scots to the game of golf but only a single relevant contemporary source, a document written with the intention to discredit her and, therefore, of questionable reliability. Royal Collection Trust/© Her Majesty Queen Elizabeth, RCIN 404408.

golfer'[285] and even a 'golf fanatic' who had a 'golfing obsession'.[286] She has been described as being 'devoted' to golf,[287] 'addicted to the game',[288] 'a keen exponent of the game'[289] and as being 'tall and tough and capable of enjoying golf in all weathers'.[290] It has been reported that Mary was 'famously enthusiastic about playing golf',[291] 'the first woman to have played golf regularly',[292] and one of the 'early female pioneering golfers'.[293] One account claims that she played golf 'very often and quite well'.[294]

It has been claimed that Mary played golf 'at many places in the east of Scotland'.[295] Locations where she is said to have played include Archerfield (East Lothian),[296] Bruntsfield Links,[297] Burntisland,[298] Craigmillar Castle (North Berwick),[299] Dunbar,[300] Edinburgh,[301] Falkirk,[302] Falkland Palace,[303] the Firth of Forth,[304] Holyrood Palace,[305] Leith,[306] Leven Links,[307] Musselburgh,[308] Perth (North Inch),[309] Perth (South Inch),[310] St Andrews,[311] Scoonie Links,[312] Seton Palace,[313] Tantallon Castle[314] and Wemyss Castle.[315] It seems that there are few places that Mary visited in Scotland that have not been proposed as sites at which she played golf, and this is a surprisingly long list of golfing locations, given that Mary's potential opportunities to play golf in Scotland were limited. Other than the first five years of her life, Mary lived in Scotland for only seven years (from 1561 to 1568). This was the brief period between her return from France and her exile in England.

The Murder of Lord Darnley

On the night of 9 February 1566/7, Mary's second husband, Lord Darnley, was murdered at Kirk o' Field in Edinburgh. It was widely believed that Mary was complicit in the plans to murder her husband and almost immediately after his death Mary's enemies in both Scotland and England set about gathering evidence that might prove her guilt. Mary's guilt or innocence is a topic that has been debated extensively but one issue that appears to be accepted by all historians is that much of the evidence presented at her trials was unreliable.

The Hopetoun Manuscript and the Book of Articles

There are a number of important documents that purport to describe events surrounding Darnley's murder. In addition to books such as *Ane Detection of the duings of Marie Quene of Scottes* (1571) that describe the case against Mary, several handwritten documents survive from this period. In terms of golf history, the document of greatest importance is the Hopetoun manuscript (Figure 6.2).[316] This manuscript is considered to be a draft of the *Book of Articles* that was presented in 1568 at Mary's trial in

Figure 6.2 George Buchanan and the Hopetoun manuscript. George Buchanan (1506–82) was closely involved in preparing the legal case against Mary Queen of Scots that led to her trial and execution in England. Buchanan is belived to have been one of the authors of the Hopetoun manuscript, thought to be a draft of the Book of Articles that was presented at Mary's trial. Left image: © National Galleries Scotland, PG 2678. Right image: © British Library; Add. MS 33531, f.60r.

Westminster as a summary of the case against her. It was translated from a Latin summary of the charges against Mary that was written more than a year after the murder by the diplomat George Buchanan (Figure 6.2).[317] There is said to be 'no reasonable doubt' that Buchanan was also an author of the Hopetoun manuscript[318] and, on the basis of comparisons with other contemporary accounts and statements, it has been concluded that Buchanan's account of events is 'demonstrably suspect' and 'constructed on a mass of falsehood'.[319] It is this document that contains the only known reference to Mary playing golf:

> Few dayes eftir the murther remaining at halyrudehouse she past to seytoun, excercing hir one day richt oppinlie at the feildis with palmall and goif, And on the nicht planelie abusing hir body with boithuell.
>
> [Staying at Holyroodhouse for a few days after the murder, she then went to Seton, taking exercise one day right openly in the fields with pall-mall and golf, and at night clearly dallying with Bothwell.][320]

The clear implication of this passage, which was undoubtedly written with the intention of discrediting Mary, is that, despite being within the official period of mourning for her husband's death, she was engaging in frivolous activities.

Pall-mall, Golf and Archery

Pall-mall (also *paillemail*, *Jeu de mail*) is a game played to a target with a mallet-shaped wooden club and a wooden ball. It is often described as being a 'royal' game that became popular in France in the fifteenth century;[321] for example, the Bishop of Ross wrote in 1574 that the King of France played 'paille maille for exercise'.[322] Consequently, it seems plausible that pall-mall (unlike golf) would have been a game that Mary might have become familiar with during the period she spent in France from the age of five to eighteen. If Mary *did* play pall-mall at Seton, it would be typical for it to have been played over a relatively short course, perhaps within the grounds of the castle itself. Interestingly, however, there are other contemporary reports of Mary's visit to Seton that make no mention of golf or pall-mall but, instead, report that Mary practised archery. Whereas the Hopetoun manuscript, in describing 'palmall and goif', appears to have been based largely on second-hand reports and is widely viewed as unreliable, we have a first-hand account of Mary's activities at Seton, written at the time of her visit (February 1566/7). William Drury was an English statesman who was appointed to Edinburgh and reported frequently on Mary's activities to William Cecil, the chief advisor to Elizabeth I. On 28 February, three weeks after Darnley's murder, Drury wrote to Cecil to say that Mary had visited Lord Seton's house and, while there, Mary and Bothwell played a 'match at shooting' [archery].[323] In contrast to the doubts that are frequently raised concerning the reliability of documents such as the Hopetoun manuscript that were intended to discredit Mary, there seems little reason why Drury would not be aiming to provide accurate information to Cecil in his regular private diplomatic correspondence. Importantly, there is also contemporary evidence to indicate that Mary had archery butts installed in the south garden at Holyrood Palace.[324] It seems significant that there are contemporary reports confirming that Mary practised archery 'often' when in St Andrews,[325] yet there are no reports dating from this period of her playing golf during her visits to the town.

Sports 'clearly unsuited to women'

The events described in the Hopetoun manuscript were restated in two subsequent texts, both linked to George Buchanan, the diplomat who was closely involved in preparing the legal case against Mary that led to her trial and execution in England. In neither case is golf specifically mentioned (as it was in the Hopetoun manuscript) but it is perhaps alluded to. In 1571 Buchanan published his famous '*Detection*', an attempt to draw together evidence that would demonstrate Mary's complicity in the murder of her husband. It was published alongside what is commonly referred to as the '*Oration*'.[326] They were published in a single volume in 1571, simultaneously in Latin[327] and in the Scottish vernacular.[328] In addition, a French translation was published the following year.[329] The Scots edition describes Mary having engaged in 'manly pastimes' during her visit to Seton ('*lusus viriles*' in the Latin edition and '*d'inuiter les hommes en leurs jeux*' in the French). Subsequently, in Buchanan's history of Scotland, *Rerum Scoticarum Historia* (1582), he describes Mary's visit to Seton and writes (in Latin) that she played sports that were 'clearly unsuited to women'.[330]

Contemporary Accounts of Mary's Sports and Pastimes

Mary's life was documented in great detail, both by members of her court and also by ambassadors reporting back to England, France and the Vatican. In addition, numerous details of her political and leisure activities were recorded in Mary's correspondence. We know the day-to-day details of the places that she visited throughout her reign in Scotland[331] and we also have detailed information about her recreational activities.[332] We know, for example, that Mary regularly participated in hunting and hawking.[333] In addition, there is evidence of her engaging in activities such as billiards, cards, dice, reading, needlework, music and dancing.[334] There are accounts recording the purchase of items that were required for Mary's sporting and musical activities. There are even records of items that were won or lost when playing games such as bowls, for example a brooch with two agates worth fifty crowns.[335] However, despite all of this evidence documenting her participation in other activities, the Hopetoun manuscript is the only document linking her to the game of golf.

Golf at Seton Palace?

Of course, it is not inconceivable that Mary played golf at Seton Palace in February 1566/7, as is mentioned in the Hopetoun manuscript, and the possibility that she did so has been mentioned in several golf histories. The possibility that Mary Queen of Scots was a golfer is also mentioned in an article written in 1898 but the author concluded that the story was 'probably apocryphal'.[336] The question of whether Mary Queen of Scots played golf is a topic that most mainstream historians (as opposed to golf historians) have either ignored or appear to have considered unimportant. Indeed, one of Mary's biographers wrote in 1901 that the question of whether she played either archery or golf while at Seton was simply a 'matter of gossip'.[337] Another historian has assessed the question of whether Mary played golf by stating 'so many baseless rumours and scandalous tales were rife that every detail of the kind must be regarded with the gravest suspicion until authenticated, or sufficiently corroborated from independent sources'.[338] Whatever the truth of the allegation that Mary played golf at Seton, it is clear that the story has been gradually embellished over subsequent years.

Golf in St Andrews?

Other than references to Seton Palace, the most widely reported story concerning Mary's golfing activities is probably that she played at St Andrews. In a chapter entitled The History of Golf, published in *Golf* (1890), Andrew Lang states that 'Queen Mary Stuart played both golf and pell mell at St Andrews after Darnley's death',[339] which is simply a mistaken interpretation of the events described in the Hopetoun manuscript. It seems likely that the story of Mary playing golf at St Andrews was propagated more widely as a result of an etching that appeared in *The Illustrated London News* in 1905, entitled *Mary Queen of Scots on the Links* (Figure 6.3).[340] It was part of a series of images depicting 'The Early Days of Sports' and it is worth quoting the caption in full:

Figure 6.3 An imagined scene of Mary Queen of Scots playing golf at St Andrews. An etching by Amédée Forestier (1854–1930), originally published in the *Illustrated London News* (23 September 1905), that helped to popularise myths relating to Mary Queen of Scots.

> Queen Mary, with Chastelard in attendance, playing at St Andrews, 1563. During the winter of 1563, Mary stayed for several months at St Andrews, occupying a house in South Street which remains to this day. There is a tradition that the Queen yielded to the inevitable spell of the place, and played golf. It may very well be believed, for it is certain that she used to play in Edinburgh. During that winter Chastelard rose to favour, presumed, and was beheaded in the market-place of St Andrews.

The fact that this image of Mary playing golf in St Andrews was based on supposition rather than evidence was soon forgotten. In *The Spirit of the Links* (1907), Henry Leach wrote that Mary 'played on golfing ground no less celebrated than St Andrews'.[341] Although Leach went on to acknowledge that the evidence supporting this claim was 'not conclusive', in *The Happy Golfer* published a few years later (in 1914), the same author retells the story but without his previous note of caution.[342] Another writer has stated that it is 'certain' that Mary played golf in St Andrews.[343] References to Mary playing golf in St Andrews are now widespread, not only in golf histories but also in publications ranging from travel guides[344] to historical novels.[345] In fact, it has been claimed that Mary played golf in St Andrews 'on several occasions'[346] and that she 'played regularly at St Andrews'.[347]

The enduring image of Mary playing golf at St Andrews, originally published in *The Illustrated London News* (1905), was reproduced in newspaper advertisements by the Scottish Tourist Board in 1992[348] and the story of Mary playing golf in St Andrews continues to the present day. This is demonstrated clearly by a 'Teachers' Pack' that was published recently by the National Trust for Scotland. It explains that Mary 'was the first woman to play golf, which she did at St Andrews'.[349] Mary has been described as being 'among the most famous people to ever play at the Old Course at St Andrews'[350] and it has been said that she 'frequently indulged in the pastime [of golf] on the windy dunes of St Andrews'.[351] It has also been suggested that Mary played golf within the campus of St Andrews University 'in St Mary's Quad off South Street near a tree she is thought to have planted there'.[352] It has even been claimed that Mary 'commissioned the building of the golf course at St Andrews'.[353]

Golf in France?

Between the ages of five and eighteen, Mary lived in France, where, until the death of her first husband François II in 1560, she was briefly Queen Consort. Although there appears to be no evidence of golf having been played in France for at least another two hundred years, there has been much speculation about Mary having played golf during the period that she lived in France. For example, it has been suggested that golf 'was introduced into France by Mary Queen of Scots'[354] and it has also been stated that 'while in France, Mary played and fell in love with the game of golf'.[355] A variation on this theme is that Mary 'learned the game at an early age and had continued to play in France'[356] and that she 'helped to popularise the sport on the continent'.[357] We are told that Mary 'first encountered the practice of using a caddie in France'[358] and it has frequently been suggested that Mary was responsible for introducing the word 'caddie' to Scotland.[359] In assessing Mary's impact on the game of golf, it has been argued that 'her legacy to golf, the caddy, is with us to this day even though largely replaced by the motorized golf cart'.[360] Another claim, also seemingly without any supporting evidence, is that, while Mary was in France, the French king 'had the very first golf course outside of Scotland built for her enjoyment'.[361]

Much of the rather tenuous story concerning Mary's involvement in the history of golf (particularly with respect to St Andrews and France) was summarised rather succinctly in the opening monologue of an episode of the BBC television programme *Antiques Roadshow* that was broadcast from St Andrews in October 2012:

> Mary Queen of Scots is well known for her turbulent life, but what you may not know is that she was also one of the first women to regularly play golf. It's said that when she arrived in St Andrews in the 1560s, she brought along her own set of golf clubs. In fact, she brought them from France, where she'd learned as a child.[362]

Father, Son and Husband

It has been claimed that Mary was taught to play golf by her father, King James V of Scotland.[363] In reality, given that she was just six days old when her father died, this is clearly incorrect. Similarly, it has been claimed that Mary's son, King James VI of Scotland (later James I of England), was 'introduced to the game by his mother, Mary Queen of Scots'.[364] While there *is* evidence to suggest that James VI played golf (as discussed later), it is implausible that his mother could have had any direct role as his golfing mentor since, although James was twenty years old when his mother was executed in 1586/7, he was just ten months old on the last occasion that Mary saw him in April 1567. One further claim, that has appeared in a biography of Mary, is that her husband Lord Darnley was 'skilled' at golf.[365] This is certainly possible, although I'm not aware of any evidence that would indicate that Darnley ever played golf, let alone that he was skilled at the game.

The Myth of the Seton Necklace

In 1894 a necklace that formed part of the Eglinton family jewels was sold at auction in London (Figure 6.4). The catalogue entry states: 'The tradition connected with these highly interesting jewels is that the necklace, together with a picture, by Holbein,

Figure 6.4 Seton Palace and the Seton necklace. Seton Palace (depicted in a painting by Alexander Keirincx, c. 1639) is the location where Mary Queen of Scots was accused of playing golf shortly after the murder of her husband Lord Darnley. It is claimed, almost certainly erroneously, that Mary gave a necklace (referred to as 'the Seton necklace'; illustrated) 'in memory of some lost golf match'. Left image: © National Galleries Scotland, PG 2696. Right image: Royal Collection Trust/© Her Majesty Queen Elizabeth, RCIN 65620.

which now hangs in Eglinton Castle, was given by Mary Queen of Scots to Mary Seton'.[366] On the face of it, this has nothing to do with golf. However, the sale was reported in the following week's issue of *Golf* magazine.[367] In an attempt to concoct a link with golf, the magazine pointed out that the queen had played golf at Seton Palace and went on to suggest, 'No doubt Mary Seton knew the game, and played with the Scots Queen at the time, and the necklace may have been given in memory of some lost Golf match.' Whereas the article in *Golf* magazine emphasised that the story was 'only conjecture', when it was retold by John Kerr in *The Golf-Book of East Lothian* (1896), he omitted this qualification and instead stated that 'the relic is therefore interesting as a gift of a royal lady golfer to one who more than likely played with the Queen at Seton'.[368] It was almost inevitable that the story of the necklace would become embellished yet further. An example of this can be found in *Golf History and Tradition* (1998),[369] which provides the following synopsis of events:

> It is recorded that Mary Queen of Scots was in the habit of playing golf with Mary Seton at Seton Palace, and that Mary Seton was a better golfer. Perhaps because Mary Stuart lost to Mary Seton, she gave her a necklace.

A recently published golf history expands the story yet further. It begins by explaining that Mary was 'an avid golfer' who is known to have 'played golf on the Links of St Andrews' and concludes with the claim that Mary 'often golfed with her ladies-in-waiting, including Mary Seton, who was given a necklace after beating the queen in a match at Musselburgh'.[370] Similarly, in 2014 the *Daily Record* (Glasgow) reported that Mary was a 'regular player' and was 'known to have forfeited a necklace after being beaten by Mary Seton, one of her ladies-in-waiting, in a match played at Musselburgh'.[371] Finally, a recently published book claims that Mary Seton was a 'regular playing partner' of Mary Queen of Scots but laments the fact that, because of her exile and imprisonment in England, the queen 'would never get the opportunity to win the Seton necklace back in a re-match'.[372] This illustrates very clearly how a story about a necklace that was described in 1894 as 'only conjecture' has, over the years, evolved into a seemingly established historical fact.

In Summary

It seems that much of what has been written about Mary's involvement in the game of golf is incorrect. It is perhaps inevitable that writers will use a degree of hyperbole in order to make history seem more vibrant. However, when assessing the importance of Mary Queen of Scots to the history of golf, it should be borne in mind that this is based entirely upon a single reference to golf in a manuscript that had the sole purpose of discrediting her. In addition, it should be remembered that, despite the large number of contemporary documents that are available from this period of history, no other supporting evidence has been identified to substantiate the claim that Mary played golf, despite strong evidence demonstrating her participation in several other sports and pastimes.

Chapter 7

King James VI, the Club-maker William Mayne and Golf in Scotland (1566–1603)

Perth and the King James VI Golf Club

There have been frequent claims that King James VI of Scotland (Figure 7.1) learned to play golf in Perth during his childhood.[373] For example, when Robert Browning discussed early golf in Perth, he stated that it was here that James VI 'learned his golf as a boy'.[374] However, there appears to be no evidence to support such a claim and the reasons why this is assumed are unclear. James had become King of Scotland shortly after his first birthday in 1567 and spent most of his childhood at Stirling Castle. The king did, however, visit Ruthven on the outskirts of Perth for a hunting expedition in 1582 at the age of sixteen, this being the occasion on which he was abducted in what has become known as the Raid of Ruthven. In addition to being the probable origin of the claim that James VI played golf in Perth as a child, the king's visit to Perth in 1582 may also explain why, when a golfing society was established in Perth in 1858, its founders decided upon the title 'King James VI Golf Club'. The earliest golf society to be established in Perth was founded in 1824, and less than ten years later (in 1833) it became the first golf society to be permitted to append the prefix 'Royal' to its name.[375] As a consequence of gaining royal patronage, the society became 'The Royal Perth Golfing Society' which, incidentally, is what appears to have prompted the more 'ancient' society of golfers in St Andrews (founded in 1754) to request permission to adopt the title 'Royal and Ancient', a request that was granted by King William IV in 1834.[376]

By 1858, due to the increasing popularity of golf in Perth and the relative exclusivity of The Royal Perth Golfing Society, a new society was established in the city. The first entry in the club's earliest minute book (dated 22 December 1858) states that it was to be called 'King James the Sixth Golfing Club'.[377] It seems entirely reasonable for a club to choose to give itself a name that

Figure 7.1 King James VI of Scotland and I of England. James VI of Scotland became King James I of England following the Union of the Crowns in 1603 and is mentioned frequently in histories of golf. © National Galleries Scotland, PG 561.

is based on a historical tradition (for example, on the assumption that James VI may have played golf in Perth as a child), particularly in a case such as this where the modern-day club's website explains clearly that the name is based on a 'tradition'.[378] As far as I am aware, the club has never attempted to claim, for example, that it was 'Instituted in 1582'[379] (or any other date within the reign of James VI) but this has not prevented others from making such claims on its behalf. For example, Horace Hutchinson commented in 1897 that James VI had 'founded also the King James VI Golf Club in Perth'.[380]

In addition to his claim that James VI 'learned his golf as a boy' at Perth, Robert Browning also speculated as to which of Perth's two current golf courses the king may have played upon in his youth, concluding that 'it is likely' to be the North Inch rather than the South Inch course.[381] This is a claim that is now often repeated. For example, it has been claimed that James VI 'was the keenest of all royal golfers, having learned the game on the North Inch (Island) at Perth'.[382] Similarly, it has been claimed that James VI 'acquired his golfing skills at North Inch, Perth'.[383] In contrast, others have claimed that, rather than playing golf on the North Inch, 'it seems beyond dispute that he [James VI] played golf on the South Inch of Perth'.[384] Many similar comments could be cited to illustrate the prevalence of claims that James VI 'learned to play golf in Perth'. Unfortunately, despite its popularity, it is a claim for which no evidence has been identified.

William Mayne, Club-maker by Royal Appointment

In 1603, following the death of the English Queen Elizabeth I, the crowns of Scotland, England and Ireland were united and James VI of Scotland was crowned as King James I on 25 July 1603 in Westminster Abbey. However, another event that year that has been commented upon frequently by golf historians is the appointment by King James VI in April 1603 of the Edinburgh bow-maker William Mayne as 'fledger, bower, clubmaker and speirmaker to his hienes' [arrow-maker, bow-maker, club-maker and spear-maker to his Highness] (Figure 7.2).[385] It has long been thought that the description 'clubmaker' was a reference to the manufacture of golf clubs but evidence to support this assumption has been elusive.

As a result of extensive research conducted by Charles Whitelaw (1869–1939), a collector of Scottish arms and weapons, we know that a number of Scottish bow-makers from the sixteenth and seventeenth centuries also made 'clubs'. Valuable sources of information for Whitelaw during his research were the testaments dative of Scottish bow-makers (these are documents providing

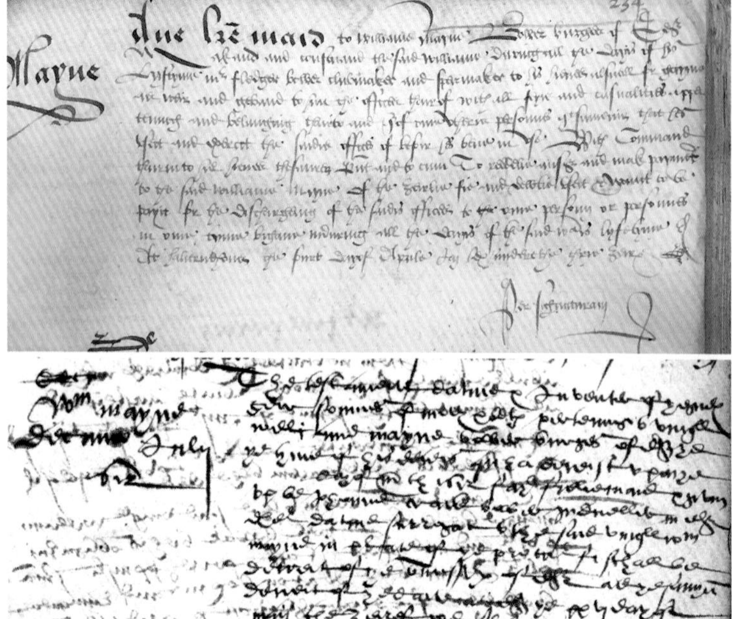

Figure 7.2 Documents relating to William Mayne, 'clubmaker' to King James VI. A Privy Seal document (1603) records the appointment of William Mayne as 'fledger, bower, clubmaker and speirmaker to his hienes' [arrow-maker, bow-maker, club-maker and spear-maker to his Highness] (top). Also shown (below) is an extract from the testament dative of William Mayne, bow-maker, containing a reference to 'club shaftis vnquhitten' [clubshafts uncut] and 'flock goiff ballis' [flock golf balls]. Top image: National Records of Scotland; PS1/73, 234. Bottom image: National Records of Scotland, CC8/8/47.

an inventory of a person's possessions at the time of their death). Whitelaw reveals that in the testament dative of a St Andrews bow-maker, Alexander Dais (1585), are listed 'club heidis and schaftis' (clubheads and shafts), in addition to items such as arrow shafts and bow-strings. Similarly, the testament dative of Beatrix Richardsone (1637), the spouse of an Edinburgh bow-maker, Donald Baine, records 'clubheids and clubschaftis ane thowsand maid and unmaid' (clubheads and clubshafts, a thousand made and unmade).[386] This provides evidence that these bow-makers were making clubs assembled from separate heads and shafts (as was typical of early golf clubs). However, the golf historian David Hamilton has pointed out, quite correctly, that there remains 'one nagging doubt', namely that nowhere in the testaments dative are the clubheads and shafts referred to as *golf* clubheads or shafts.[387] Among early Scottish bow-makers, William Mayne has attracted particular attention from golf historians, largely as a consequence of the importance attributed to his patronage by King James VI. However, despite this interest, little additional information about William Mayne has been uncovered. Indeed, this lack of biographical information is something that has been commented upon by golf historians.[388] However, some years ago I came across several original documents that help to provide a much clearer picture of William Mayne and confirm his importance in the history of golf.

The accounts of the Lord High Treasurer of Scotland provide extensive information about expenditure by the Scottish Exchequer. The handwritten accounts from the period 1473–1580, spanning the reigns of five Scottish monarchs (from James II to James VI), have been transcribed and published in thirteen volumes. An extensive index was included in the printed accounts and, as a consequence, this has provided a readily accessible source of information for historians. For example, it is from these printed accounts that evidence has previously been found indicating that James IV (great-grandfather of James VI) played golf in 1503/4.[389] Although handwritten treasury accounts cover the entire period of James VI's reign in Scotland (1567–1603), only those up to 1580 were included in the thirteen printed volumes. As a consequence, the handwritten accounts from the later years of James VI's reign are less well known. However, they contain the following entry dated April 1603:

> Item be his hienes speciall comand and direccion foirsaid payit and delyuerit to william mayne bower for certane fer speiris and golf clubbis furnisit be him to his maiesteis vse as the particular compt & ducet beris — j^{c} £
>
> [Item, by his Highness' special command and direction aforesaid, paid and delivered to William Mayne bower, for certain sound spears and golf clubs furnished by him to his Majesty's use, as the particular account and docket bears — £100][390]

This leaves no doubt that the clubs made by William Mayne were golf clubs and, in addition, it provides evidence that William Mayne made golf clubs for James VI's personal use. That golf clubs were purchased for the king's own use is important because, although it is widely assumed that James VI played golf, finding convincing documentary evidence to confirm this has been challenging. In addition to the unsubstantiated claims discussed earlier that James VI played golf in Perth, it has also been suggested that accounts dating from 1624 indicate that the king played golf in England. However, as will be discussed in more detail later, the relevant accounts relate to expenditure by the Duke of Buckingham, rather than to the king himself. Perhaps the strongest evidence cited previously to support the possibility that James VI played golf is a reference to a gift of '2 golf cloubbis' that James received when a child in Scotland from the Laird of Rosyth.[391] Of course, although this provides evidence that James possessed golf clubs, it does not confirm that he ever used them. Consequently, the treasury accounts from 1603 are important because they confirm that golf clubs were purchased for 'his Majesty's use'. There are several other payments recorded in the handwritten treasury accounts that support the conclusion that James VI played golf in Scotland. For example, an entry in September 1600 records the payment of four pounds for 'twa golf clubbis'.[392] Further entries in the accounts from December 1601 record purchases by the king of 'ane dozen of golf ballis' and of 'tua golff clobbis'.[393] However, it is debatable whether this is sufficient justification for James VI to have been described by modern-day golf writers as being 'an ardent devotee of the sport'[394] or having an 'addiction to golf'.[395]

William Mayne, Purveyor of Golf Clubs to the King

The royal decree that appointed William Mayne as 'fledger, bower, clubmaker and speirmaker' was issued by James VI in Edinburgh on 4 April 1603, the day before he left Scotland to take up the English throne. It was in the same month that the Scottish treasury accounts record the payment of £100 from James VI to William Mayne for 'speirs and golf clubbis'. Although the Scots pound was worth less than the pound sterling, this was a large sum of money in 1603.[396] This, and the fact that the payment was recorded as being 'by his Highness's special command and direction', might indicate that it was a parting gift from the king in recognition of several years of loyal service. A possible explanation for why the king made a payment to William Mayne at this time and why he bestowed the honour of a royal appointment just days before departing for London is that it appears William Mayne remained in Edinburgh rather than joining the extensive entourage of Scots that accompanied the king to England.

Several pieces of information indicate that William Mayne remained in Edinburgh after the king's departure for England. The Edinburgh *Register of Marriages* records that on 15 June 1603, just two months after his royal appointment and after receiving £100 from the king, William Mayne married Katharine Young in Edinburgh (he is recorded in the register as 'William Mayne, bower').[397] In addition, birth records indicate that William and Katharine subsequently had three children, all of whom were born in Edinburgh. Katharine was born on 6 April 1604, Robert was born a year later on 12 May 1605 and Barbara was born on 5 March 1609. This would seem to confirm that, despite the king having appointed William Mayne as his club-maker shortly before travelling to London on his accession to the English throne, Mayne remained in Scotland after the king's departure. Further evidence that William Mayne remained in Edinburgh comes from the Edinburgh *Register of Apprentices*,[398] which provides detailed records of those apprenticed to various professions in Edinburgh.

William Mayne, Supplier of Golf Balls

A testament dative of William Mayne was written in 1612 (Figure 7.2)[399] and provides further evidence that he was still living in Edinburgh at the time of his death. This document, which is preserved in the National Record of Scotland, provides further insights into William Mayne's life and of his importance in the history of golf. Importantly, it provides evidence of him possessing 'thriescoir club shaftis vnquhittin' [three score clubshafts unwhittled] and, given the evidence that Mayne supplied golf clubs to James VI (as discussed earlier), it seems reasonable to conclude that these were golf club shafts. What is perhaps even more significant and unexpected is a further entry from the Mayne's testament dative that describes 'five scoir tuell flok goiff ballis at xxxijs the dosane' [five score and twelve flock golf balls at thirty-two shillings the dozen]. This would suggest that William Mayne may have been supplying the golfers of Edinburgh with both golf clubs and balls. This description of 'flok goiff ballis' was cited in *A Dictionary of the Older Scottish Tongue* (1951) as being an early example of a written reference to golf balls but was listed without any further comment.[400] The term 'flok' (or flock) was used widely at this time to describe material such as wool or cotton that was used as stuffing in quilting or bedding and perhaps derives from the Latin *floccus* (a tuft, for example of wool).[401] It may be that the use of the term 'flok' was used to distinguish these golf balls from more expensive feather-filled balls. Leather balls filled with wool or animal hair are said to have been used in the Low Countries for games such as *caets* (hand tennis) and also for stick-and-ball games such as *colf*.[402]

It is generally assumed that the manufacture of early golf clubs and leather golf balls were distinct trades. Whereas it might be expected that golf clubs would be made by those with wood-working skills such as bow-makers, there is evidence of stuffed leather golf balls being made by shoemakers. It may be more likely that the bow-maker William Mayne identified an opportunity to supply cheaper 'flok' golf balls (manufactured by others) to the golfers that he was supplying with golf clubs. With regard to this, it may be significant that there is evidence that golf balls were being imported into Scotland at this time, as is discussed in Chapter 12.

In Summary

Scottish treasury accounts dating from 1603 confirm that the Edinburgh bow-maker William Mayne also made golf clubs. Importantly, this same source confirms that he supplied golf clubs for the personal use of King James VI. A testament dative reveals that at the time of his death, William Mayne's possessions included, in addition to clubshafts, a large quantity of golf balls. Because the manufacture of leather golf balls would have required skills that are distinct from those of a bow-maker or club-maker, it seems probable that the golf balls would have been purchased by William Mayne from a specialist ball-maker and resold to those golfers who bought his clubs.

Chapter 8

King James VI/I, Early Golf in England and the Blackheath Golf Myth

As was discussed in Chapter 4, based on a letter written by Catherine of Aragon, it has been suggested (incorrectly) that golf had been played in England (as opposed to Scotland) in 1513. However, what seems much more plausible is that golf was introduced to England by the Scottish courtiers who accompanied King James VI of Scotland to London in 1603, following the Union of the Crowns and his accession to the English throne as James I.

The Blackheath Golf Myth

There is certainly evidence for golf having been played in England in the early seventeenth century, shortly after the arrival in 1603 of King James VI/I, the son of Mary Queen of Scots. There is also evidence that the Blackheath Golf Club, the earliest known golf society in England, was in existence some one hundred and fifty years later (in 1766). It is perhaps because of the acknowledged seniority in England of the Blackheath Golf Club (latterly the Royal Blackheath Golf Club) that it is widely assumed that the earliest known instance of golf being played in England was in the vicinity of Blackheath. The scenario that is most often advanced is that golf was played by Scottish courtiers at Greenwich Palace, the royal palace that lies in closest proximity to Blackheath. Indeed, this has led to the frequently repeated claim that the Royal Blackheath Golf Club was 'instituted in 1608',[403] as is discussed in Chapter 14.

It is probably safe to say that most golf historians now acknowledge that it is difficult to justify the claim that anything resembling a modern-day golf club was in existence at Blackheath (or anywhere else) in 1608.[404] This was certainly the opinion of the respected golf historian Charles Clapcott.[405] However, even though there is no documentary evidence for the formation of a golf club at Blackheath in 1608, the possibility that golf was played at this time at Greenwich or Blackheath is still widely accepted and, as will be discussed later, is based on a claim that golf was played there in the early seventeenth century by James I's son, Henry Stuart, Prince of Wales (Figure 8.1). I will argue that not only is there no evidence that a golf club was instituted in 1608 but that the evidence points to Prince Henry having played golf at Richmond in Surrey, rather than at Greenwich or Blackheath.

In 1955 Robert Browning dismissed the claim that Blackheath Golf Club had been 'instituted in 1608', suggesting that the idea had been concocted by the 'barrow-boys of Fleet Street'. Nevertheless, he went on to say, 'I have no doubt that Prince Henry's games were played in the park of the royal manor at Greenwich.'[406] Similarly, in 1975 Geoffrey Cousins regarded the evidence of Prince Henry playing golf as having 'no significance in the history of the Royal Blackheath Golf Club' but remained confident that 'James and his courtiers played over Blackheath in 1608, when the Court was at Greenwich'.[407]

Because of the widespread assumption that golf was being played in the vicinity of Greenwich and Blackheath in the early seventeenth century, it may be helpful to review the evidence used to support this claim. Two contemporary documentary sources are frequently cited, both of which provide evidence that golf was played in England by James I's son Henry, Prince of Wales. As will be discussed, these are the Harley manuscript[408] and a letter written by the French ambassador, Monsieur de la Boderie.[409] One immediate concern in identifying the location as Greenwich (or Blackheath) is that, although Prince Henry occasionally visited Greenwich Palace, he did not live there. Similarly, when James I was in London his court was based at the Palace of Whitehall. In contrast, it was the queen (Anne of Denmark) who based her own household at Greenwich Palace. Ever since his earliest years in Scotland, Prince Henry had been brought up separately from both the king and the queen. In Scotland he was raised at Stirling Castle (rather than in Edinburgh) by the Earl and Countess of Mar. After the Jacobean court relocated to England in 1603, Prince Henry lived for most of his life at either St James's Palace in Westminster or Richmond Palace in Surrey. In addition, he is known to have spent periods of time at other palaces in Surrey, such as Nonsuch and Oatlands.

Figure 8.1 Henry, Prince of Wales. The earliest evidence of golf being played in England, as opposed to Scotland, dates from 1606 and concerns Prince Henry (1594–1612), son of King James VI/I. © National Galleries Scotland, PGL 240.

The Harley Manuscript

The most commonly cited document describing Prince Henry playing golf is a manuscript now held in the British Library (Harley MS 6391, frequently referred to as the 'Harley manuscript') that is thought to have been written no later than 1608 (Figure 8.2).[410]

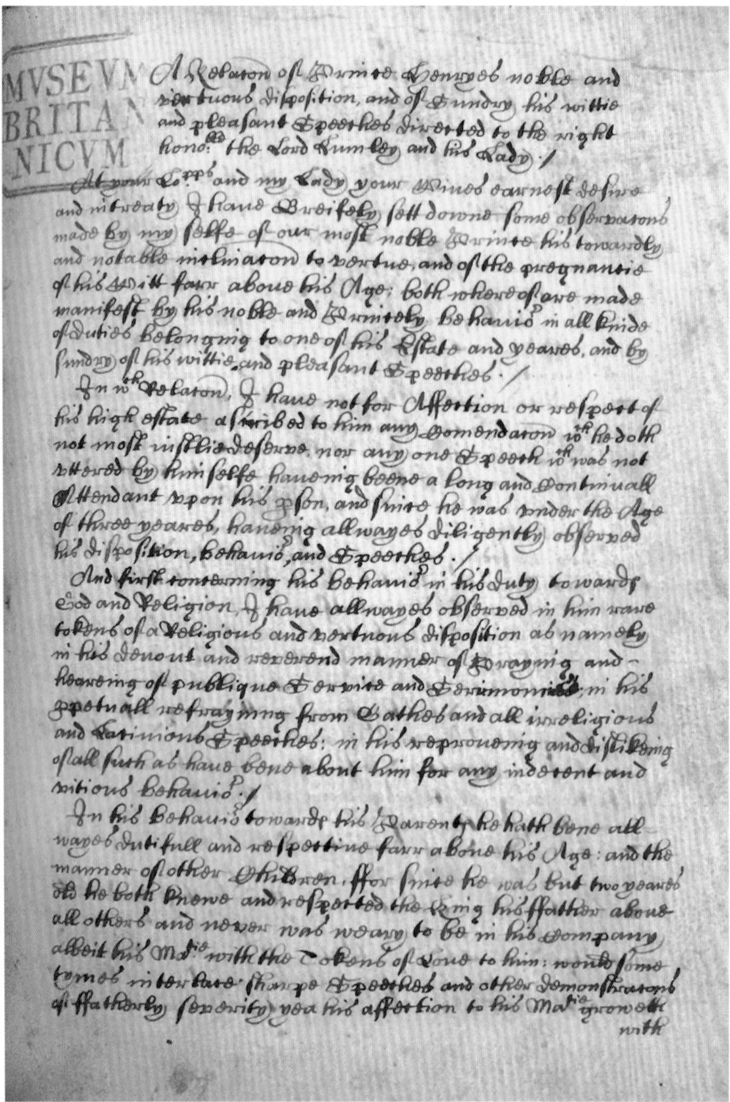

A Relation of Prince Henryes noble and vertuous disposition, and of sundry his wittie and pleasant speeches directed to the right hono^ble the Lord Lumley and his Lady./

At your Lo^pps and my Lady your wives earnest desire and intreaty I have breifely sett downe some observations made by my selfe of our most noble Prince his towardly and notable inclination to vertue, and of the pregnancie of his witt farr above his Age; both wherof are made manifest by his noble and Princely behavio^r in all kinde of duties belonging to one of his Estate and yeares, and by sundry of his wittie and pleasant speeches./

In wch Relation, I have not for Affection or respect of his high estate ascribed to him any commendation wch he doth not most iustlie deserve, nor any one speech wch was not uttered by him selfe haveing beene a long and continuall Attendant upon his person, and since he was under the Age of three yeares, haveing allwayes diligently observed his disposition, behavio^r, and speeches./

And first concerning his behavio^r in his duty towards God and Religion, I have allwayes observed in him rare tokens of a Religious and vertuous disposition as namely in his devout and reverend manner of praying and hearing of publique Service and Ceremonies; in his perpetuall refrayning from oathes and all irreligious and Lacivious speeches: in his reprooving and disliking of all such as have beene about him for any indecent and vitious behavio^r./

In his behavio^r towards his Parents he hath beene allwayes dutifull and respective farr above his Age: and the manner of other Children. For since he was but two yeares old he both knewe and respected the King his ffather above all others and never was weary to be in his company albeit his Matie with the tokens of Love to him: would some tymes interlace sharpe speeches and other demonstrations of ffatherly severity yea his affection to his Matie growe with
with

Figure 8.2 An account of Prince Henry playing golf in England (c. 1606). The earliest evidence of golf being played in England (as opposed to Scotland) can be found in the 'Harley manuscript' (c. 1606). It describes the young prince 'playing at Goffe' and using 'his Goff-Club to strike the Ball'. © British Library Harley MS 6391.

The identity of the writer is not identified but he describes himself as a 'long and continual attendant' of the prince. The manuscript contains a collection of about ninety brief and unrelated anecdotes that appear to span a twelve-year period of Henry's short life (from the age of two to fourteen), including incidents from his early years in Scotland. Henry was nine years old when he moved from Scotland to England in 1603 and was only eighteen when he died at Richmond Palace in 1612. However, contained within the Harley manuscript is a brief description of Prince Henry playing golf:

> At another tyme playing at Goffe (a play not unlike to Palemaille) whilest his Schoolmaster stood by talking with an other, and marked not his highness, warning him to stand further offe; the Prince thinking he had gon aside, lifted up his Goff-Clubb to strike the Ball. In the meane tyme one standing by said to him; beware that you hitt not Mr Newton.[411]

Importantly, there is no indication in this document of *where* Henry was playing golf. Consequently, we cannot be certain that it occurred at Greenwich or even whether it occurred in England or Scotland. The schoolmaster who is identified as being present when the prince played golf (Adam Newton) was a Scotsman who was first appointed as Henry's tutor in Scotland c. 1600, several years before Henry moved to England. I suspect the reason why this incident concerning golf has traditionally been associated with Greenwich is because a separate unrelated anecdote in the manuscript *does* mention Greenwich (in an incident concerning a meal the prince attended at which insufficient food was served).

The French Ambassador's Letter

In contrast to the lack of an identifiable date or location for the golf described in the Harley manuscript, a second document providing evidence of early golf in England can be dated precisely. It is a letter written by the French ambassador, Monsieur de la Boderie (Figure 8.3), and it is dated '*ce dernier Octobre 1606*' (31 October 1606).[412] The letter contains the following passage:

Lettre dudit Sieur de
La Boderie
a Monsieur de
Puisieux.
De Richement ce dernier
Octobre 1606.

Monsieur

Celle quil vous a pleu mescrire du xx.e
arriua icy le xxvi.e mais comme elle
ne contient rien ou il eschee grande
response, et que cette mauldite peste de
Londres tient tout le monde escarté

Figure 8.3 Golf at Richmond in 1606. A letter written by the French Ambassador, Monsieur de la Boderie (31 October 1606), provides evidence of golf being played by Henry, Prince of Wales at Richmond Palace in Surrey (rather than at Blackheath in Greenwich, as has been widely assumed). Also shown is a painting of Richmond Palace (1638). Left image: © *Bibliothèque nationale de France*; *Français* 7108, f.180v. Right image: Royal Collection Trust/© Her Majesty Queen Elizabeth, RCIN 703013.

> *Il joüe volontiers à la paulme, et à un autre jeu d'Escosse qui est quasi semblable au pallemail*
>
> [He plays willingly at tennis and at another Scottish game that is quite similar to pall-mall.]

There seems little doubt that the 'Scottish game' is golf. Whereas pall-mall (or *jeu de mail*), a croquet-like game, was popular in France, there is no evidence of golf being played in France at this time and, consequently, it would be unfamiliar to the French ambassador, hence his use of a sport he was familiar with to describe it. This report of Henry playing golf at Richmond is the earliest documented instance of the game being played in England that can be accurately dated. It occurred almost exactly a year after the infamous Gunpowder Plot which aimed to blow up the House of Lords during the State Opening of Parliament in 1605 and which, had it been successful, might have resulted in the assassination not only of James I but of Prince Henry himself.[413]

Richmond Palace, Surrey

When living in England, Prince Henry spent much of his time at either St James's Palace in London or Richmond Palace in Surrey. Although the king made use of Richmond Palace for hunting and had expanded the deer park for that purpose, by 1605 Richmond Palace was being used primarily as the home for his sons, Prince Henry and Prince Charles.[414] Contemporary documents record Henry's movements in some detail and indicate that he was living at Richmond Palace in October 1606, when bubonic plague had broken out in London.[415] The king had left London to visit his hunting lodges and, with the king away, the French ambassador travelled to Richmond in Surrey to visit the young prince. This in itself provides strong evidence that the ambassador observed Henry playing golf at Richmond during his visit in October 1606.

Following the ambassador's appointment to England in April 1606, he wrote a total of thirty-three letters to France that year.[416] All except two of these letters indicate that they were sent from London ('*De Londres*'). In contrast, the two letters that he wrote towards the end of October 1606 were sent from Richmond ('*De Richemont*').[417] So, not only is there evidence that Prince Henry was living at Richmond Palace in October 1606 and that the French ambassador visited Henry at Richmond Palace in October 1606, there is also evidence that the letter describing Henry playing golf was written at Richmond. Consequently, it seems reasonable to conclude that this early instance of golf being played in England occurred in the vicinity of Richmond Palace, rather than at Greenwich Palace or Blackheath. Richmond Palace was demolished in the 1650s, during the Interregnum following the abolition of the monarchy, but was located on the Surrey bank of the Thames adjacent to the existing location of Richmond Green and Old Deer Park.[418]

Adam Newton and Charlton House

Another argument that has been used somewhat tentatively to support the idea that Prince Henry played golf at Blackheath is that Henry may have lived at Charlton House.[419] Charlton is an impressive Jacobean mansion, some two miles from Blackheath, between the towns of Greenwich and Woolwich. Although there is a tradition that Charlton House was built for Prince Henry, the respected architectural historian, Avray Tipping, has argued very convincingly that the house was built for Adam Newton, Henry's tutor.[420] Tipping also concludes that it is 'impossible' that Prince Henry ever lived at Charlton House. Of course, it could be argued that Henry may have played golf while visiting his tutor at Charlton House. However, Adam Newton did not buy the manor of Charlton until 1607 and the construction of Charlton House was not completed until 1612, the year of Prince Henry's death. This is four years after the latest plausible date for the incident in which Henry is reported to have played golf in the presence of his schoolmaster 'Mr Newton' (1608) and six years after the golf incident that was observed by the French ambassador (1606).

One of the anecdotes in the Harley manuscript provides some evidence of where Adam Newton lived. In response to a gift of some plums from the prince, Newton comments that he would 'rather entertain your Highness at my house, if I had one'. He also continues, 'I have a wife and no house for her'. Presumably Newton's comments about not having a house of his own were because Charlton House had not yet been completed and because Newton, like other members of the prince's inner circle, lived as part of the prince's household. Supporting this conclusion are the surviving deeds relating to Adam Newton's purchase of Charlton in 1607.[421] In the deeds the purchaser is described as being 'Adam Newton of Richmond, Surrey'. Therefore, although it is not possible to identify conclusively the location of the incident in which Henry played golf while Mr Newton 'stood by talking', Richmond seems to be a plausible location. Richmond is a place where both the prince and his tutor Adam Newton are known to have lived at the time that the incident is thought to have occurred (c. 1608). In addition, as described earlier, there is evidence that the prince played golf at Richmond in 1606 when he was observed by the French ambassador.

A Blackheath Postscript

There is a long and established tradition that golf was played in the vicinity of Greenwich and Blackheath shortly after the arrival in London of James VI/I's court in 1603. It is not my intention to state categorically that golf was not played at this location. Indeed, given the number of Scots that came south with the Royal court, it could be seen as inevitable that golf would have been played at numerous different locations. It is certainly possible that Greenwich or Blackheath was one of the sites at which early golf in England was played but as far as I am aware no evidence has been identified that directly supports this conclusion. Similarly, there is no evidence that James VI/I ever played golf at Blackheath, despite frequent claims that he did so. For example, it has been claimed (but without any reliable evidence having been cited) that James VI/I played golf 'with gusto on Blackheath',[422] that 'he built a course at Blackheath'[423] and that 'he founded the Royal Blackheath Club'.[424]

Prince Henry's Purchase of 'clubbes' and 'balles'

I have come across one other contemporary document that provides support for the conclusion that Prince Henry played golf. The prince's expenditure was recorded in accounts drawn

Figure 8.4 The Privy Purse accounts (1610–12) of Henry, Prince of Wales. The accounts, drawn up by Sir David Murray, Keeper of the Prince's Privy Purse, record the purchase of 'clubbes' and 'balles'. National Archives, E351/2794.

up by Sir David Murray, a Scotsman who was educated in St Andrews and who was the Keeper of the Prince's Privy Purse. In the Prince's Declared Accounts, preserved in The National Archives at Kew, is a document describing Henry's purchase of 'clubbes' and 'balles' (Figure 8.4).[425] It is uncertain where this expenditure occurred but it is from a set of accounts dated 1610 to 1612, covering the last two years of Henry's life, after he had been invested as the Prince of Wales and when he spent most of his time at either St James's Palace or Richmond Palace. Of course, the accounts do not mention whether these were *golf* clubs and balls but this may be a reasonable conclusion, given the evidence that he had played the game in 1606.

The Duke of Buckingham and Golf at Royston (1624)

Another document recording early golf in England during this period is an account book maintained by Sir Sackville Crowe that reports the following expenditure:

> Paid to the Gofball keep[er] for clubbs and balles at Roiston 4 october [1624] 1. 11. 0 [£ s d].
> Lost to Sr Robert Deale at Goff the 4th October [1624] 2. 0. 0. [£ s d].
> Paid to the Gofman for Balles and Battes [December 1624] 1. 5. 0. [£ s d].
> Given to the Gofman at Royston 15th [January 1625] for balls & battes 0. 10. 0. [£ s d].[426]

It has been suggested that this provides evidence that King James VI/I played golf in England. This is unlikely, given that the expenditure listed in Sackville Crowe's account book occurred in 1624, just a few months before the king died (aged fifty-seven) and at a time when the king was seriously ill. Indeed, these are not the accounts of the king but of George Villiers, the 1st Duke of Buckingham, who was one of a series of handsome young men that James promoted and lavished his favours upon (Figure 8.5). So, although these accounts do not provide evidence that James VI/I himself played golf in England, they nevertheless provide clear evidence that golf was played at Royston, Hertfordshire in 1624 by one of his inner circle. Significantly, George Villiers was an Englishman, so this

Figure 8.5 George Villiers, Duke of Buckingham and evidence of golf at Royston (1624). The account book of Sir Sackville Crow (1624) provides evidence of golf being played at Royston, England by George Villiers, Duke of Buckingham. © National Galleries Scotland (left)/British Library, Add MS 12528, f16v.

also represents an early example of golf having been transferred from Scottish to English members of the king's court in England.

Historical references to golf such as this are frequently seized upon and perhaps misinterpreted. There seems to be no justification in thinking that evidence of golf having been played somewhere in the vicinity of Royston in 1624 should have any direct connection to a golf course that was built two hundred and fifty years later. Nevertheless, when I first presented these findings concerning evidence of golf being played at Royston in 1624 (in a magazine article published in 2016),[427] it appears to have been received enthusiastically by members of the current Royston Golf Club. The *Cambridgeshire News* published an article entitled 'Discover the history behind the oldest 18-hole golf course in England', in which they also reported that the story had been discussed on the BBC television programme *Look East*.[428] However, as of yet, Royston Golf Club (which was founded in 1892) has not adopted the claim 'Instituted in 1624'.

In Summary

Reliable evidence exists to indicate that golf was being played in England during the first half of the seventeenth century, notably by Henry, Prince of Wales in 1606. The evidence supports the conclusion that the game of golf was exported from Scotland to England following the accession of King James VI of Scotland to the throne of England in 1603. In addition to the evidence of golf being played at Richmond (in 1606) and Royston (1624), further evidence will be presented in subsequent chapters of golf being played in England at Newcastle (1646) and Tothill Fields, Westminster (1655 and 1658/9). As discussed in this and subsequent chapters, where the identity of the golfers can be established, a pattern emerges of early golf in England being a game that was played initially by royalty (for example, at Richmond in 1606), by nobility (Royston in 1624) and by the gentry (Westminster in 1655). Of course, it is quite possible that the game may have had a wider appeal, even at this early stage of its adoption in England, but, if so, such records have not as yet come to light.

Chapter 9

King Charles I, the Countess of Mar and Golf at Leith and Newcastle

King Charles I and the Dunfermline Golf Myth

Charles, the second son of King James VI of Scotland (Figure 9.1), was born on 19 November 1600 in Dunfermline Palace, Fife. It is perhaps because of this link to Dunfermline that stories have emerged suggesting that Charles played golf there in his youth. For example, the golf historian Robert Browning wrote in 1955 that Charles 'first tried his hand at the game as a boy in his native Dunfermline'.[429] Another golf writer has concluded that Charles 'learned the game at Dunfermline and was said to enjoy it'.[430] However, the possibility that Charles played golf in Dunfermline in his youth is highly unlikely.

Although Charles was born in Dunfermline, he was only three years old when, following James VI's accession to the English throne, Charles left Dunfermline and Scotland to travel to England. What makes the story even more implausible is that Charles was a notoriously sickly child, suffering from what we would probably now diagnose as rickets, a bone disorder associated with a deficiency of vitamin D. Indeed, the boy's departure from Scotland to England was delayed by several months because of his poor health. Contemporary documents record that Charles was only considered to be strong enough to travel after he was able to walk unaided. His departure for England was finally approved after his tutor, Dr Atkin, wrote to the queen in July 1604 to confirm that the boy could now walk 'all the length of the great chamber at Damfermelinge like a gallant soldier all alone'.[431]

Stories relating to Charles playing golf in Dunfermline appear to have originated in a history of Dunfermline Golf Club that was published in 1899. The author mentions that there is a 'tradition' that Charles played golf at Dunfermline and goes on to conclude that 'the chances are that the tradition is correct'.[432] A local newspaper in 1900 provided rather weak supporting evidence,

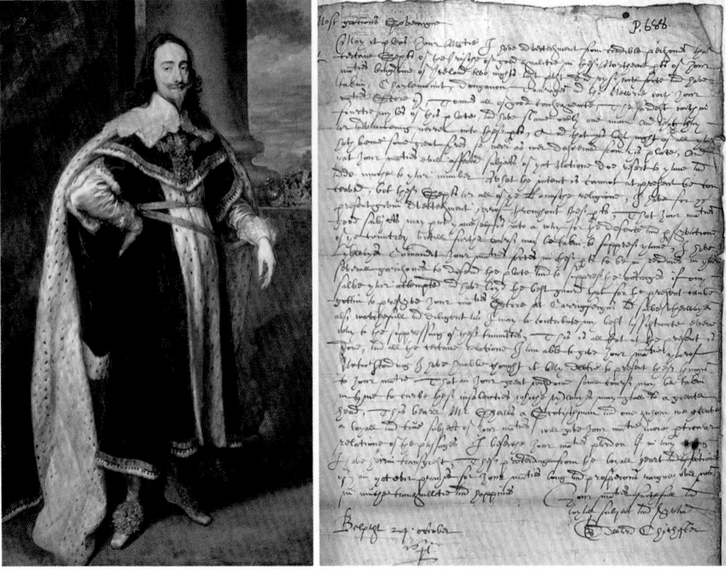

Figure 9.1 King Charles I and a letter informing him of the Irish Rebellion. King Charles I (r.1625–48/9) is said to have received this letter when playing golf on the Links of Leith in 1641. Left image: Royal Collection Trust/© Her Majesty Queen Elizabeth, RCIN 404398. Right image: © National Records of Scotland; PA6/5.

by commenting that 'what gives strength to the tradition' is that there is a street in Dunfermline called 'Golfdrum' (meaning golf hill).[433] The article continues with the suggestion that it was on Golf Hill that Charles 'wielded the driver and the cleek'. A more recent history of Dunfermline Golf Club, published in 1987, states confidently that Charles 'played on occasions' in Dunfermline'.[434]

Clearly, it is implausible that Charles played golf as a three-year-old boy who was struggling to walk unaided but perhaps it could be argued that he played golf during a subsequent visit to Dunfermline. However, Charles returned to Scotland only twice in his lifetime and to Dunfermline for only one night. He returned to Scotland first at the age of thirty-two for his delayed Scottish coronation in 1633 and on a second occasion to negotiate with the Scottish Parliament in 1641. Contemporary records of these two brief visits reveal that Charles' only visit to Dunfermline as an adult was on 4 July 1633. Examination of the king's itinerary confirms that it is highly unlikely that he would have had time during this brief visit for recreations such as golf. On 4 July Charles travelled from Stirling to Dunfermline (about twenty-two miles) and then the following day, after presiding over the investiture of six Scottish nobles, he continued his journey from Dunfermline to Falkland (about twenty miles).[435] These journeys, which he would have undertaken by horse and carriage, are likely to have taken much of the day. Additionally, there appears to be no evidence in any of the contemporary records to suggest that Charles played golf during this overnight stay in Dunfermline (or, indeed, anywhere in Scotland during his coronation visit in 1633).

It may be useful to note that the original story describing a 'tradition' that Charles played golf in Dunfermline first appeared some two hundred and fifty years after the king's death. In addition, neither this nor any of the subsequent versions of the story provide any supporting evidence to substantiate the claim. As a consequence, it seems reasonable to conclude that this story, like many others in the early history of golf, should be classified as a rather fanciful myth.

Golf Balls for 'his Majesty's use'

While there is no evidence that King Charles I played golf in Dunfermline as a child, there is clear evidence that he did play golf in his later life, for example at Newcastle in 1646 (as will be discussed later). In addition, there is a reference from 1629 to golf balls being made for 'his Majesty's use'. An entry in the records of the Scottish Privy Council dated 1629 records a complaint made by William and Thomas Dickson, 'makers of gowffe ballis in Leith', that a monopoly on the manufacture of golf balls that had been issued to James Melvill in 1618 (see Chapter 13 for more details) had never been ratified. The document from 1629 records that James Melvill had illegally taken possession of 'ane greate number of gowffe ballis' that had been made 'for his Majesteis use'.[436]

Charles I and Golf at Leith in 1641

One of the most frequently told stories concerning Charles I is that he was playing golf on Leith Links when he was brought news of the Irish Rebellion in 1641. For a story to become so well established in the history of golf it probably helps if there is a suitable image to illustrate the story (as has been discussed

Figure 9.2 King Charles I on Leith Links receiving news of the Irish Rebellion. An etching by John Gilbert depicting Charles I on Leith Links in 1641 was published in 1875. It is an image that has been repeated frequently, including on the base of the original Havemeyer trophy awarded to the winner of the US Amateur Championship. This is a replica (from the USGA museum) of the original trophy that was destroyed in a fire at East Lake Country Club in 1925. Right image: © United States Golf Association.

previously, this certainly seems to be the case with myths relating to Mary Queen of Scots, as discussed in Chapter 6). In the case of Charles I, it was an etching by John Gilbert that appeared as the frontispiece in *Golf: A Royal and Ancient Game* (1875) alongside the caption 'Charles I while playing golf on Leith Links receives news of the breaking out of the Irish Rebellion' (Figure 9.2).

The documentary source that is commonly cited by golf historians to support the story of Charles playing golf at Leith is an article that was published in 1792, more than one hundred and fifty years after the event was supposed to have occurred. The original account, published in *Archaeologia Scotica*, is as follows:

> King Charles I is said to have been fond of the exercise of the golf. The following anecdote I have been told of him: That, while he was engaged in a party at golf on the Green or Links of Leith, a letter was delivered into his hands, which gave him the first account of the insurrection and rebellion in Ireland. On reading which, he suddenly called for his coach; and, leaning on one of his attendants, and in great agitation, drove to the Palace of Holyroodhouse, from whence next day he set out for London.[437]

It is significant that the story is described as being an 'anecdote'. Of greater concern is that some aspects of the account are clearly incorrect (such as Charles departing for London the next day).[438] It could be concluded that the story is based upon rather weak evidence. However, there is an earlier, and largely overlooked, account of Charles playing golf at Leith in 1641 that lends credence to the story. Reverend Robert Wodrow (1679–1734) was a Scottish historian, noted for his history of the Church of Scotland, but he is also the author of a series of handwritten manuscripts that have been preserved in the National Library of Scotland. An entry in one of these journals, dated 1713, records:

> Mr Steuart informs me, that he has this accompt from very good hands: That when King Charles the First was here in Scotland, the leaders of the Irish Rebellion, or some from them, wer with him at the Abbey, and wer led to him covertley, and by the back-stairs: That when the expresse came to him with letters giving accompt of the Irish Massacre, he was playing at the gouf in the Links of Leith.[439]

Although this account was written in 1713 (seventy-two years after the event), there are reasons for thinking that it is substantially more credible than the account dating from 1792. Wodrow was a respected historian and, importantly, his information is attributed to a named source. Other entries in Wodrow's journals suggest that 'Mr Steuart' is Robert Steuart, 4th Baronet of Coltness (1677–c. 1758) who, significantly, was the grandson of Sir James Steuart of Coltness (1608–81). Sir James (who became Lord Provost of Edinburgh in 1648) would have been a prominent local figure during Charles' visit to Edinburgh in 1641 and he is likely to have been aware of the king's activities during his stay in the city.

There are detailed contemporary records of the king's activities during his visit to Edinburgh in 1641.[440] For example, he attended church each Sunday (usually twice) and he is recorded as being 'present in parliament' on sixty-seven days of his three-month visit. There are only about ten days during the king's visit when no activities are recorded. However, it may be significant that one of those days was Wednesday 27 October 1641, which was the day immediately before it is recorded in the parliamentary records that 'His majesty produced a letter [. . .] regarding some commotion in Ireland'. Furthermore, the letter concerning the Irish Rebellion was sent from Belfast on 24 October 1641,[441] so the dates fit. The letter's journey from Belfast to Edinburgh, by sea and horseback, would have taken several days. This, together with Robert Wodrow's account, would seem to lend credibility to the possibility that Charles may have been playing golf on Leith Links when he received the letter from Ireland.

Inevitably, the story has been embellished. There has been speculation, for example, that Charles used the arrival of bad news as a convenient excuse to end a golf match that he was losing. When writing about the story in 1890, Andrew Lang suggested 'possibly he was four down with six to play'.[442] Another author, making essentially the same joke, has suggested that the king may have been 'six down with eight to play'.[443] A variant of the story is that Charles chose to finish his game of golf before departing. As one writer put it, 'following the example of Sir Francis Drake, who completed his game of bowls before dealing with the Spanish Armada, Charles did likewise and played on'.[444] Another writer has claimed that Charles 'proceeded to finish his match, which of course he lost'.[445]

Charles I and Golf at Newcastle in 1646

While there may still remain some doubt about stories concerning Charles I playing golf at Leith in 1641, there is clear evidence that he played golf towards the end of his life, while incarcerated at Newcastle. In April 1646, at the end of the first English Civil War, Charles surrendered to the Scots at Newark. He was taken one hundred and fifty miles north to Newcastle, which was currently under Scottish control, where he was detained for almost nine months. It was while Charles was in Newcastle that we find several contemporary accounts of him playing golf in Shieldfield, an area to the east of the town centre. There are several printed accounts of Charles playing golf here, all of which were published between 1646 and 1647. Typically, they are short printed pamphlets reporting recent events, with titles such as *Papers from the Scots Quarters* and *A Letter from New-Castle*. They report, for example, 'seeing the King at Goffe',[446] that the king 'tooke a little recreation at Goffe'[447] and that 'His Majesty came from Goffe'.[448] One publication mentions that 'The King seldome goes out to goffe'[449] and another that 'His Majestie hath played little at Goffe'.[450] The story was also retold in the early English newspaper *Mercurius Diutinus*, which reported 'The King was then at Goffe',[451] and also in a pamphlet with the wonderful title *The Scots Treacherous Designes Discovered*, which describes the king's 'priviledges to play at Goffe or Bowles' while he was in Newcastle.[452]

The Countess of Mar and John the Bairn (1638)

A further reference to golf from the reign of Charles I that has attracted attention concerns Marie Stewart, the Countess of Mar (Figure 9.3). The extent to which women may have played golf during the game's early history has attracted a considerable amount of speculation. Much has been written about the possibility that Catherine of Aragon and Mary Queen of Scots may

Figure 9.3 Marie Stewart, Countess of Mar. Based on an entry in her household accounts concerning the purchase of a golf club (1638), it has been suggested that Marie Stewart, Countess of Mar was an early woman golfer. However, a reassessment of the accounts suggests that it was purchased for her grandson. © National Galleries Scotland, PG 2214.

have played golf in the sixteenth century. However, as has been discussed in previous chapters, we can confidently dismiss any such claims about Catherine of Aragon and it would appear that much of what has been written about Mary Queen of Scots are exaggerations based on a single historical document of questionable reliability. Another prominent figure who has been proposed as being an early woman golfer (but seemingly erroneously) is the Countess of Mar (c. 1573–1644). Prior to her marriage to John Erskine, Earl of Mar, in 1592 she had been a lady-in-waiting to Anne, the Queen Consort of Scotland. The earl and countess were very much a part of the Scottish court's inner circle, to the extent that the king entrusted them to raise his long-awaited first-born son, Prince Henry. This arrangement, whereby the prince would reside in Stirling Castle, was put into place from the moment Henry was born in 1594 and continued until the Scottish court relocated to London in 1603, indicating the extent to which the Earl and Countess of Mar were trusted by the king. The decision concerning the upbringing of his young son and heir appears to have been motivated by a need to ensure that Henry could not be seized by any of the king's political or religious opponents.

Selected extracts from the Countess of Mar's household accounts were transcribed and published in 1883 and included an entry from 23 September 1638 in which five shillings were 'paid for ane golf club to John the Baun'.[453] However, it seems that this is another example of a handwritten document having been transcribed incorrectly. The transcription of the Countess of Mar's household accounts came to the attention of the golf historian John Kerr, who assumed that the club had been bought by the countess for her own use. In the *Golf-Book of East Lothian* (1896), Kerr comments that it is 'not unlikely' that the countess was a golfer. He even speculates that she may have played near Dunbar, at 'Tyninghame links'.[454] Amy Pascoe, who wrote an article on ladies' golf in 1898, became aware of the story from Kerr's book and stated confidently that the purchase of the golf club in 1638 indicated that the Countess of Mar could be considered as being a 'seventeenth-century player' of the game.[455] Pascoe interpreted the entry in the accounts as indicating that the countess had purchased the golf club from a club-maker by the name of 'John the Baun'. Indeed, Pascoe went on to speculate that the golf club 'was what the noble lady would call finely fashioned and of most excellent workmanship; Master John Baun would see to that.'[456] It seems likely, however, that 'John the Baun' was a transcriptional error.

There is another more detailed and extensive transcription and analysis of the Countess of Mar's household account book that was published in 1815. Importantly, in this case the handwritten accounts are transcribed as 'Payit for ane golf club to John the bairne'.[457] The editor of the text also comments that 'John the bairne appears to have been Lady Marie's grandson, John',[458] suggesting that it was a club bought for a boy ('John the bairne'), rather than having been purchased from a club-maker by the name of 'John the Baun'. Indeed, there are several other payments recorded in the household accounts that pertain to 'John the bairne'. These include a payment to 'John the bairne to give the Doctor for his rashes'[459] and for a red scarlet riding coat ('ane rid skarlott ryding coat for John the bairne').[460] Thus, it would seem that on the basis of these household accounts from 1638, it would be inappropriate to conclude that the Countess of Mar was one of the earliest known female golfers. However, in contrast, it *would* appear that her grandson (John Erskine) should be added to what is a relatively short list of golfers who have been identified prior to the eighteenth century.

In Summary

While claims that Charles I played golf in Dunfermline appear to lack any credible evidence, it is certain that he did so at Newcastle in 1646. In addition, a reassessment of documents relating to the king's visit to Edinburgh in 1641 provides support for the frequently reported story that he was playing golf at Leith in 1641 when he received news of the Irish Rebellion. Finally, claims that the Countess of Mar played golf in 1638, during the reign of Charles I, can be dismissed due to what appears to be an error in transcribing her household accounts.

Chapter 10

King Charles II, a 'Goffe-Club-maker' and Golf in Restoration Britain

King Charles II

A frequent theme in several of the preceding chapters of this book has been the exaggerated claims that some golf historians have made concerning the role of various kings and queens in the early history of golf. Somewhat paradoxically, it seems that the opposite situation has arisen in the approach that many golf historians have taken when assessing the possible role of King Charles II in the history of golf (Figure 10.1). The prevailing view appears to be that Charles II was disinterested in the game of golf and that he was not a golfer.

Charles II is known to have had links to the game of pall-mall (or paille-maille, another stick-and-ball game that has some similarities to croquet) and it is probably because of these links with pall-mall that some golf historians have drawn conclusions such as 'Charles preferred paille maille to golf'[461] and that he was 'probably more of a mailer than a golfer'.[462] A further source states that 'there is no account of his having formed any attachment to the game of golf'.[463] Others have been considerably more emphatic. For example, it has been reported that Charles II 'detested' golf,[464] that 'he was not as keen on golf as his brother James'[465] and that he 'had other things on his mind than golf'.[466] It has also been stated, without any explanation or justification, that Charles II 'would not practise his golf, although constantly urged to do so'.[467] However, as was perhaps inevitable, a minority of golf historians have adopted a dramatically opposing view; claiming, for example, that Charles II was 'partial' to golf[468] or that he was a 'devotee' of golf.[469] In addition, it is common to see claims that Charles II played golf at Leith[470] but these claims appear to have arisen simply as a result of confusion over whether it was the first or second 'King Charles' that was involved in the often-retold story concerning a game of golf being interrupted by news of

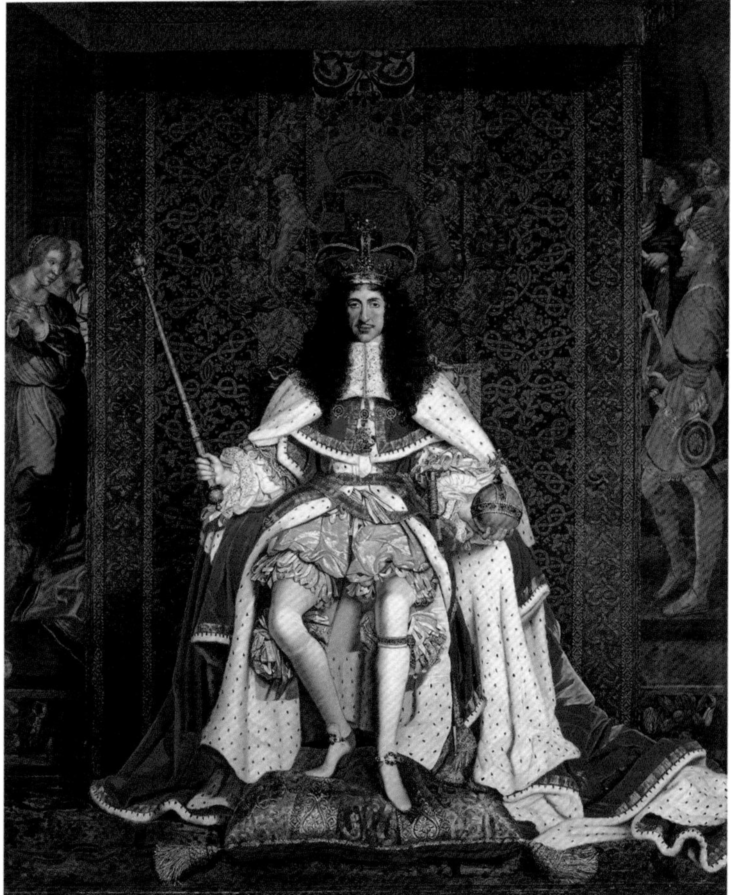

Figure 10.1 King Charles II. Despite a widespread belief that Charles II was not a golfer, contemporary documentary sources indicate that he played golf in both Scotland and England. Royal Collection Trust/© Her Majesty Queen Elizabeth, RCIN 404951.

the Irish Rebellion in 1641 (discussed in the previous chapter). Alongside these contradictory points of view as to whether or not Charles II was a golfer, the authoritative *Encyclopædia Britannica* has for many years stated that 'nothing whatever is known' about Charles II's involvement in the game of golf.[471]

I will argue that several independent contemporary documentary sources now help to provide clear and unambiguous evidence of Charles II's extensive involvement in the game of golf and, indeed, reveal that he had a 'golf club-maker' in his Royal Household and that he played golf in both Scotland and England.

Golf at Scone

There is clear evidence that Charles II played golf during a visit to Scotland in 1651 for his Scottish coronation, which took place at Scone in Perthshire. Charles's visit occurred at the time of the Interregnum, following the Second English Civil War that was precipitated by the execution of his father, King Charles I. A Commonwealth had been declared in England but Charles made a brief and clandestine visit to Scotland from his exile in France to be crowned King of Scotland. The evidence of Charles having played golf comes from a memorandum that was written by the Earl of Lothian on 9 January 1651, eight days after Charles's Scottish coronation. The document was transcribed and published in 1875[472] and it is this published version that has been relied upon by subsequent golf historians. The passage relating to golf states 'That the Kyng have constantly a proportion of his gardes to waitt upon him to and garde att the church, as also when he goeth to the fields to walke or goff.'

While this account was published more than two hundred years after the memorandum was written, it is believed to be a direct transcript of the original document. It is mentioned in the book's preface (in 1875) that 'the original letters are preserved at Newbattle Abbey', which was the home of the Marquess of Lothian. However, subsequent to the book's publication, Newbattle Abbey was converted into an adult education college and, as a consequence, it no longer holds the Lothian archives. The original document has, however, been preserved in the National Records of Scotland and it confirms the accuracy of the text that was published in 1875,[473] providing unambiguous evidence that Charles II played golf in Scotland.

Golf in London during the Interregnum

During the Interregnum, the period between the execution of Charles I and the restoration of the monarchy in England (1649–60), there is evidence of golf being played in London. The earliest account (1655) concerns Lord Strathnavar (later the Earl of Sutherland) who, with his younger brother, visited London from their home at Dunrobin Castle in the Scottish Highlands. They arrived in September 1654 and stayed in London for almost two years. An account of the visit is provided in *The Sutherland Book* (1892), which mentions that 'their amusements included golf, tennis, and bowls'.[474] In support of this, the author of *The Sutherland Book* cites contemporary handwritten accounts recording Lord Strathnavar's expenditure. These accounts, now deposited in the National Library of Scotland, confirm expenditure by Lord Strathnavar of two shillings in March 1655 'for playing at gowffe'.[475] The precise location of the golf is not recorded but another entry in the handwritten accounts indicates that Lord Strathnavar was living in King Street, which the author of *The Sutherland Book* suggests probably refers to the street of that name in St James, Westminster. Based on the evidence of golf being played at Westminster in 1658/9 and 1661/2 (as discussed below), a plausible location for Lord Strathnavar's golf would be Tothill Fields.

Evidence of golf having been played at Tothill Fields (Westminster) in 1658/9 can be found in a letter written by Thomas Harbottle, the 'Keeper of Tuttlefeilds' (Figure 10.2). In his letter, Harbottle mentions that golf by 'the gentry' was being disrupted by various undesirable activities. The original letter survives in the Library of Westminster Abbey[476] and describes several activities that were causing 'the hindrance of the meeting of the Gentry for their recreation at Bowles, Goffe, and Stowball'. The importance of this letter in the history of golf was discovered in 1901 by Edward Scott of the British Museum.[477] Harbottle's letter is quite specific about who was disrupting the gentry's golf. For example, William Curtis and George Hanly were described as leaving night soil 'unburyed to the general Hurt of the Inhabitants'. In addition, William Baker and Thomas Kennet were criticised for disposing of dead horses and leaving them 'unburyed tending to the infection of the Inhabitants'.

Restoration Golf at Tothill Fields, Westminster

With the restoration of the English monarchy in 1660, Charles II returned to London from his exile in Europe for his English coronation. In addition to the documentary evidence that Charles II played golf in Scotland during his Scottish coronation (discussed earlier), there is also evidence that he played golf in England.

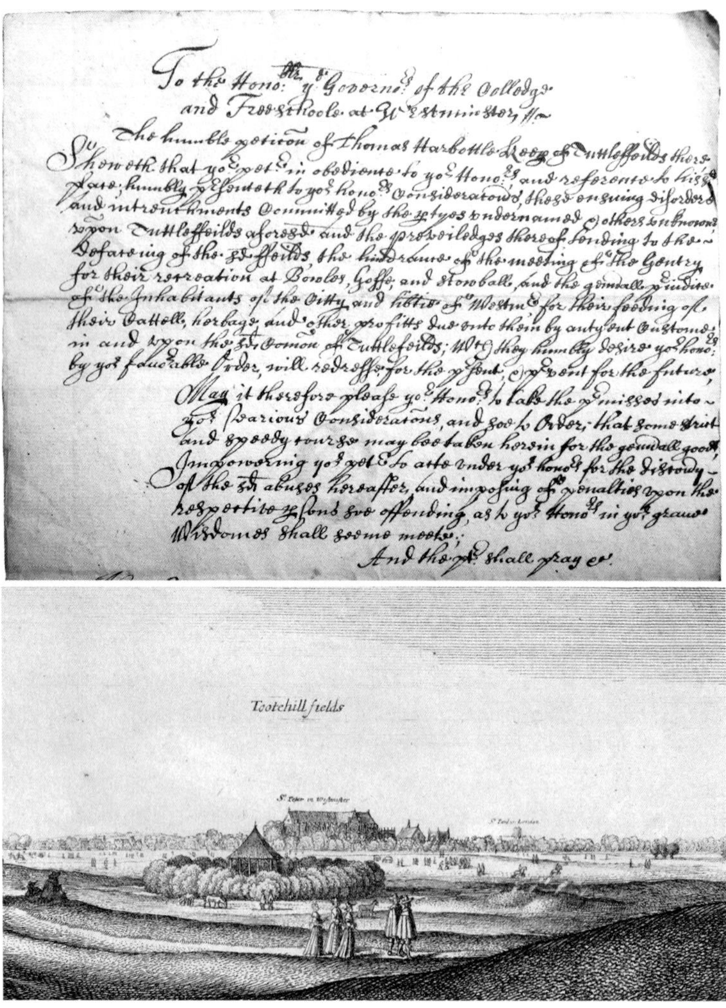

To the Hono:ble ye Governo:rs of the Colledge
and Free Schoole at Westminster &c

The humble petition of Thomas Harbottle keeper of Tuttlefeilds there

Sir
Showeth that yor petr in obedience to yor Hono:rs and reference to his
care; humbly presenteth to yor hono:rs Consideracions, these ensuing disorders
and intrenchments Committed by the partyes undernamed & others unknowne
upon Tuttlefeilds aforesd and the priviledges thereof tending to the
defaceing of the sd ffeilds, the hindrance of the meeting of the Gentry
for their recreation at Bowles, Goffe, and Stowball, and the generall prejudice
of the Inhabitants of the Citty and liberties of Westmr for their feeding of
their Cattell, herbage and other proffitts due unto them by antient Customes
in and upon the sd Comon of Tuttlefeilds; wch they humbly desire yor hono:rs
by yor favourable Order, will redresse for the present, & prevent for the future;

May it therefore please yor Hono:rs to take the premisses into
yor serious Consideracons, and see to Order, that some strict
and speedy course may bee taken herein for the generall good,
Impowering yor petr to atte under yor hono:rs for the discovery
of the sd abuses hereafter, and imposing of penalties upon the
respective persons soe offending, as to yor Hono:rs in yor grave
Wisdomes shall seeme meete:

And the petr shall pray &c

Figure 10.2 Golf at Tothill Fields, Westminster (1658). A letter written by Thomas Harbottle describes 'goffe' being played on 'Tuttlefeilds' in 1658 and an etching (c. 1643) of 'Tootehill fields' by Wenceslaus Hollar. Top image: Reproduced by kind permission of the Dean and Chapter of Westminster, WAM 25188. Bottom image: Royal Collection Trust/© Her Majesty Queen Elizabeth, RCIN 802718.

The evidence comes from a contemporary documentary source that was transcribed and published some two hundred years after the event and is to be found in the diaries of Alexander Brodie (1617–80), a Scottish Lord of Session.[478] It is clear that Brodie was himself a golfer since there are two entries in his diaries in which he mentions playing golf near the 'well of Riuus',[479] which is near the Moray coast of Scotland. In the published version of Brodie's diary he describes visiting London on 7 February 1661/2[480] and comments, 'The King went to goulf in Titl [Spittle] Feilds.' The insertion of '[Spittle]' in the published version of Brodie's diary is the transcriber's interpretation of the handwritten word 'Titl'. When transcribing Brodie's handwritten diary, it was assumed that 'Titl Feilds' was a reference to Spitalfields (in the east of London) and this interpretation of the entry in Alexander Brodie's diary has been accepted by golf historians.[481] However, a more likely location is Tothill Fields in Westminster. In addition to the close proximity of Tothill Fields to Charles's Palace at Whitehall, there is evidence of golf being played at this location two years earlier (as just mentioned). This conclusion is supported by an earlier transcription of Brodie's diaries that transcribes the relevant passage as 'The King went to Goulf in Totl Fields.'[482] That 'Totl Fields' is an abbreviation of Tothill Fields would be consistent with Brodie's style of writing, which is said to have made 'free use of contractions' and 'every other sentence written in a kind of shorthand', in addition to being 'wretched handwriting'.[483] Tothill Fields is referred to as 'Tuttle Fields' in a 1673 map of London and as 'Tootehill Fields' in an etching from the same period. Today, the only area of Tothill Fields that has not been built upon is Vincent Square, the playing fields of Westminster School.

Angliæ Notitia and a 'Goffe-Club-maker'

There is, therefore, strong evidence that Charles II played golf in both Scotland (near Scone in 1651) and in England (at Tothill Fields, Westminster in 1661/2). A further contemporary source providing evidence that Charles II was a golfer comes from published lists of the members of his Royal Household. An extensive list of servants was published in *Angliæ Notitia* in 1669 and indicates that among the king's servants was a 'Goffe-Club-maker'. It appears that this was a full-time occupation, given that this was included in a list of servants holding distinct roles but followed by the words 'one of each'.[484] That the king had among his household someone with such a specific job title would seem to suggest a substantial demand for golf clubs, presumably for use by a wider group of people than just the king himself. Interestingly, it was common for servants in the king's household to have very specific roles. For example, other servants listed in *Angliæ Notitia* have titles such as button-maker, coffee-maker, coffer[trunk]-maker, comb-maker, cross-bow-maker, hand-gun-maker, peruque[wig]-maker and watch-maker.

During the final fifteen years of Charles II's reign, fifteen editions of *Angliæ Notitia* were published (1669–84) and it is interesting to see how the title of 'Goffe-Club-maker' was recorded in *Angliæ Notitia* over this period. It remains as 'Goffe-Club-maker' throughout the first seven editions (1669–73)[485] but in the eighth edition (1674) a typographical error occurred, which resulted in the king's servant being described as a 'Coffe-Club-maker'[486] Understandably, the typesetter of the following (ninth) edition in 1676 appears to have been confused by the meaning of 'Coffe' and, presumably because of this, the job title was changed to 'Coffee-Club-maker'.[487] This error (concerning the king seemingly having a 'Coffee-Club-maker') persisted for a few more editions of *Angliæ Notitia*[488] before it was corrected back to 'Goffe'.[489] Of course, as is often the case when errors appear in print, they tend to be repeated and, indeed, there are at least four other publications (spanning more than two hundred years, from 1681 to 1903) that have perpetuated a myth that Charles II employed a 'Coffee-Club-maker',[490] although, incidentally (and as was mentioned earlier), he *did* have a servant with the role of 'Coffee-maker'. However, what may be of particular interest is that in the fourteenth and fifteenth editions of *Angliæ Notitia* (1682 and 1684), the name of the king's golf-club-maker was included for the first time. He was 'David Gastiers' (Figure 10.3).[491] A summary of the relevant changes that occurred in the various editions of *Angliæ Notitia* between 1669 and 1684 are as follows:

First edition (1669)	Goffe-Club-maker
Second edition (1669)	Goffe-Club-maker
Third edition (1669)	Goffe-Club-maker
Fourth edition (1670)	Goffe-Club-maker
Fifth edition (1671)	Goffe-Club-maker
Sixth edition (1672)	Goffe-Club-maker
Seventh edition (1673)	Goffe-Club-maker
Eighth edition (1674)	**Coffe**-Club-maker

Ninth edition (1676)	**Coffee**-Club-maker
Tenth edition (1677)	**Coffee**-Club-maker
Twelfth edition (1679)	**Coffee**-Club-maker
Fourteenth edition (1682)	Goffe Club-maker, **David Gastiers**
Fifteenth edition (1684)	Goffe-Club-maker, **David Gastiers**

The surname 'Gastiers' is unusual and is certainly not a common English or Scottish name. However, a recently discovered document suggests that 'Gastiers' may have been a typographical error for the Scottish surname of 'Carstairs'. Several original documents concerning Charles II's household have survived, including lists of the king's servants. An examination of those held in the National Archives at Kew has revealed evidence, from 1663, of a 'Goffe Clubmaker' by the name of James Carstairs (Figure 10.3).[492] In addition to 'Carstairs' being remarkably similar to

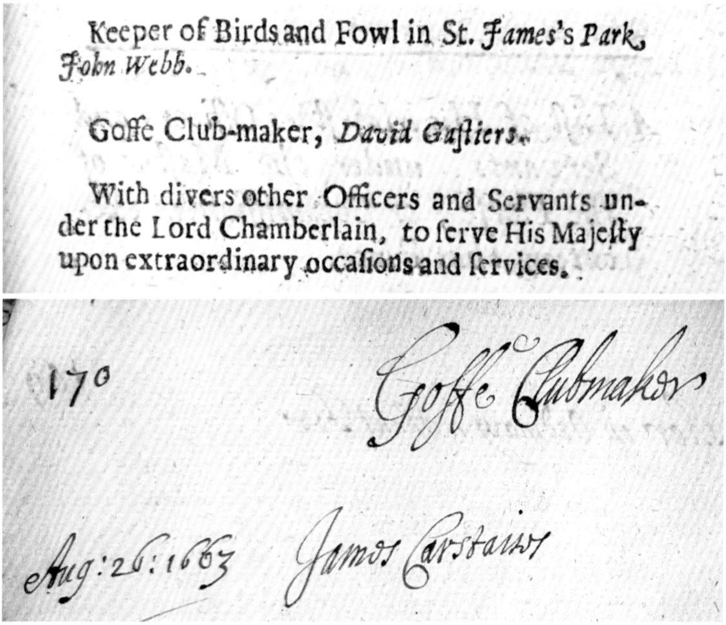

Keeper of Birds and Fowl in St. *James's Park*, *John Webb*.

Goffe Club-maker, *David Gaſtiers*.

With divers other Officers and Servants under the Lord Chamberlain, to ſerve His Majeſty upon extraordinary occaſions and ſervices.

170 Goffe Clubmaker

Aug:26:1663 James Carstairs

Figure 10.3 Golf club-makers to King Charles II. *Angleæ Notitia* (1682) identifies David Gastiers as a 'Goffe Club-maker' in the king's household and earlier handwritten household accounts of King Charles II record (1663) James Carstairs as a 'Goffe Clubmaker'. It seems possible that the two club-makers were related and that 'Gastiers' may have been a typographical error. Bottom image: National Archives, LC 3/25, 170.

'Gastiers', it is also the name of a village in South Lanarkshire. It is clear that the typesetters of *Angliæ Notitia* were error-prone, as is illustrated by their transposition of the word 'Goffe' into 'Coffe' (and then, subsequently, into 'Coffee'), so it seems entirely possible that 'Gastiers' was a typographical error. It also seems plausible that James Carstairs, who was the king's club-maker in 1663, may have been followed in this role by David Carstairs (rather than 'Gastiers'), perhaps a son or relative.

Given the established links between Scottish bow-makers and early golf club-makers (as was discussed in Chapter 7), it is interesting to note that there are records from 1641 of an Edinburgh bow-maker by the name of Thomas Carstairs (who was associated with the Marquis of Argyll).[493] A further point of interest is that the Marquis of Argyll was the very person who placed the crown on the king's head during Charles's Scottish coronation in 1651.[494] Whether James Carstairs (1663) and David Gastiers [but perhaps 'Carstairs'] (1682–4), both of whom were the king's golf club-makers, had any direct ancestral link to Thomas Carstairs (1642), the Edinburgh bow-maker, remains to be established.

The Privy Purse Accounts of Baptist May

There is one further piece of evidence that provides support for an association between Charles II and the game of golf that, as far as I am aware, has not been discussed previously by golf historians. It comes from the accounts of Baptist May, Keeper of the Privy Purse to Charles II. Although some of Baptist May's accounts survive in The National Archives, the Privy Purse records from this period are incomplete. However, handwritten copies of May's accounts were made by Edmund Malone (1741–1812), a noted biographer and literary scholar. Malone's handwritten copies of May's Privy Purse accounts have survived and were acquired by the Bodleian Library, Oxford in 1893.[495] Significantly, Malone's copy of Baptist May's Privy Purse accounts reveals that among Charles II's expenditure were the following entries:

April 1666	P^{d} Mr Forbes for Goffe Clubbes	7 14 0 [£ s d]
August 1668	To Mr Forbes for Goffe Balles	1 2 0 [£ s d]
September 1668	To ye Goffe Man	12 0 0 [£ s d][496]

It is interesting that Master Forbes (another Scottish surname) was supplying both clubs and balls to the king, with separate payments recorded for 'Goffe Clubbes' (in April 1666) and for 'Goffe Balles' (in August 1668). The identity of the 'Goffe Man', who was paid in September 1668, is unclear but the payment that was made to him is within a month of the payment that was made to 'Mr Forbes' for golf balls, so it seems reasonable to assume that all three of these golf-related payments may have been to the same person. What is less clear is the location where the payments were made. It seems that during this period the king's court moved regularly. For example, to avoid the Great Plague of 1665–6, the king relocated to Hampton Court and then, subsequently, to Salisbury and Oxford. It also appears that the king settled into a semi-regular routine of spending summers at Windsor and winters at Whitehall but with visits to Newmarket in the spring and autumn to attend the horse racing.[497] Given that the king had a servant within his household who was a golf club-maker, one possibility is that these payments to a 'Goffe Man' occurred when Charles II was away travelling. While it may be a coincidence, the year of the first of these golf payments (1666) was the first year since the restoration of the monarchy in 1660 that the king visited Newmarket.[498] It may also be significant that the three months of the year in which the payments were made (April, September and October) broadly coincide with the times of year (spring and autumn) that the king visited Newmarket to attend the horse racing. Further evidence of a possible link between the golf payments and Newmarket is that the payment to the 'Goffe Man' (September 1668) occurred in the same month and just two entries prior to a separate payment for 'cutting the Ditch at Newmarket'. In addition, in the following month (October 1668) a payment was made to 'the poor at Newmarket'.

Early Golf in America?

It has been claimed that events during the reign of Charles II have relevance to the history of golf in America. For example, it has been suggested that the earliest evidence of golf being played in America can be dated to either 1657[499] or 1659.[500] In both cases these claims concern the North American Dutch Colony of New Netherland (subsequently renamed New York) and can be traced back to contemporary documentary sources that were written in Dutch rather than English. It was a period when this region of North America was under the control of the Dutch, prior to British control from 1664 when the province was gifted by Charles II to his son the Duke of York (hence it being renamed New York). Although it has been widely assumed that these seventeenth-century documents refer to the game of golf, it seems almost certain that they concern the Dutch game of *colf/kolf* (the two spellings were used somewhat interchangeably at this time). To understand the Dutch documents it may be useful to point out that *kolven* is the verb form of the noun *kolf* (club) and that *gekolft* is the past participle of the verb *kolven*. The document from 1657 refers to a game being played on ice ('*op t ijs gekolft hadden*')[501] and the document from 1659 refers to a game being played in the streets ('*het kolven langs de Straeten*').[502] There seems little doubt that the game that was being played on ice and in the streets by Dutch settlers in New Netherland was the Dutch game of *colf/kolf* (a game that is known to have been played in Holland both on ice and in the streets), rather than the Scottish long-game of golf. The confusion may, at least in part, be a consequence of the influential golf historian Steven van Hengel's tendency to use the terms '*colf*' and 'golf' interchangeably. For example, van Hengel described how the 1659 ordinance was aimed at 'prohibiting colf' in Albany, New Netherland but then continued by concluding, 'So, Albany can beat any other part of the United States in regard to claims about the earliest golf there.'[503]

In Summary

Despite the concerns that were expressed in the *Encyclopædia Britannica* that 'nothing whatever is known' about Charles II's involvement in the game of golf, it is clear that there are multiple independent sources of information confirming that he was a golfer. This includes evidence that he played golf at identifiable locations in both Scotland (Scone) and England (Tothill Fields, Westminster). In addition, there is evidence of there being golf club-makers among his household servants (James Carstairs and David Gastiers/Carstairs) and that he made payments to a 'Goffe Man'. Consequently, it seems reasonable to conclude that King Charles II was indeed a golfer.

Chapter 11

King James VII/II: the 'First International Golf Match' or an Enduring Myth?

The 'First International Golf Match'?

One of the most popular and enduring stories relating to early golf concerns an event that is said to have taken place in 1682 and which is frequently described as being the 'first international golf match'.[504] The story, as it is most commonly retold, concerns a visit to Scotland by James, Duke of York (later King James VII of Scotland and James II of England and Ireland). It is said that the Duke of York (Figure 11.1) was challenged to a golf match by two Englishmen and that he selected as his partner the best local player, John Paterson, an Edinburgh shoemaker. We are told that the duke and the shoemaker were victorious and that Paterson was handsomely rewarded, thereby enabling him to build a house in Canongate, Edinburgh.

It is a story that has been repeated in more than a hundred published accounts of the history of golf but on no occasion have any contemporary documentary sources been cited. The story appears to have originated in 1824 (more than a hundred and forty years after the golf match is said to have taken place) and was seemingly an attempt to interpret an ambiguous Latin poem of just twenty-six words. The origin of the story will be described, as will an earlier but different explanation of the Latin poem that has been almost entirely overlooked. This earlier interpretation, first published in 1774, fifty years before the emergence of the popular golf legend, states that the poem concerns a game of archery (rather than golf).

The Latin Poem

The poem at the heart of this story (*In Ædes Joan. Patersoni.*) was written by the Edinburgh physician Archibald Pitcairne (1652–1713) and was first published in *Selecta Poemata* in 1727 (Figure 11.2). It is reproduced below, together with an English translation:

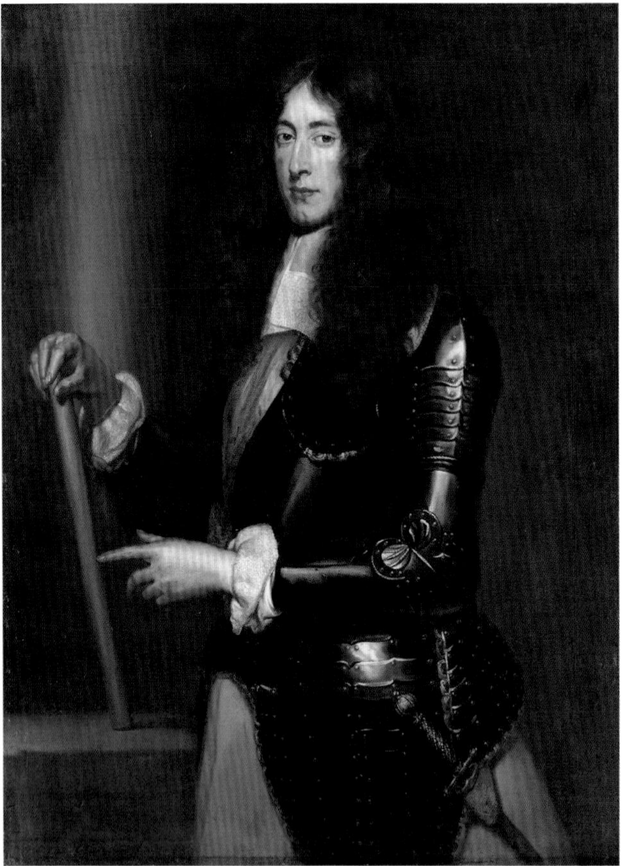

Figure 11.1 James, Duke of York. This portrait (c. 1656–60) depicts James as Duke of York (b.1633–d.1701), prior to his coronation as King James VII/II in 1685. There is a popular tradition (but no reliable evidence) that the duke played golf in 1682 with an Edinburgh 'shoemaker' in what has been described as 'the first international foursome'. Royal Collection Trust/© Her Majesty Queen Elizabeth, RCIN 402572.

Cum victor ludo, Scotis qui proprius, esset,
Ter tres victores post redimitus avos,
Patersonus, humo tunc educebat in altum
Hanc, quae victores tot tulit una, domum.

[Since he became champion in the game which belongs to the Scots and was crowned as had thrice three of his champion ancestors before, Paterson then raised from the ground to its present height this house which on its own had produced so many champions.][505]

POEMATA. 33

Vos condi voluit, facetiasque
Omnes in Stygio ablui fluento.
Quare in perpetuum valete, Manes,
Conditi sale plurimo, valete.

In Ædes JOAN. PATERSONI.

CUM victor ludo, Scotis qui proprius, esset,
Ter tres victores post redimitus avos,
Patersonus, humo tunc educebat in altum
Hanc, quæ victores tot tulit una, domum.

GEORGIUS FERCHARD *ad uxorem demortuam.*

QUâ mihi non vixit vexatior altera conjunx,
Nec potuit nostro dignior esse jugo,
Me sine, securam per secla silentia vitam,
Esse solet qualis Manibus, uxor, age;
Impositumque tuo saxum prægrande sepulchro,
Non leve præteriti pignus amoris, habe.

In

Figure 11.2 Archibald Pitcairne and a Latin poem from *Selecta Poemata*. Archibald Pitcairne (1652–1713) was an eminent Scottish physician but also noted for his often-obscure Latin poetry, for example as published in *Selecta Poemata* (1727). Pitcaire's brief epigram *In Ædes Joan. Patersoni* was the basis for the frequently retold nineteenth-century golf story concerning 'the duke and the shoemaker'. Right image: © Royal College of Physicians of Edinburgh, OBJ/PAI/55.

It should be noted that golf is not mentioned explicitly in Pitcairne's Latin poem. Similarly, there is no explicit reference to the Duke of York (or to a shoemaker or to two Englishmen).

The Origin of the Golf Story

The first identified written account of the story concerning a golf match involving the Duke of York can be attributed to Robert Chambers, a young and ambitious Edinburgh author who went on to establish the successful Chambers publishing empire. One of his first ventures into printing was *Traditions of Edinburgh* (1824), a book that had the aim of collecting oral traditions relating to the buildings and the people of Edinburgh (Figure 11.3). In a section of the book entitled 'Old Houses', Chambers quotes Pitcairne's Latin epigram that had been published in 1727 and mentions it as being engraved on the second floor of a building in Edinburgh's Canongate.[506] Interestingly, while this is the first

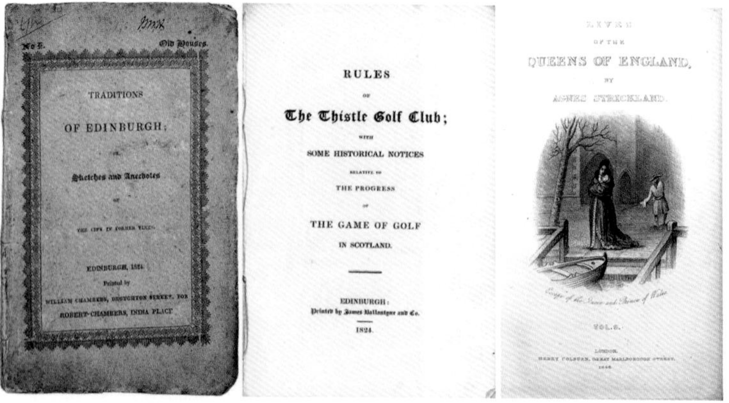

Figure 11.3 Three differing accounts of a golf match involving James, Duke of York. They describe him playing with either a brewer from Leith (Chambers, 1824) or a shoemaker from Edinburgh (Cundell, 1824) and against either the Scottish Duke of Lauderdale (Chambers, 1824) or two Englishmen (Cundell, 1824). A later account (Stickland, 1846) combines aspects of these two earlier versions but differs from both.

written account suggesting that the poem describes a golf match, Chambers's account differs somewhat from the version that subsequently became popular. In the first (1824) edition of *Traditions of Edinburgh*, Chambers explains that 'the report of tradition' is that the poem describes a golf match between the Duke of York and the Scottish Duke of Lauderdale, in which the Duke of York took as his partner a brewer from Leith. The Duke of York and the brewer were victorious and Chambers goes on to explain that, following their victory, the duke's 'plebeian friend' purchased the house in Canongate with his winnings.[507]

A second, somewhat modified, account of the story appeared in the same year. In *Rules of the Thistle Golf Club* (1824), John Cundell included an introductory chapter entitled 'Historical Account of the Game of Golf' that contained what has become the more enduring version of the story (Figure 11.3).[508] Cundell, like Chambers, quotes Pitcairne's Latin poem. In addition, like Chambers, he mentions that it is engraved on a house in Canongate and suggests that it contains a reference to a golf match. However, in contrast to Chambers, John Cundell states that the Duke of York was partnered by an Edinburgh shoemaker (rather than a brewer) and that they triumphed over two Englishmen (rather than the Scottish Duke of Lauderdale).[509] It is clear that, prior to publishing a second edition of *Traditions of Edinburgh* the following year (in 1825), Robert Chambers had become aware of Cundell's version of the story and that he adopted it 'in preference' to his earlier version.[510] Perhaps this was because the 'England vs. Scotland' aspect of Cundell's story was too attractive to resist. By way of explanation, Chambers commented that among the many stories that he had heard, the version concerning the duke and the shoemaker 'seems most probable'. However, it is important to note that in a subsequent edition of *Traditions of Edinburgh* (published in 1847) Chambers states that 'it must be admitted there is some uncertainty about this tale' and continues by observing that 'the tradition, nevertheless, seems too curious to be entirely overlooked, and the reader may therefore take it at its worth'.[511]

A third variant of the story was published in 1846 by Agnes Strickland, an English writer and historian (Figure 11.3). It was, in effect, a composite of the previous two published accounts and was described as being based on the 'oral traditions of Edinburgh'.[512] Strickland describes the Duke of York playing golf with a shoemaker (as had John Cundell). However, as was the case in Chamber's original version, their opponent was said to have been the Duke of Lauderdale rather than the two Englishmen. In a surprising embellishment, Strickland describes how the duke 'handed the gold to Paterson' with the words 'through your skill I have won this game, and you are, therefore, entitled to the reward of victory'.[513] However, despite three different versions of the story having been published in the first half of the nineteenth century, the version that has been repeated most frequently involves the Duke of York being partnered by a shoemaker against two English opponents. It is a story that probably gained even greater popularity due to a painting by Allan Stewart (c. 1919) entitled *The First International Foursome* (Figure 11.4) that has been reproduced frequently, including on the dust jacket of Robert Browning's *A History of Golf* (1955).

An Alternative Interpretation

Whereas the earliest written account claiming that Pitcairne's poem referred to golf did not appear until the nineteenth century (1824), an article that was published fifty years earlier (in 1774)

Figure 11.4 An imagined scene of James, Duke of York playing golf at Leith. Allan Stewart's painting (c. 1919) entitled *The First International Foursome* has been reproduced frequently, including on the dustcover of Robert Browning's *A History of Golf* (1955), and this has helped to popularise the story of the 'duke and the shoemaker' that is said to have taken place in 1682.

provided a different and largely overlooked interpretation of the poem; that it concerned the game of archery. The 1774 article, which was published in *The Edinburgh Magazine and Review*,[514] stated that the poem 'imports that John Paterson built the house [in Canongate] in the year in which he carried the prize of Archery'. The author of the article is thought to be Lord Hailes (David Dalrymple) and there is evidence that he had extensive knowledge of Archibald Pitcairne and of Pitcairne's Latin poems. Lord Hailes was the grandson of Sir David Dalrymple (Baronet of Hailes), an Edinburgh advocate who defended Pitcairne at a trial before the Privy Council in 1700.[515] Pitcairne is also reported to have treated Sir David Dalrymple for rheumatism[516] and, in addition, one of Pitcairne's Latin poems is addressed to Dalrymple (*Ad. D. Davidem Dalrymplium Equitem &c.*).[517] Collectively, this suggests that Lord Hailes and his family were likely to have had a detailed knowledge of the poet. Further evidence that Hailes considered himself to have a genuine insight into the meaning of

Pitcairne's poems is provided by the author's observation that 'Dr Pitcairn frequently alludes to circumstances of private history'. He goes on to explain that Pitcairne's poems 'have become obscure, and, unless they meet with a commentator, will, in a short time, become unintelligible.' Lord Hailes began his analysis of Pitcarine's poems by stating, 'I am able to explain but a few of these obscure passages.' This comment is important because it suggests that the poems that Lord Hailes did choose to comment upon were those that he felt confident in interpreting. It is also notable that, in discussing the poem, Hailes suggested that it had been written 'in jest', despite it having been misinterpreted by Paterson as a serious and flattering eulogy. Again, this is important because it indicates that the poem should not be interpreted too literally. Hailes does not mention which 'John Paterson' Pitcairne wrote his poem about but I suspect that this is because Hailes considered it to be self-evident (the possible identity of John Paterson will be discussed later).

Two Competing Claims (Golf and Archery)

We have two differing interpretations of Pitcairne's poem; a claim concerning golf that appears to have originated in 1824 and which has attracted popular attention, and also an earlier claim, from 1774, that it concerns archery. Since the golf story has been accepted so uncritically, it may be useful to explore whether the alternative explanation (concerning archery) seems plausible.

It is perhaps significant that Archibald Pitcairne was a member of the Royal Company of Archers and that he is known to have written several Latin poems that are unambiguously about archery. Two such examples are *In Davidem Drummondum in certamine Sagittariorum Edinburgensi Victorem* (On David Drummond, Victor in the Archery Contest held in Edinburgh)[518] and *Roberto Fribarnio, Typographo Regio, in certamine Sagittariorum Regiorum Victori* (Robert Freebairn, Typographer Royal, Victor in the Competition of the Royal Company of Archers).[519] Both of these poems are written as quatrains and are in a similar style to *In Ædes Joan. Patersoni*. There are also interesting similarities between phrases that are used by Pitcairne in his poem to John Paterson and those he used in his poems that are known to be about archery. A poem addressed to Robert Freebairn begins with the phrase '*Prisca pharetratis quae & propria Gloria Scotis*' (The ancient quiver and Scotland's own glory), suggesting that Pitcairne was associating archery with 'Scotland's own glory'. This would seem to support the possibility that Pitcairne's use of the phrase '*ludo Scotis*' (Scotland's game) in his poem to John Paterson may also be a reference to archery. Pitcairne's poem to Robert Freebairn contains the phrase '*per te ter faustum*' (through you, thrice fortunate). This may be a reference to the fact that competitions such as the Musselburgh silver arrow were determined on the basis of the best of three arrows or because it reflected the fact that the trophy was retained if it was won three times successively. Whether or not this is the case, Pitcairne's poem to John Paterson contains a very similar phrase: '*ter tres victores*' (thrice three victories).

'*Ludo Scotis*' (Scotland's Game)

It seems likely that what led writers such as Robert Chambers in 1824 to conclude that Pitcairne's poem concerned golf was the phrase '*ludo Scotis*'. A prevailing view in the nineteenth century was undoubtedly that golf was 'Scotland's game' but it seems much less certain that golf would have been regarded as being 'Scotland's game' at the time that Pitcairne wrote this poem (the late 1600s/early 1700s). There is no doubt that golf was played in Scotland at this time but it was a much less well-established pastime in Scotland than other sports, including archery. The earliest established Scottish golf societies date from the mid-1700s and the earliest identified golf trophy (a silver club donated by the Edinburgh City Council) dates from 1744. In contrast, the Royal Company of Archers have records dating back to 1676[520] and there are several examples of archery trophies from early in the seventeenth century, including the Musselburgh Arrow (1603), the St Andrews Arrow (1618) and the Peebles Arrow (1628). It is also notable that archery games such as papingo were considered to be 'familiar and meaningful in sixteenth-century Scotland'[521] and have been referred to as 'this old Scottish pastime'.[522] However, as has been pointed out, it is probably a mistake to attempt to interpret the poem too literally. It seems unlikely that Pitcairne would have been implying that any sport (whether golf or archery) was truly 'Scotland's game', particularly since it is unlikely that he would have had any meaningful global perspective on the relative popularity of sports in different countries. All he could really be confident of was that a sport was popular in Scotland. Thus, on the basis of the phrase *ludo Scotis*, it seems no more plausible to assume that Pitcairne was referring to golf than to other sports such as archery.

John Paterson

There is evidence of leather workers (shoemakers or cordwainers) by the name of Paterson working in Canongate in the late 1600s,[523] but this is not particularly surprising, given that Paterson is one of the most common Scottish surnames. There is also evidence (from the 1686 Edinburgh Burgh Records) of a John Paterson who was a maker of golf clubs and it seems likely that such evidence played a strong part in the origins of the golf story that emerged in the nineteenth century as an attempt to explain Pitcairne's poem.[524] Nevertheless, if one accepts the possibility that Pitcairne's poem may be about archery rather than golf, a useful question might be whether a 'John Paterson' can be identified who would be a plausible subject of a poem written by Pitcairne about archery. It is clear that Archibald Pitcairne was firmly established among the Edinburgh intelligentsia. Among Pitcairne's poems in *Selecta Poemeata* there are a small number that are addressed to his wife, to his daughters or to his female acquaintances. However, other than these, almost all of the people who are the subjects of Pitcairne's poems are either fellow members of the Edinburgh intelligentsia or people of high status (these include kings, queens, princes, dukes, earls, viscounts, barons, physicians, surgeons, professors, advocates and members of the clergy). Indeed, this is probably not surprising, given that such people are more likely to have received a classical education and to have understood Latin. Many of Pitcairne's Latin poems were addressed to his acquaintances and at least a dozen of them, like Pitcairne, were members of the Royal Company of Archers.[525] It is, therefore, of particular interest that another notable member of the Royal Company of Archers was the Archbishop of Glasgow, John Paterson (1632–1708), who is known to have lived in Edinburgh and who was also appointed as Bishop of Edinburgh. As a consequence, Archbishop John Paterson would seem to be at least as plausible a candidate to be the subject of a poem by Pitcairne than the 'poor shoemaker'. In addition, both Archibald Pitcairne and Archbishop John Paterson are listed as being subscribers to a 1710 translation of Virgil's *Æneis*,[526] suggesting that these two men may have shared similar literary interests.

Perhaps an even more convincing link between Pitcairne and the archbishop is that one of Pitcairne's Latin poems describes an incident involving Archbishop John Paterson. Pitcairne was an ardent Episcopalian (a supporter of the Scottish church that, in contrast to the Presbyterians, recognised the authority of bishops). In one of Pitcairne's longer Latin poems (*Ad Georgium Buchananum*)[527] he describes Archbishop John Paterson's return to Scotland following a period of exile in England.[528] Another link between Pitcairne and Archbishop John Paterson can be found in a document, handwritten by Pitcairne, that survives in the British Library.[529] In describing his time at college in Edinburgh, Pitcairne writes that he was 'graduated by Sir Wm Paterson'. This is believed to be a reference to Sir William Paterson of Granton, who acted as Pitcairne's regent (tutor) in Edinburgh. The significant point is that Sir William Paterson, who was a tutor to the young Archibald Pitcairne, was also the brother of Archbishop John Paterson.[530] These various pieces of information, taken together, would seem to provide a strong argument that Pitcairne was closely associated with Archbishop John Paterson and that Archbishop John Paterson is a plausible subject of the poem *In Ædes Joan. Patersoni.*

The Ambiguity of Pitcairne's Latin Poems

It remains unclear why Pitcairne's poem was engraved on a house in Canongate and why the poem is entitled *In Ædes Joan. Patersoni.* (On John Paterson's House). There is, however, evidence that Archbishop John Paterson had lodgings in Canongate around the time that Pitcairne is likely to have written the poem. A handwritten document dating from 1692 preserved in the Edinburgh City Archives records that 'John archbishope of Glasgow' occupied rooms on the second storey of a tenement.[531] The document reveals that he was living with his son Alexander Paterson in accommodation comprised of eight rooms (four chambers, two closets, a dining room and a kitchen).

As has been discussed, it seems possible that Pitcairne's poem has been misinterpreted by those who considered it to be about golf. If so, this is perhaps not particularly surprising, given that much of Pitcairne's poetry is thought to have been deliberately obtuse and ambiguous – a feature that may have been an attempt by Pitcairne to hide his Jacobite and Episcopalian sympathies. For example, it has been claimed that 'even his closest friends sometimes found Pitcairne's poetry difficult' and that some of Pitcairne's poems 'might have been obscure even to a Scot in the early eighteenth century'.[532] Consequently, it is perhaps unsurprising that one of his poems has been interpreted in two different ways (as being a reference to either archery or golf). A writer in 1760 remarked that Pitcairne frequently wrote about 'private occurrences' and sometimes did so in a manner that was 'hardly intelligible'.[533] However, for the reasons outlined, it seems plausible that Pitcairne's poem to John Paterson concerns the game of archery and may have been addressed to Archbishop John Paterson, rather than describing a golf match involving the Duke of York and a shoemaker.

A Coat of Arms and a Golfing Motto

Undoubtedly, one of the reasons why many have linked the game of golf with the poem engraved on a house in Canongate was the poem's proximity on the building to a coat of arms featuring a hand grasping a golf club and containing the golfing motto 'far and sure'. However, it seems possible that the poem was engraved on the building prior to the subsequent addition of features such as a golf club and motto, perhaps being added whimsically in the nineteenth century, having been inspired by an oral tradition linking the poem to the game of golf. Support for this possibility is provided by Lord Hailes's account of the poem in 1774 (in which he states that the poem is about archery). Hailes describes the poem as being 'recorded in gold letters on the house itself' but it is notable that he makes no mention of either a coat of arms containing a golf club or the motto 'far and sure'. Perhaps a more compelling reason for assuming that these features were added to the building at a later date (and most probably in the early nineteenth century) is that there is no evidence of the motto being used in a golfing context prior to it being adopted by the Edinburgh Burgess Golfing Society in 1802.[534] Thus, while it is certain the poem was engraved on the building before 1774, it seems possible that features such as the motto were added between 1802 (when the motto was adopted by the Burgess Society) and 1824 (the date when the golf legend was first published). It also seems implausible that a shoemaker would have been entitled to a coat of arms and, indeed, previous golf historians have concluded that there is no evidence of one having been granted.[535] Another possibility is that a coat of arms was added to the building at an early date but that it was subsequently altered by the addition of a golf club and the nineteenth-century golfing motto. In support of this possibility is a description of the coat of arms that was provided by Daniel Wilson in *Memorials of Edinburgh in Olden Times* (1848). Wilson describes the coat of arms as containing a 'defaced crest, said to be a hand grasping a golfer's club'[536] (the 'crest' being the heraldic feature placed above a helmet at the top of a coat of arms). Wilson's use of the expression 'defaced crest' provides support for the possibility that an earlier (bona fide) coat of arms may have been subsequently altered (or defaced) by the addition of elements such as a motto and a hand grasping a golf club.

Paterson's Land, Canongate

Following the emergence of the story of the duke and the shoemaker, Daniel Wilson examined Council records in 1848 and suggested that the property in Canongate had been in existence long before the emergence of a golf legend claiming that a 'poor shoemaker' had built it with his winnings from a golf match in 1682. Wilson describes the property as having been acquired in 1608 by a 'maltman', Nicol Paterson, and, as a consequence of this, expressed doubts about aspects of the story of the duke and the shoemaker. It is clear that Wilson was being sarcastic in stating that he was sorry 'to disturb a tradition backed by such incontrovertible evidence'.[537] Nevertheless, perhaps not wanting to dismiss the legend entirely, he suggested that the property may have been 'lost, instead of won by the gaming propensities of its owner'.

The house in Canongate has often been described as 'Golfer's Land' but this is a relatively recent phenomenon. I am not aware of any instance of the house being called 'Golfer's Land' prior to 1848 (a date that is after the first appearance of the golf legend in 1824) In contrast, there are frequent earlier instances of the house

Figure 11.5 Golfer's Land, Canongate. An etching of 'The Golfer's Land, Canongate' from Daniel Wilson's *Memorials of Edinburgh in Olden Times* (1848). The building was demolished in 1960 and a new bronze reproduction of a golf-related coat of arms was added to a new building that was built on the same site. Left image: © National Galleries Scotland, PGP EPS 644.366.

being referred to as 'Paterson's Land', for example in the records of the Edinburgh Dean of Guild during the 1700s. The building in Canongate was demolished in 1960 and was replaced by a new building to which a bronze reproduction of the coat of arms and the motto 'far and sure' has been attached (Figure 11.5). While Pitcairne's Latin poem that initiated the golf legend is no longer present, an additional bronze plaque has been added to the new building that provides a potted history of the story of the duke and the shoemaker. It seems almost inevitable, therefore, that the story will continue to be retold.

A Popular Story

There are undoubtedly elements within the golf legend that are plausible. For example, there is evidence that the Duke of York played golf during a visit to Edinburgh in 1679 and 1682 (as is discussed later). Although doubts about the story's reliability have occasionally been expressed,[538] the duke and the shoemaker's golf match is almost universally accepted as being an established historical fact. For example, one writer commented that 'no one doubts the authenticity of the account',[539] whereas another observed that, in comparison to some other aspects of early golf history, this story is 'much more verifiable'.[540] In addition to John Kerr's description (from 1896) of it being 'the first international golf match',[541] the legendary golf match has been described subsequently as being 'the first recorded match between two competing nations'[542] and a 'forerunner to the present Walker Cup and Ryder Cup duels'.[543] An interesting variation of the story, which places it in England rather than Scotland, is that it has been described as 'a high-stakes money match at Blackheath.'[544] However, one of the most bizarre versions of the story claims that 'King Charles I played on the course [at Leith] as host of the first international golf match between two English noblemen, George Patterson and the Duke of York, in the early 1680s'.[545] It is probably stories concerning the Duke of York playing in the 'first international golf match' that led one author to conclude that James was 'the keenest golfer of all the sovereigns',[546] and why another has claimed that he was 'one of the best golfers in Scotland'.[547] It should be remembered, however, that no contemporary evidence has ever been cited to support the tradition that the Duke of York played golf with a shoemaker in 1682, or that he rewarded his humble golfing partner with the means to build a house in Canongate.

James Duke of York Played Golf in Scotland (but not in America)

Despite there being no evidence that James, Duke of York played in 'the first international golf match', there *is* evidence that he played golf during his visits to Scotland, for example during the time he served as Lord High Commissioner of Scotland. The best-known evidence is perhaps a letter that was written from Edinburgh by James on 31 January 1682 in which he mentions that, due to the lack of opportunities for hunting in Scotland, 'playing at Goffe' has been his only outdoor activity.[548] However, further evidence of golf being played by James in Scotland has come to light recently, as a result of the acquisition by the National Library for Scotland of a pocketbook that belonged to Sir John Werden, who was secretary to the Duke of York. In his pocketbook, Werden records several items of expenditure under the heading 'Moneys Disbursed by JW [Sir John Werden] by the Dukes Order'. Of particular interest is an entry from 4 February 1679:

> To John Douglas a Bill for Goff Balles & stickes, allsoe for 12 Dozen of Goffe Balles at 5d each – 06 09 02 [£ s d][549]

However, in contrast to this evidence of golf in Scotland, one of the more implausible claims concerning James, Duke of York is that he 'brought the game [of golf] to the United States' and that he 'played golf on the land that would become Bethpage State Park in 1688'.[550] Another version of this story describes how in 1688 three men (including the Duke of York) met at Bethpage in Long Island, where 'the first round of golf in America was about to be played'.[551] Although the province of New Netherland (subsequently renamed New York) had been granted to the Duke of York by King Charles II in 1664, there is no evidence that the Duke of York ever visited America, let alone that he played golf there. Indeed, by 1688 James, Duke of York had been crowned King James VII/II and it is almost inconceivable that he travelled from England to America in what was the final year of his reign without this event having been documented or commented upon by historians of the period.

In Summary

There is evidence that James, Duke of York played golf in Scotland (in 1679 and 1682) but, in contrast, no evidence that he did so in America in 1688. Concerning Pitcairne's Latin poem that is so frequently considered to refer to golf, it is not my aim to state categorically that it is about archery or that it may refer to Archbishop John Paterson. However, it seems appropriate to draw attention to this being no less plausible than the frequently repeated claims about the 'duke and the shoemaker'. The story linking the poem to a golf match appears to have first surfaced (at least in written form) in 1824, more than one hundred and forty years after the golf match is said to have taken place. It is also of interest that an earlier explanation of the poem stated that it concerned archery. However, given the notoriously ambiguous style of Pitcairne's poetry, it is probable that we will never know with certainty the meaning of the poem or why it was engraved on a building in Canongate.

Part II

A Thematic History of Early Golf

Chapter 12

Early Golf Balls and Golf-ball Myths

Early Golf Balls

There is evidence to indicate that early balls for the 'long game' of golf (the forerunner of the modern-day game) were made of leather stuffed with material such as feathers and, as a consequence, such balls are commonly referred to as 'feather balls' or 'featheries' (Figure 12.1). However, there is also evidence for the use of materials such as wool or cotton[552] and, for that reason, the more generic term 'leather balls' is also used. These balls were expensive and difficult to make but they are believed to have been the most common type of ball used for golf, at least for affluent golfers, up until the realisation (c. 1848) that cheaper and more resilient balls could be produced from gutta-percha, a rubber-like product from the sap of the Malaysian tree of the same name (Figure 12.1).[553] Gutta-percha balls were used widely in the second half of the nineteenth century until the widespread adoption of rubber-cored balls, such as the Haskell ball, at the turn of the century.[554] An informative description of the manufacture of feather golf balls can be found in *Delineations of St Andrews* (1807):

> They are made of strong alumed leather, and stuffed with feathers. The feathers are forced in at a small hole left in the covering, by a blunt pointed iron instrument, which the maker applies to his shoulder, and the operation is continued till the ball acquires a degree of hardness and elasticity scarcely credible to those who have not seen it. The balls are afterwards boiled, and when dry painted with white oil paint to exclude the water and render them easily seen.[555]

A more poetic description of the art of the feather-ball maker (and also one of the earliest descriptions) can be found in *The Goff* (1743),[556] a poem that describes the skills of the golf-ball maker 'Bobson', who is assumed to be one of a dynasty of St Andrews ball-makers by the name of Robertson:

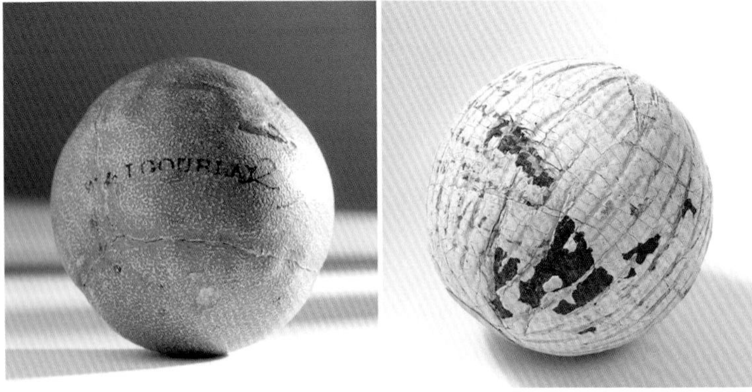

Figure 12.1 Early golf balls. A feather-filled leather golf ball by W. & J. Gourlay of Musselburgh (c. 1840) and an early painted gutta-percha ball (c. 1850) with hand-hammered markings designed to improve aerodynamic properties. Reproduced with kind permission of the Royal and Ancient Golf Club of St Andrews, RNA 04 013 and RNA 04 026.

The work of Bobson; who with matchless art
Shapes the firm hide, connecting ev'ry part,
Then in a socket sets the well-stitch'd void,
And thro' the eyelet drives the downy tide;
Crowds urging Crowds the forceful brogue impels,
The feathers harden and the Leather swells;
He crams and sweats, yet crams and urges more,
Till scarce the turgid globe contains its store:
The dreaded falcon's pride here blended lies
With pigeons glossy down of various dyes;
The lark's small pinions join the common stock,
And yellow glory of the martial cock.

The occupational hazards associated with the manufacture of feather-filled balls are illustrated by a post-mortem that was conducted in 1725 on a 'maker of golf balls' by Thomas Simson, Professor of Medicine in St Andrews. The date of the autopsy is recorded as 20 May 1725, but it was not published until some twenty years later in *Medical Essays and Observations*, perhaps the earliest medical journal. Simson's post-mortem account of the ball-maker contains the following description:

> The Side of his Breast he leaned his Instruments upon, in beating in the Stuffing of his Balls was much deprest through its whole Extent, and the other was thrust out as much: In the deprest Side no Lobes of the Lungs could be distinguished, and the Lungs were of as deep a Red, and as firm a Substance as those of a boiled Fowl, and were quite united to the different Parts surrounding them.[557]

While it is certain that early golf was played with leather balls, it is not accepted universally that these were the only type of early golf ball. For example, it has been argued that golf balls may have been made from materials such as wood. This possibility will be examined and, in addition, some popular golf-ball myths will be discussed.

'A top hat full of feathers'

It is frequently stated that a feather golf ball contained the quantity of feathers that would fill a top hat. For example, it has been suggested that golf balls contained 'a top hat full of wet feathers',[558] 'a top-hat full of boiled feathers',[559] 'a top hat full of chicken feathers'[560] or 'a top hat full of goose feathers'.[561] In 1998 the golf historian David Stirk set about making some feather golf balls, using traditional techniques, and concluded that 'a feather ball contains a much greater quantity of feather than would fill an old top hat'.[562] It seems likely that the originator of the feathers-in-a-hat story may have been the golf writer and noted amateur golfer Horace Hutchinson, whose information was certainly not first-hand, given that he was born in 1859, after the end of the feather-ball era. Hutchinson wrote in 1893 that balls were 'stuffed so tightly with feathers that when taken out the feathers filled a hat'.[563] However, a few years later (1898) Hutchinson wrote a newspaper article in which he stated that the feathers in a golf ball would 'fill a top hat'.[564] It seems likely that Horace Hutchinson was simply using the image of a hat (or top hat) as a metaphor to indicate that a large quantity of feathers was required but the image has been enduring and has been taken literally. For example, it has been suggested that a ball contained a 'precise top hat full' of feathers[565] and that a 'top hat contains the exact quantity of feathers' required for a golf ball.[566] It has also been claimed that 'the accepted formula for one ball was a hatful of feathers'[567] and that 'a top-hat full of feathers was the general measure'.[568] Perhaps to make the metaphor more understandable to a North American audience, the quantity of feathers has been described in 1968 as being the amount that would fill 'a tall beaver hat'.[569] In 1992 the magazine *Popular Science* provided an explanation of how feather golf balls were manufactured and included the following instructions: 'Fill a top hat with feathers, stuff the feathers into a wet leather pouch, and wait for the leather to dry.'[570] The likelihood of an artisan ball-maker measuring a quantity of feathers in something as upmarket as a top hat seems implausible but, nevertheless, it is an appealing image.

Speculation about Pebbles and Stones

It is probably Sir Walter Simpson, author of *The Art of Golf* (1887), who should be acknowledged as being the originator of a popular story concerning a Scottish shepherd hitting a pebble into a rabbit hole with his shepherd's crook.[571] It is a deliberately fanciful story that Simpson proposed as the origin for the game of golf and, while it has been repeated endlessly, it is not usually promoted as being a reliable or established part of the history of golf. However, occasionally the story is retold in a way that might seem to imply that it is supported by documentary evidence. For example, it has been stated that 'Hundreds of years ago, Scotch shepherds invented golf.'[572] It has even been argued that there are 'four periods' in the development of the golf ball and that the earliest of these (described as 'c. 1150–1648') relates to 'the shepherd's stone and wooden balls',[573] a conclusion that would seem to be attributing too much historical importance to Walter Simpson's light-hearted comment.

Wooden Golf Balls?

If we ignore speculation such as 'the first golf balls were probably stones knocked around by bored shepherds',[574] the most common hypothesis concerning the nature of the earliest golf balls (other than that they were leather balls) is that they may have been made of wood. The evidence that has been cited to support this claim, at least concerning the 'long game' of golf (see Chapter 1), is relatively weak but, nevertheless, it has been claimed that 'there is no question that the first games of golf we know today were played using wooden balls'.[575] It is certainly possible that inexpensive wooden balls may have been used by those unable to afford expensive leather balls, particularly since wooden balls are known to have been used for a variety of other stick-and-ball games, including games such as *colf*, *crosse* and *mail*, that were popular in France and the Low Countries.[576] In addition, wooden balls were used for the Scottish team game of shinty, a game played with a wooden club that was shorter than a golf club,[577] and it seems very likely that it is a game such as shinty that was being described in 1698 by a visitor to the remote Scottish islands of St Kilda in the Outer Hebrides.[578] The author describes how the islanders 'use for their diversion short clubs and balls of wood'. He also goes on to say that the players are 'so keen for victory, that they strip themselves to their shirts to obtain it', which certainly sounds more like an energetic and vigorous game, such as shinty, rather than the more leisurely game of golf.

The most commonly cited reason for thinking that early golf balls may have been made of wood is based on a comment that was made in a letter written in 1614 by the Earl of Caithness. The first person to discuss the significance of this letter in the context of golf history was Andrew Lang in his book *A History of Britain* (1902). Lang drew attention to a comment made in the letter in which cannonballs that had been used in the siege of Kirkwall Castle in the Orkney Islands were described as having been 'broken like golf balls, and cloven in two halfs'.[579] It is this description of broken cannonballs that led Andrew Lang (and subsequently many others) to conclude that golf balls from this period were made of wood. Lang's assessment of the Earl's comment was:

> a feather golf-ball, such as was used in the eighteenth and early nineteenth centuries, cannot break into two fragments, as a gutta-percha or a wooded golf-ball does. Hence we may infer that the golf-balls of King James's reign were wooden.

However, Andrew Lang's quotation from the letter is not entirely accurate. The original letter, written by the Earl of Caithness in 1614, is available for consultation in the National Library of Scotland[580] and it differs subtly but perhaps significantly from Lang's published quotation. The wording of the original letter is 'cannone billetts both brokkin lyk goulfe balls upoune the castelle and clovin in twa halffis'. The writer's use of 'both' in this sentence seems to indicate that he is describing cannonballs that were broken in two distinct ways. That is, on the one hand, cannonballs that were 'cloven in two halves' and, on the other, those that were 'broken like golf balls'. If so, this would weaken the argument that was used by Lang when he postulated that golf balls from this era must have been wooden, an argument that is based entirely on the assertion that a leather ball cannot break into two fragments. Leather balls did, of course, frequently 'break' and perhaps it is the particular way in which leather balls break that provided a useful simile with which to describe those cannonballs that were 'broken' but which were not 'cloven in two halves'. This is not to say that balls made of wood have never been used for golf. Due to a scarcity of rubber in the Second World War, there is evidence of golf balls being made from wood. The *Sunday Post* (Glasgow) reported in 1944 that, 'So short are supplies of rubber that an English firm is placing a wooden golf ball on the market.'[581] A report in the *Nottingham Evening Post* the same year mentioned that 'Golf balls made of a very tough wood are being used on South African courses owing to the great scarcity of the more orthodox products.'[582] The balls were described as having 'mesh markings and are enamelled white'. Another English newspaper reported in 1943 that wooden balls being produced by a firm in Southern Rhodesia were registered under the trademark 'Fleetwood' and were being sold at two shillings each.[583] Consequently, there is evidence of wooden balls having been used for golf in unusual circumstances, such as during the Second World War.

John Daly and a Wooden Golf Ball (1550)

A surprising claim concerning wooden golf balls has emerged in recent years. It is a claim that golf was played with wooden balls in 1550 and is a story that has been mentioned in several golf books, as well as on numerous websites. However, on no occasion has a documentary source ever been cited and, in that respect, it would appear to have many of the characteristics of the more well-established myth concerning a golf ball in 1452 (discussed in Chapter 1). The earliest example of the claim that I have come across is in *Golf's Book of Firsts* (2002),[584] which mentions that 'one documented reference tells of a man named

John Daly playing with a wooden [golf] ball (possibly beechwood) in 1550'. In 2005 the story was repeated in Nepal's English-language newspaper the *Nepali Times* (Kathmandu),[585] where it was explained that this was not a reference to the 'John Daly' of modern-day golf fame. In 2012 a pared-down version of the story appeared in the school textbook *Principles of Engineering*,[586] in which it was stated that 'documents dating as far back as 1550 reference the use of wooden golf balls'. Among the numerous websites that have repeated this story can be found comments such as, 'The history of golf balls is back dated to 1550 where some claim that a John Daly used a wooden ball.'[587] It is hard to imagine what could be the basis of this story. I am unaware of any references to a 'John Daly' in any documents relating to early golf or of any early documents that describe the use of wooden balls in 1550. One possibility is that it is a corruption of a story that was first recorded in *Neederlandsche Histoorien* (1642). In this history of the Netherlands there is recorded an account (in Dutch) of a visit by John of Glymes, Marquess of Berghes, to Spain in 1556. It describes John of Glymes being wounded after being hit on the leg by a wooden ball (probably in connection with a game of pall-mall).[588] Perhaps a garbled version of this obscure reference from a seventeenth-century Dutch text may have become corrupted into a golf myth concerning John Daly. It is possible that a story concerning John of Glymes being struck on the leg by a wooden ball during a game of pall-mall in 1556 somehow morphed into a story in which John Daly played golf with a wooden ball in 1550. Further research may be required but this story has all the hallmarks of a modern golf myth.

Leather Balls and Common Balls

While there appears to be no direct evidence for golf balls having been made of wood in the early history of 'long golf', there is very clear evidence to indicate that early golf balls were made of leather and that golf-ball making was a trade that was linked to that of shoemakers and leather-workers (cordiners or cordwainers). The earliest example is a handwritten document from 1554 concerning the 'Cordiners and Gowf-ball makers of North Leith'[589] but a series of other sources dating from 1639 to 1654 establish clear links between cordiners or shoemakers and the manufacture of golf balls.[590] Another argument that is sometimes advanced when suggesting that at least some early golf balls may have been made of wood comes from a letter that was written in 1585 and which mentions as a postscript, 'Ye will remember to bring with you ane dossen of common golf ballis.'[591] This would suggest that there was more than one type of golf ball in the late sixteenth century. An argument that is sometimes made is that this reference to 'common golf balls' may be a reference to inferior wooden balls. However, it is clear from contemporary accounts that there were superior and inferior varieties of leather balls, perhaps made by highly skilled and by less-skilled ball-makers.

Some of the clearest evidence indicating that different qualities of golf balls were used comes from the accounts of three students from St Andrews between 1712 and 1716. This is a period that is universally considered to be the 'leather-ball era', at a time when there are numerous references to leather balls and no evidence of wooden golf balls having been used for golf. These accounts, which record expenditure incurred by three students at St Andrews (sixteen-year-old Alexander and his twelve-year-old twin brothers Kenneth and Thomas), were maintained by their tutor James Morice and have been discussed at length elsewhere.[592] Over a twelve-month period (from November 1712 to October 1713) James Morice purchased a total of 110 balls for the two younger boys and seventy-six balls for Alexander, who appears to have played golf more frequently. Significantly, the accounts reveal that Alexander, who was presumably a better and more experienced golfer, always received golf balls costing four shillings, whereas the two younger boys always played with cheaper balls, costing two shillings each. The frequency with which the balls were purchased suggests they typically lasted for just one round of golf, which suggests that both types are likely to have been fragile leather balls. Indeed, it has been estimated that the boys' golf was costing more than their tuition at St Andrews,[593] which provides further evidence that golf was primarily a game for the wealthy during the leather-ball era.

Further evidence for the existence of differing qualities of early golf balls was uncovered recently[594] from the testament of John Dickson, a Leith ball-maker, who died in 1729.[595] Among the inventory of his possessions is evidence of five different qualities of golf ball (presumably leather balls)[596] of differing value. The 'gooff balls' are described as: 'very coarse' (16d/dozen), 'the coarser sort'

(18d/dozen), 'another sort' (22d/dozen), 'finer' (two shillings/dozen) and 'fine' (three shillings/dozen).[597]

Imported Golf Balls

Evidence for the importation of golf balls into Scotland in the early seventeenth century is provided by a decree that was issued by King James VI (also now James I of England). On 5 August 1618, James VI/I granted a monopoly to James Melvill and his associates to manufacture and sell golf balls (Figure 12.2).[598] As justification for issuing the monopoly, the document referred to the considerable cost to the Scottish economy that was passing 'yeirlie out of his hienes kingdome for bying of golf ballis'. It stated that, for a period of twenty-one years, no one else in the kingdom would be permitted to 'mak or sell anie golf ballis'. The king's motive in issuing the monopoly to Melvill appears to have been largely financial; the document makes clear that a proportion of the profits would be retained by the king ('half of the benefitte aryssing thairby to come to our soverane Lordis use, and the uther half to the use of the said James Melvill'). The document also instructs Melvill to use a 'particular stamp' to mark his

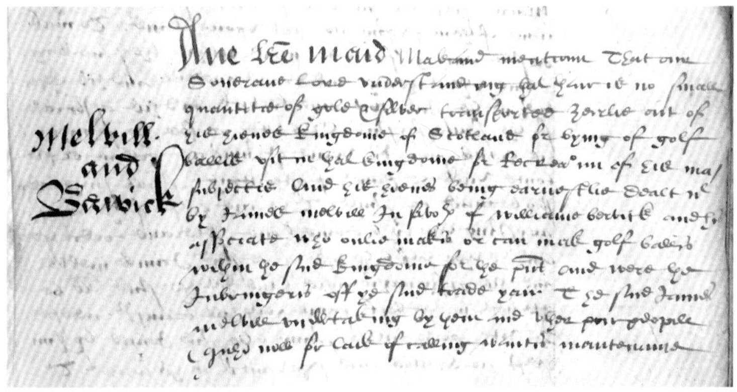

Figure 12.2 Licence granted to James Melvill in 1618. King James VI/I granted a monopoly to James Melvill (on 5 August 1618) to manufacture and sell golf balls. The stated purpose of the licence was to reduce the amount being spent on importing balls into Scotland. It is this event in 1618 that perhaps explains why the date of 1618 is so frequently (but incorrectly) suggested as being the date that the feather golf ball was 'invented'. © National Records of Scotland; PS1/87, ff.169–70.

golf balls and that any balls stamped otherwise would be confiscated ('all ballis maid within the kingdom found to be utherwayis stamped shall be escheated'). Whereas Melvill's monopoly was intended to last for twenty-one years (until 1639), there is evidence of it having been challenged in 1629, a few years after the death of James VI/I, at a time when his son Charles I had acceded to the throne. In 1629 a complaint was issued by William and Thomas Dickson, 'makers of gowffe ballis in Leith', in which they complain of unfair taxes being imposed by James Melvill.[599] It appears that Melvill had sent a number of 'lawlesse' thugs who were making 'manie threatning and execrable oathes' and who confiscated a 'greate number of gowffe ballis'. Melvill was ordered to pay five pounds for the nineteen golf balls that had been seized but it is unclear if this indicated the end of his twenty-one-year monopoly.

Balls Imported from Holland?

Robert Clark, in *Golf a Royal and Ancient Game* (1875), assumed that the golf balls referred to in the decree issued by James VI in favour of James Melvill were being imported from Holland, which is certainly possible. However, golf historian Robert Browning dismissed this idea, stating, 'I do not believe that in 1618 Scotland was importing golf balls either from Holland or anywhere else.'[600] Browning argued that the 'specious' suggestion that revenue was being lost to Scotland due to the importation of golf balls had been concocted by the king simply to justify the granting of a monopoly (the granting of monopolies being a recognised method by which the king raised funds).

In 1982 Steven van Hengel described evidence that balls (though not necessarily golf balls) were being exported from Holland to Scotland as early as 1486.[601] Reference to the source that was cited by van Hengel confirms that Scotland was one of several countries with which the Dutch were trading at this time, for example by importing Scottish wool (*Schotsche wol*), but it doesn't provide direct evidence that it was to Scotland that the balls were being exported.[602] Because of this remaining uncertainty, I was interested to discover evidence that balls *were* being imported into Scotland in the period 1597–1612 and, importantly, that they were referred to as being 'golf' balls. The evidence comes from the Scottish 'Book of Rates', in which the rateable value of goods imported into Scotland is recorded, although the location from which the goods were imported is not identified. In 1597 custom duties were imposed on all goods imported into Scotland, rather than only on wine and English goods as had occurred previously.[603] These rates were revised in 1611 and again in 1612 due to concerns that some goods had been either over- or under-rated. All three of the books concerning Scottish import rates from this period contain the rateable value for imported golf balls.[604] Throughout this period (1597–1612) the rateable value of a dozen golf balls fluctuated somewhat, being twenty shillings in 1597,[605] thirty-two shillings in 1611[606] and twenty-six shillings and eight pence in 1612.[607] The entries in the import rate books for 1597, 1611 and 1612 are, respectively:

> Golf Ballis the do[zen] — xx s.
> Balles called Golf balls the dozen — xxxij s.
> Ballis called Golf ballis the dozen — xxvi s. viii d.

It is notable that the rateable value of a dozen imported golf balls in 1611 is identical to the assessed value of the golf balls that were listed in William Mayne's testament at the time of his death in 1612 (thirty-two shillings per dozen; Chapter 7). It is certainly possible that the 'flok' golf balls that were supplied by William Mayne were imported balls, rather than balls that were manufactured in Scotland. It is also possible that imported/flok balls may be an example of the 'commoun golf ballis' that are known to have existed in Scotland at this time.[608] In 1597 a dozen imported balls had an assessed value of twenty shillings, whereas the treasury accounts from a similar time (1601; see Chapter 7) show the king buying a dozen golf balls for forty shillings. If two types of golf balls were available in Scotland at this time – common golf balls (perhaps imported/flok-filled) and better-quality balls (perhaps locally produced/feather-filled), it seems likely that the king would use the best quality that was available to him.

In addition to listing golf balls, the 'Imports' section of the Scottish Book of Rates also lists 'raket balls' (in 1597), 'catchpule balls' (1611) and 'catchpoole ballis' (1612), all of which are probably references to balls used for playing tennis-like games. Catchpull/caichpule is defined as hand tennis in the *Dictionary of the Scots Language* and it has been suggested that it may derive from the Flemish word *caetsspel/kaatspel*, literally 'chase-game'.

The Books of Rates for England and Wales from this period (1604–57) list imported 'tennis balls' but make no mention of golf balls.[609] Interestingly, whereas golf balls were rated by the dozen in the Scottish Books of Rates, imported tennis/catchpull balls are almost always rated by the thousand (in both the Scottish and English Books of Rates).[610] This presumably reflects the popularity of tennis in Scotland and England but also the requirement for multiple balls during games of tennis. In addition, it seems likely that tennis balls might be particularly susceptible to damage, being repeatedly struck against the hard surface of the court during a game. Whereas golf balls were listed in the Scottish rate books for 1597, 1611 and 1612, a later edition of the Scottish Book of Rates (1657) lists tennis balls but no longer lists imported golf balls.[611] This absence of a reference to golf balls being imported into Scotland in 1657 could be seen as being consistent with the royal decree, mentioned earlier, in which a monopoly on the manufacture of golf balls was issued in 1618 to James Melvill and, at the same time, imposing a ban on the importation of golf balls.

A 1618 Golf Ball Myth

Given the absence of any direct evidence for the existence of wooden golf balls being used for the traditional long game of golf, together with the strong evidence that early golf balls were made of leather, it is surprising to see frequent claims that the feather golf balls were 'introduced' or 'invented in 1618'. What is frequently linked to such statements is the claim that, prior to this date, balls were made of wood. For example, it has been suggested that 'golf balls were originally crafted of wood, but in 1618 the golfing world was introduced to the "featherie" golf ball'.[612] This idea appears to have originated as a result of a comment made by Robert Browning in *A History of Golf* (1955). An appendix in that book entitled 'A Chronological Table of Leading Events' identifies the date of the 'introduction' of the feather golf ball as '1618(?)', with the question mark presumably indicating a degree of uncertainty. It is a claim that has been restated frequently and uncritically in a variety of contexts. For example, it is claimed that 1618 is the date that the feather golf ball was 'created',[613] 'debuted',[614] 'first handcrafted',[615] 'first made',[616] 'first manufactured',[617] 'invented'[618] and 'introduced'.[619] Similarly, it is said to be the date that the feather ball 'began coming into use[620] and 'came into existence'.[621] This illustrates how a statement, such as the one made with a slight degree of caution in 1955, can have a significant influence on how others view the history of golf. I suspect that Robert Browning, when first he made the claim in 1955, had in mind the date that King James VI/I issued a monopoly in 1618 to James Melvill for the manufacture and sale of golf balls. It may also be appropriate to point out that not all golf writers have adopted the dubious claim that feather balls were introduced in 1618. For example, it has been suggested that feather balls were in use 'from about the year 1400',[622] 'in the 1400s',[623] 'around 1440',[624] 'from 1440–1848'[625] and '1450 to the 1880s'.[626] Somewhat less seriously, the writer and broadcaster Alistair Cooke described the era of the feather balls as spanning two thousand years (which he expressed as '55 BC–AD 1845').[627] Similarly, James Balfour wrote in 1887 that balls 'made of leather stuffed with feathers' have been used by golfers 'from time immemorial'.[628] All of these authors, although they have expressed it in different ways, would appear to agree that the feather ball was in existence long before 1618 and that it continued to be used until the introduction of gutta-percha in the 1840s.

In Summary

There is no clear evidence that early golf balls used for the 'long game' of golf were made of wood, whereas there is extensive evidence to indicate that balls made of leather filled with feathers were used extensively until the introduction of gutta-percha balls in the 1840s. Even if it could be argued that some early golf balls were made of wood (which is possible), there is still no reason to conclude that 1618 should be considered the date that the feather golf ball was 'invented', particularly since there is evidence from 1554, some sixty years earlier, of trade being conducted by 'Cordiners and Gowf-ball makers of North Leith'. There is also evidence of golf balls being imported into Scotland in the late sixteenth and early seventeenth centuries.

Chapter 13

Early Clubs and Caddies

Evidence of Early Clubs from Paintings and Documents

There is relatively little reliable information concerning the earliest types of clubs that were used to play the game of golf. The earliest unambiguous written reference to the purchase of golf clubs dates from 1503/4 when King James IV of Scotland paid nine shillings for 'golf clubbes and balles' (as discussed in Chapter 3).[629] However, this and other early documentary sources provide no specific information about the type of golf clubs that were in use at that time. Unfortunately, none of the very earliest golf clubs appear to have survived and accurate dating of early surviving golf clubs is challenging. While some rare examples may date from the latter part of the seventeenth century, there are several golf clubs that can be dated with reasonable confidence to the early part of the eighteenth century (Figure 13.1). Information about early golf clubs is also available from paintings depicting golf and from portraits of golfers. However, the earliest of these dates from c. 1740 (Figure 13.2). In marked contrast, there has been a much longer tradition of painting rural scenes in the Low Countries and, as a consequence, there are several earlier examples of paintings depicting sports such as *colf*, as has been well documented in books such as *Golf & Kolf* (1993),[630] *Golf Through the Ages* (2004)[631] and *Serendipity of Golf* (2010).[632]

The Use of Multiple Clubs and Differing Designs

There has been much discussion of possible links between early Scottish golf and other stick-and-ball games (something that will be examined in Chapter 16) but something that appears to set golf apart from most other early stick-and-ball games is the varied terrain over which it is played and, as a consequence, the requirement for multiple clubs with differing playing characteristics. This is in contrast to what has been described as 'short golf' that is thought to have been played in locations such as churchyards, or

Figure 13.1 Early golf clubs. It is unlikely that any of the very earliest golf clubs have survived and, although dating early clubs can be a challenge, these are examples of what are thought to be some of the earliest surviving golf clubs (c. 1700–50). Illustrated from left to right are a long spoon/scraper, a putter, a light iron and a heavy iron. For further details of these clubs, see Ellis (2007), Vol. I, 25–9, 33–9, 40–1, 116–17. Images © Jeffrey B. Ellis.

for hockey-like games such as shinty.[633] A single type of club is also normally considered sufficient for croquet-like games, such as pall-mall, that are played on flat courts and indoor games such as *kolf* but also for outdoor games such as *colf*, which was often played on ice. So the use of multiple types of clubs, typically carried by caddies, appears to be a characteristic feature of Scottish 'long golf' and something that may distinguish it from other contemporary stick-and-ball games.

Figure 13.2 Early golfers, golf clubs and caddies in eighteenth-century paintings. A painting (c. 1740) depicting golfers and caddies at St Andrews is believed to be one of the oldest images depicting golf (top); a portrait (c. 1749) of two boys, one of whom (Alexander MacDonald) is holding a golf club (bottom left); and a portrait by David Allan of William Inglis, who was Captain of the Edinburgh Company of Golfers from 1782 to 1784 (bottom right). Top image: Reproduced with kind permission of the Royal and Ancient Golf Club of St Andrews, RNA 14 018. Bottom images: © National Galleries Scotland, PG 2127 and PG 1971.

While it has been argued on occasion that early golf may have been played with just a single club,[634] this does not appear to be supported by the weight of evidence. The varying terrain and unpredictable lie of a ball on a Scottish links course is not well-suited to a player who attempts to rely upon a single club. Indeed, the obvious desirability of having a variety of different types of golf club may explain why it is common for early records to describe the simultaneous purchase of multiple clubs. For example, James IV is recorded as having bought 'golf clubbes and balles' in 1503/4[635] and there are records of the Duke of

Buckingham buying 'clubbes and balles' in 1624.[636] However, some of the clearest evidence that early golf was played with multiple clubs can be found in a letter written in 1691 by a professor at St Andrews who describes 'ane sett of Golfe-Clubs consisting of three, viz. an play club, ane scraper and ane tin fac'd club' (Figure 13.3).[637] The possible meaning of a 'tin-faced' club will be discussed subsequently but it is interesting that this 'set' of golf clubs (an expression that might be assumed to be an exclusively modern-day term) makes no mention of a putting club. There is, however, evidence of 'putting clubs' being used at this time. A letter written in 1690 refers to a 'short putting club' and, interestingly, appears to contrast the use of this club to what is required for 'long gauff'.[638] It is possible, however, that specialist putting clubs were not always considered necessary due to the likelihood that early golf was not played on manicured putting greens. Evidence to support this conclusion is provided by the early Rules of Golf. For example, the Leith Rules of 1744 state that the ball must be teed 'within a club length of the hole'.[639] Even when the concept of a separate 'teeing ground' was introduced in 1875, players were still being advised to tee their ball between eight and twelve club-lengths from the hole if a teeing ground had not been marked out.[640]

An entry in the accounts of Sir John Foulis from 1703 concerns a visit from Edinburgh to Leith to play golf when he paid three shillings 'for a loan of 3 clubs'.[641] In addition to providing evidence that clubs were available for hire at Leith at this time, this provides additional evidence for the use of multiple clubs to play a round of golf and, perhaps, that three clubs were considered to be sufficient. Further evidence that multiple types of clubs were used by early golfers is provided by a document from 1629 that makes reference to '2 bonker clubis, a iyrone club, and twa play clubis'.[642] The description 'bonker club' [bunker club] is of particular interest, since it suggests that clubs had been designed with the specific aim of facilitating the play of a ball from a bunker as early as 1629.

Caddies

To an extent, it is probably the use of multiple clubs for a round of golf that might necessitate the employment of a caddie to carry a player's clubs. The golf caddie as a profession is perhaps as old as

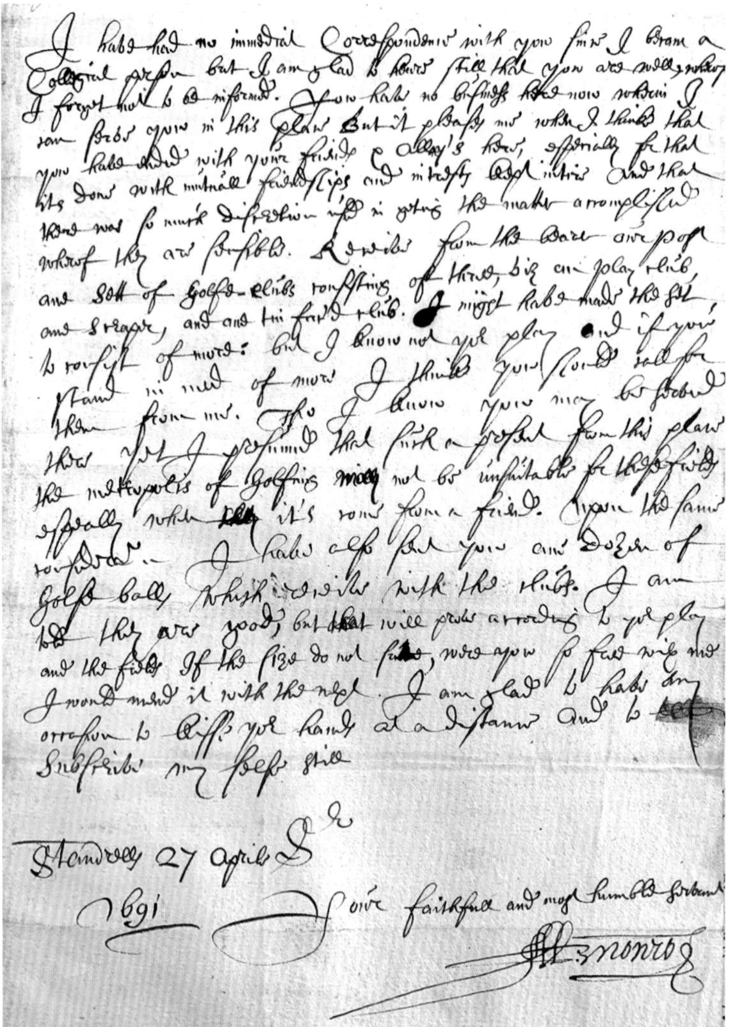
I have had no immediat Correspondence with you since I became a
Collegiat person but I am glad to hear still that you are well, whom
I forget not to be informed. You have no business here now when I
can see you in this place but it pleases me when I think that
you have ended with your friends in Abbey's house, especially for that
its done with mutuall friendships and in trust acquaintance And that
there was so much discretion used in getting the matter accomplished
whereof they are sensible. Herewith from the bearer ye receive
ane Sett of Golfe-Clubs consisting of three, viz. an play club,
ane Scraper, and ane tin fac'd club. I might have made the set
to consist of more: but I know not your play and if you
stand in need of more I think you should call for
them from me. Tho I know you may be served
there yet I presumed that such a present from this place
the metropolis of Golfing may not be unsuitable for these fields
especially when it's come from a friend. Upon the same
consideration I have also sent you ane Dozen of
Golfe balls which come with the clubs. I am
told they are good, but that will prove according to your play
and the fields. If the size do not sute, were you so free with me
I would mend it with the next. I am glad to have any
occasion to kiss your hands at a distance and to
subscribe myself still

Sr

St Andrews 27 April
1691

Your faithfull and most humble servant
Al: Monro

Figure 13.3 A letter sent from St Andrews in 1691 describing a set of golf clubs. In the letter, dated 27 April 1691, Alexander Monro of St Andrews mentions that he has sent 'ane Sett of Golf-Clubs consisting of three, viz. an play club, ane Scraper, and ane tin fac'd club'. He also mentions that he has sent 'ane Dozen Golfe balls' and states that 'I am told they are good'. National Library of Scotland, MS.1393, 177.

the game of golf itself. However, the earliest documented instance of a golfer having employed an assistant to carry his clubs probably dates from 1628 and is recorded in the accounts of James Graham, the sixteen-year-old Earl of Montrose.[643] While studying at St Andrews University, Montrose spent much of his time engaged in recreations such as archery and golf and is recorded as making frequent payments to boys for carrying either his arrows or his golf clubs. For example, the accounts, recorded by his assistant John Lambye, show that Montrose was something of a philanthropist, making frequent donations to 'the poor'. Indeed, in a biography of Montrose, published in 1848, it was suggested that he rarely engaged in any activity 'without bestowing something on the poor'.[644] In addition to describing the Earl of Montrose's expenditure on golf balls and clubs, John Lambye records three payments in 1628 to boys who had carried Montrose's golf clubs:

to the boy who carried my Lords clubs to the fields	3 sh.
to the poor, and boys who carried my Lords clubs that week	8 sh.
to the poor and the boy who carried my Lords clubs that week	8 sh.[645]

These payments took place in November and December 1628 and would appear to be the first documented examples of someone being employed to carry golf clubs. It has been claimed that these payments may have occurred when the Earl of Montrose was playing golf in the town of Montrose, but they almost certainly occurred when he was golfing in St Andrews.[646] Further examples of payments for carrying clubs are documented in the account books of Sir John Foulis of Ravelston (1671–1707).[647] For example, Foulis records having paid four shillings 'to the boy that caried my clubs' after playing golf at Leith (in 1672)[648] and two shillings 'to the lad [who] carried the clubs' (in 1692).[649] Similar payments are mentioned in the diaries of Thomas Kincaid, who paid three shillings 'to the boy' in 1688, on a day when Kincaid had visited Leith to play both archery and golf.[650] Kincaid does not state explicitly that the payment of three shillings was to a boy for carrying clubs, but this would be a reasonable conclusion.

At first sight, Montrose (1628), Foulis (1672–92) and Kincaid (1688) may seem to have paid rather large amounts of money to those who carried their clubs, particularly since, as will be discussed later, golfers in the 1700s are recorded as paying caddies only a few pence per round of golf. One author commented in 1989 on the apparent generosity of seventeenth-century golfers and speculated on why they may have paid 'over the odds'.[651] In fact, golfers were paying broadly similar amounts to their caddies in the late 1600s and in the 1700s. Prior to the Acts of Union (1707), the currency of Scotland (the Pound Scots) was worth only one-twelfth of the Pound Sterling (the currency of England prior to 1707 and the currency of Britain after 1707).

Early References to Caddies

While the previously mentioned financial accounts of Montrose (1628), Foulis (1672–92) and Kincaid (1688) are perhaps the earliest documented examples of payments to boys for carrying golf clubs, none of these use the word 'caddie'. It has been suggested that the 'first use of the word caddie is in the account of Andrew Dickson of Leith, ball-maker and caddie (1655–1729), who ran forward to mark the balls for the Duke of York'.[652] However, this conclusion is potentially misleading, since Andrew Dickson himself does not appear to have left any first-hand account of this incident. Instead, we have an anecdotal report from 1792 (long after Andrew Dickson's death) by someone who claimed 'in his youth' to have 'conversed with an old man named Andrew Dickson'.[653] This account from 1792 does not use the word caddie, nor does it indicate that Dickson himself used the term. However, the anecdote was reported in newspapers published in 1792 that suggested that 'Dickson was then performing the duty of what is now commonly called a *fore-cadie*'.[654]

An obvious place to look for early written references to golf caddies would be within the minute books of the earliest golf societies and indeed the first minute book of the Gentlemen Golfers of Leith records the following entry dated 11 March 1771: 'when a Golf Ball lyes half in Water in the Green, the player shall be at liberty to take out the Ball and cause his Cadie to drop the Ball behind the hazard'.[655] Similarly, the St Andrews minutes of 27 June 1771 mention that the caddies 'are to get four pence sterling for going the length of the holl called the Holl of Cross and if they go further than that hole they are to get six pence and no more'. The minutes continue by specifying, 'Any of the

Gentlemen of this Society transgressing the rule are to pay two pint Bottles of Claret at the first meeting they shall attend.'[656]

From 1771 onwards, references to golf caddies appear with some regularity in the minute books of early golf societies, particularly in entries relating to the Rules of Golf. The general impression conveyed by references to caddies in these minute books is of a desire to discourage members from being overly generous in their payment to or their treatment of caddies. This is illustrated clearly in the first minute book of 'The Society of Golfers in and about Edinburgh at Bruntsfield Links' (dating from 1773). In a set of rules adopted in 1773 it is stated, 'No Golfer shall under any pretence whatever give any old Balls to the Cadies, if they do, they shall for every such Ball given away forfeit sixpence to the Treasurer.'[657] The same source emphasises that 'no member of this Society pay the Cadies more than one penny p. round'.

Handwritten entries in the minute books of golfing societies would have been accessible to only a handful of people and do not indicate that the word was in common use among non-golfers. There is, however, evidence from the late eighteenth century that 'golf caddie' was a widely understood term, at least in Scotland. As far as I am aware, the earliest reference demonstrating a more widespread use of the word, and also the earliest verifiable example of the word in printed (typeset) form, dates from 1787. In a newspaper advertisement for an evening of theatrical entertainment entitled 'Away for Leith Links or A Golfing we Will Go!', it is stated, 'The Golfers will be dressed in the uniform of the Golf Club, attended by Cadies.'[658]

In Tobias Smollett's novel *The Expedition of Humphry Clinker* (1771), it is mentioned that 'There is at Edinburgh a society or corporation of errand-boys, called cawdies, who ply the streets at night with paper lanthorns, and are very serviceable in carrying messages.'[659] Although this description comes immediately after a description of golf being played at Leith, Smollett does not use the term 'cawdies' in a golf context. It is clear that the term caddie (or cawdie, or cady, etc.), as used to describe someone employed to carry golf clubs, was in widespread use in the eighteenth century. Interestingly, there is evidence that the word was used simultaneously by members of early golf societies to describe those undertaking a variety of other menial tasks. This is illustrated by entries in the account books of the Gentlemen Golfers of Leith. An entry from 6 December 1782 describes a payment to 'Cadys for collecting 35 Subscriptions at 6d each'.[660] This perhaps supports the suggestion, put forward by others, that the use of caddie to describe a carrier of golf clubs derives from its more general and older usage in Scotland to describe messengers and errand-boys.[661]

The Design of Early Golf Clubs

Thomas Kincaid, an Edinburgh medical student, recorded in his diary in 1687:

> The shaft of your club most be of hazell. Your club most be almost straight, that is, the head most make a verie obtuse angle with the shaft, and it most bend as much at the handle as it doth at the wooping, being very supple and both long and great.[662]

The limited evidence that is available concerning early golf clubs suggests that they were fragile and more prone to damage to their shafts than was the case after the importation of hickory for use in shafts in the nineteenth century. Indeed, there is evidence of golf clubs being repaired in the sixteenth, seventeenth and eighteenth centuries. For example, there are references to 'ane club mending' (in 1599),[663] 'dressing some auld clubs' (1629),[664] 'mending my play club' (1686)[665] and 'mending a club' (1713).[666] There is also evidence that the heads of early wooden clubs were protected by the addition of animal horn, presumably to protect the lower leading edge, as continued to be a feature of many wooden clubs up until the early twentieth century. There are several instances of the purchase of horn for early golf clubs, presumably for their repair, for example in the accounts of Sir John Foulis in 1686[667] and those of St Andrews students in 1712.[668] In 1771 golf clubs were described by one observer as being 'curious bats, tipt with horn'.[669]

It is of interest that the previously mentioned 'set' of golf clubs sent from St Andrews in 1691 included 'ane tin fac'd club'.[670] There is also a reference in accounts of Sir John Foulis (also from 1691) to two 'new tin heads to clubs'[671] and a much earlier reference (from 1599) to a 'tene adge [tin edge?] and ane club mending' in accounts detailing payments to a bow-maker for items such as 'goulff clubs'.[672] Whereas references to 'iron clubs', mentioned previously, are likely to be clubs with wooden shafts attached to solid iron clubheads, it seems less likely that a clubhead might have been made entirely from a soft metal such as tin. It seems possible that tin (or more probably a harder alloy of tin such as pewter) may have been applied to a wooden clubhead for protection, much in the same way that horn was used to protect the leading edge of a wooden club, or as brass soleplates were used on 'brassie' clubs up until the twentieth century. Another possibility that has been suggested previously is that tin-faced clubs might be a reference to the tinning of an iron clubhead to prevent rusting.[673] Indeed, there is evidence of items such as keys, nails, spurs, stirrups and swords being tinned in sixteenth-century Scotland.[674]

Just as twentieth-century wooden-headed golf clubs often had weight added to the clubhead by pouring molten lead into a cavity, it appears that a similar approach may have been used to add weight to early golf clubs. The description of the golf club provided by the *Encyclopædia Britannica* in 1797 is 'a slender and elastic club of about four feet long, crooked in the head, and having lead run into it, to make it heavy'.[675] However, one of the most detailed descriptions of early golf clubs, which mentions the use of both horn and lead, is provided in *Hoyle's Games* (1790):

> The Club is taper, terminating in the Part that strikes the Ball, which is faced with Horn, and loaded with Lead. But of this there are six Sorts used by good Players; namely, the *Common Club*, used when the Ball lies on good Ground; the *Scraper* and *Half-Scraper*, when in long Grass; the *Spoon*, when in a Hollow; the *Heavy Iron Club*, when it lies deep amongst Stones or Mud; and the *Light Iron ditto*, when on the Surface of chingle or sandy Ground.[676]

Hoyle's Games describes 'six sorts' of golf club in 1790, which is more than the previously described 'set' of three mentioned in 1691. However, further evidence that early golfers may have considered three clubs to be sufficient comes from a letter written in 1735 in which golf clubs were ordered from an Edinburgh club-maker and which states, 'Tell him to provide me with nine clubs viz three play clubs, three scrapers, one of which a half scraper or spoon and three putting clubs.'[677] Although nine clubs were requested, it is possible that this may have been three sets of three clubs. There has been some debate about the term 'scraper' and whether this might describe a club used to drag (or 'scrape') a ball from a bad lie without the need for a backswing. What seems more likely is that the term 'scraper' described a commonly used club that had more loft than a standard 'play club'. This seems to be supported by the request for clubs in 1735 in which 'half-scraper' or 'spoon' were given as examples, perhaps being 'scrapers' with differing degrees of loft. A 'lead scraper club' is mentioned in 1686,[678] which may perhaps have been a lofted wooden club that contained lead to increase its weight.[679]

In Summary

A characteristic feature of golf is that it is played over varying terrain and therefore requires a variety of different clubs, something that in turn led to the employment of caddies to carry a player's clubs. Evidence suggests that early wooden clubheads were often weighted with lead and protected by the addition of material such as horn, as was the case with clubs that were produced up until the twentieth century. There is also evidence of early clubs with iron heads, the forerunner of modern-day 'irons'.

Chapter 14

Early Golf Societies and Early Women's Golf

Early Golf Societies

It is not until almost three hundred years after the first written reference to golf that there is evidence for the establishment of organised golf competitions or organised golf societies. On 7 March 1744, the minutes of the Town Council of Edinburgh describe an agreement to provide a silver club as a trophy for an annual golf competition that was to be played on the links of Leith.[680] The Act records that the silver club had been presented by the City of Edinburgh in response to a request from 'Several Gentlemen of Honour, Skilfull in the Ancient and Healthfull Exercise of Golf'. A copy of this agreement was included in the first minute book of the Gentlemen Golfers of Leith and those minutes confirm that the first competition for the silver club was held on 2 April 1744 and that it was won by Mr John Rattray, a surgeon from Edinburgh.[681] One of the regulations of the competition was that the winner of the competition would be considered 'Captain of the Golf' and that he would be required to attach 'a gold or silver piece' to the club (Figure 14.1). Although captains are now elected, the tradition of attaching an engraved replica of a golf ball to the silver club has continued, as it has in several other golf societies.

There is little evidence that prior to the nineteenth century golfers paid much attention to the relative antiquity of their golf societies. For example, the Edinburgh Company of Golfers had been listed in directories such as *The Edinburgh Almanack* and *The Universal Scots Almanack* since the 1780s[682] but it wasn't until almost thirty years later (c. 1812) that the society included its foundation date of 1744.[683] What may have changed this apparent sense of disinterest among golfers about the relative antiquity of their golf societies was the first appearance in the *Edinburgh Almanack* (in 1830) of the Blackheath Golf Club. Somewhat unexpectedly, given that it was a London Club, the Blackheath Golf Club requested in 1830

Prize of the Silver Golf. at Edn. 1787.

Figure 14.1 The silver golf club presented by the City of Edinburgh in 1744. This painting, *Prize of the Silver Golf [Club] at Edn.*, by David Allan (1787) depicts a procession displaying a silver golf club that was presented by the City of Edinburgh in 1744 for an annual golf match at Leith. Silver replica golf balls were appended to the trophy by the winner of the competition, a tradition that has continued by annually elected captains. © National Galleries Scotland, D 387.

that it be listed in the *Edinburgh Almanack*[684] and, significantly, it included the claim 'Established prior to 1745'.[685] This claim appears to have prompted a flurry of activity by the Edinburgh societies, now wanting to assert their own foundation dates. Over the next few years, the *Edinburgh Almanack* included foundation dates for the Bruntsfield Links Golfing Society (1761)[686] and the Musselburgh Golf Club (1774).[687] These dates were either supported by reliable evidence or were relatively uncontroversial[688] and, consequently, may have caused little comment. In contrast, the Edinburgh Burgess Golfing Society announced in 1834 that it had been 'Instituted about 1735',[689] an approximate foundation date that was ten years earlier than that of the Edinburgh Company of Golfers. In the following year's *Edinburgh Almanack* (1835) the foundation date of the Edinburgh Burgess Golfing Society was stated simply as '1735'.[690] The earliest minute book of the Edinburgh Burgess Golfing Society is dated 1773 but it includes a comment concerning 'the present state of the said Society' that suggests it had existed prior to 1773.[691] The precise date (1735) that was claimed in the *Edinburgh Almanack* is harder to explain. A cynic might suggest that, by proposing a foundation date of 1735 in the year 1834, it would enable the society to hold a centenary celebration the following year. However, an entry in the society's minute book from 1835 suggests that it was having financial difficulties at the time and there are no records of any celebrations having taken place the following year.[692] The Burgess Society did, however, celebrate its 'bicentenary' in 1935 and its '250th anniversary' in 1985.[693]

The Edinburgh Company of Golfers had been somewhat distracted during this period and had initially remained quiet. Like the Burgess Society, they were experiencing financial problems and this resulted in the society selling most of their assets in 1833 (including portraits, silver and furniture). Additionally, in the following year they sold 'Golf House', their clubhouse at Leith.[694] After several years, seemingly in abeyance, the club resurfaced at a new home in Musselburgh. The society subsequently reappeared in the 1839 *Edinburgh Almanack*, after a five-year absence, and was now described as the 'Honourable Company of Edinburgh Golfers'.[695] It appears that they now felt the need to respond to Blackheath's claim of having been established prior to 1745, not to mention the claim by the Burgess Society of having been instituted in 1735. In 1839 the reinvigorated Honourable Company of Edinburgh Golfers made the following announcement in the *Edinburgh Almanack*:[696]

> HONOURABLE COMPANY OF EDINBURGH GOLFERS.
> The period at which the Company was formed cannot now be ascertained; but the first of a regular series of minutes, signed by President Forbes of Culloden, bears date 1744.

The following year, perhaps as a result of the reappearance of a newly emboldened Honourable Company, the Blackheath Golf Club disappeared from the *Edinburgh Almanack* and did not reappear.

The 1830s could be seen as the decade that marked the beginning of an era in which golf societies began attributing importance to their relative antiquity or seniority. In addition to the activities of the Blackheath Golf Club, it was a decade in which the Perth Golfing Society (founded as recently as 1824) became the first golf society to be granted permission (in 1833) to use the prefix 'Royal', an event that prompted the more 'ancient' Society of St Andrews Golfers to request royal patronage and permission to adopt the title 'Royal and Ancient' (a request that was granted in 1834).[697] It is probably only after these events in the 1830s that chronological lists of the earliest golf societies began to appear. One of the first was in the *Fifeshire Journal* of 1855,[698] which listed the oldest golf societies as:

The Edinburgh Burgess Golf Club	1735
The Blackheath Golf Club, London	1744
The Edinburgh Company of Golfers	1744
The St Andrews Royal and Ancient Golf Club	1754

The foundation dates included in this list were almost certainly based on the dates that these clubs had claimed in *The Edinburgh Almanack*. That Blackheath and the Edinburgh Company of Golfers were both identified as having been founded in 1744 was perhaps an attempt to deal diplomatically with Blackheath's claim of being founded 'prior to 1745'. It was not long after such chronological lists began to appear that a new claim concerning the antiquity of the Blackheath Golf Club emerged: namely that it was 'instituted in 1608'. The earliest instance of this claim may have been in 1863.[699] It is a foundation date that has been repeated frequently up until the present day[700] but, as was discussed in Chapter 8, it is a claim that is not supported by any contemporary documentary evidence. Following the appearance of the claim 'instituted in 1608' it has become very common for this to be reflected in chronological lists of golf societies, as is illustrated by the following example published in 1895:[701]

Royal Blackheath Golf Club	1608
Edinburgh Burgess Golfing Society	1735
Hon. Company of Edinburgh Golfers	1744
St Andrews	1754

The person who has perhaps devoted most thought to the relative seniority of golf clubs is Charles Clapcott, an English lawyer and noted collector of golf books.[702] Clapcott wrote a letter to *The Scotsman* in 1938 rebutting a claim the newspaper had made concerning Royal Blackheath and Royal Burgess being 'the two oldest golf clubs in the world'.[703] Additionally, in an essay written in 1939 Clapcott explained in some detail the basis for having arrived at the following chronological list:[704]

Honourable Company of Edinburgh Golfers	previous 1744
Royal and Ancient Golf Club of St Andrews	1754
Royal Burgess Golfing Society	previous 1760
Bruntsfield Links Golfing Society	1760
Royal Blackheath Golf Club	1766

The logic behind some of the dates that Clapcott arrived at (in particular 'previous 1760') is somewhat convoluted, albeit clearly explained.[705] More recently, a well-researched golf history website[706] has come to the following conclusion about the probable foundation dates of the oldest golf societies:

Royal Burgess Golfing Society	1735
Honourable Company of Edinburgh Golfers	1744
Royal and Ancient Golf Club of St Andrews	1754
Bruntsfield Links Golfing Society	1761
Royal Blackheath Golf Club	1766
Royal Musselburgh Golf Club	1774
Fraserburgh Golf Club	1777 (1881)
Royal Aberdeen Golf Club	1780
Crail Golfing Society	1786
Glasgow Golf Club	1787
Earlsferry Golf Society	1787 (1858)

However, if relying solely on the availability of documentary evidence to identify the oldest golf societies (an approach that one golf historian has described as 'Gradgrindian'),[707] this would probably lead to the following chronology (but with some qualifications, discussed below and in the notes):

The Honourable Company of Edinburgh Golfers	1744
The Royal and Ancient Golf Club of St Andrews	1754
Royal Blackheath Golf Club	1766[708]
Royal Burgess Golfing Society	1773[709]
Royal Musselburgh Golf Club	1774
Crail Golfing Society	1786
Bruntsfield Links Golfing Society	1787

This approach does, however, have its challenges and may be controversial. For example, there is evidence of golf clubs that existed briefly at dates earlier than some of those listed above but that have either not survived or have no clear direct link to an existing club or society. These include, for example, a fleeting reference to 'Bray Goff Club' (1762),[710] Fraserburgh Golf Club (for which a minute book exists for the period 1777 to 1786)[711] and Earlsferry Golf Society (1787).[712] There is evidence of a Society of Golfers at Aberdeen in 1780–3 but no further records until 'the establishment of a Golf Club' at Aberdeen in 1815.[713] Similarly, there are records of Glasgow Golf Club dating back to 1787 but the club appears to have been inactive in the periods 1794–1809 and 1835–69.[714] Additionally, some have argued that The Honourable Company of Edinburgh Golfers was in a period of abeyance in the 1830s (something that could potentially enable the Royal and Ancient Golf Club of St Andrews to claim to be the oldest club in continuous existence) and this is something that clearly troubled Charles Clapcott,[715] a man who had great affection for the Honourable Company and who was subsequently elected as one of their honorary members.[716] However, the most pragmatic assessment of this contentious topic is probably that offered by Alastair Johnston, who edited a volume of Charles Clapcott's writings in 1985 and who concluded: 'The Honourable Company possesses written evidence of its existence and proceedings over a longer period than any other golf club.' He then went on to suggest that we should perhaps 'leave it at that!'.[717]

Early Women's Golf

There is very little evidence of golf having been played by women prior to the nineteenth century. Claims relating to Catherine of Aragon (1513) and the Countess of Mar (1638) have been dismissed (in Chapters 4 and 9) and claims relating to Mary Queen of Scots (1542–87) have been shown to be either incorrect or questionable (Chapter 6). This raises the question of when *did* women begin to play golf? Other than a single questionable reference to Mary Queen of Scots playing golf in 1566/7, no evidence has been identified of women playing golf prior to the eighteenth century. The earliest identified evidence of women playing golf in the eighteenth century is a newspaper article from 1738 concerning women playing golf on Bruntsfield Links. It provides the following limited information:

> Early last Tuesday Morning two married Women of this City stept out to Burntsfield [*sic*] Links to a concerted Match at Golf, followed by their Husbands carrying the Clubs. Curiosity led thither a great Crowd, who were charmed with seeing the half-naked Virago's [*sic*] tilt the Balls so manfully, and their Dexterity in holing. Considerable Wagers were laid; but charming Sally carried the Prize.[718]

The comment 'Curiosity led thither a great Crowd' would suggest that the sight of two women playing golf in 1738 was considered unusual and the reference to 'half-naked Viragos' is clearly intended to be disparaging. A further example of women playing golf in the eighteenth century was reported in *The Statistical Account of Scotland* (1795)[719] and concerned the fishwives of Fisherrow, a village near the Scottish town of Musselburgh. Again, it was a very brief account but provides the following description of the Fisherrow fishwives: 'they do the work of men, their manners are masculine, and their strength and activity is equal to their work. Their amusements are of the masculine kind. On holidays they frequently play at golf.'[720] It is notable that the author, the Reverend Dr Alexander Carlyle, comments on the women golfers' masculinity, in much the same way that this was emphasised in the report of the women playing golf at Bruntsfield Links in 1738. Carlyle was seemingly intimidated by the golfing fishwives, as is indicated by him describing them as having 'an extreme facility in expressing their feelings by words or gestures, which is very imposing'.[721] He also comments that 'a considerable degree of licentiousness appears in their freedom of speech'.[722]

It seems reasonable to conclude that there is very little evidence of women playing golf before the nineteenth century. The earliest golf societies were exclusively for men, having been formed in the mid-eighteenth century at a time when golf was generally seen as being an entirely male pursuit. This is illustrated by the game being described in 1787 as one of the 'manly exercises'[723] and in 1792 as a 'healthful and manly diversion'.[724] Perhaps it is as a consequence of such views that there appear to have been no golf clubs or societies with women members prior to the establishment of the St Andrews Ladies' Golf Club in 1867, later renamed the Ladies' Putting Club (Figure 14.2).[725] In 1868 a ladies' golf club was formed in England at Westward Ho! that was associated with the Royal North Devon Golf Club. Here, as at St Andrews, the women played on a separate short putting course.[726]

An article published in 1872 explained that golf was typically played (by men) using 'seven to twelve or more clubs', whereas 'the golfing lady carries but one club, a putter'.[727] By the 1880s and 1890s, golf clubs for women or with female members were becoming increasingly common, as was the provision of separate shorter courses at established golf clubs for use by women golfers (but that were frequently also available for use by boys or 'juveniles').[728] For example, a report concerning the Troon Ladies' Golf Club (established in 1882) mentioned that 'the ladies have a course of their own, over which boys are allowed to play'.[729] There is increasing evidence of women playing on longer golf courses, particularly in the 1880s and 1890s (Figure 14.3). The nine-hole course used by the Lundin Ladies' Golf Club had holes ranging from 60 to 170 yards and was described in 1892 as being 'by no means a mere putting course'. Similarly, the nine-hole course used by the Blackheath Ladies' Golf Club had holes 'varying from 80 to 170 yards' and was described in 1890 as being 'a driving and not a putting course'.[730] However, what has been referred to as a 'defining moment' in the development of women's golf was the foundation in 1893 of the Ladies' Golfing Union and the establishment in that year of the first Ladies' Championship, on a 'specially lengthened' course of 2,112 yards at Lytham and St Annes.[731] Subsequently, women's golf flourished and has increased greatly in popularity in recent years.

Figure 14.2 Early women's golf at St Andrews. A watercolour by Thomas Hodge (1827–1907) depicting members of the St Andrews Ladies' Golf Club (later renamed the Ladies' Putting Club) on the short Himalayas putting course in 1870 (top). This is thought to be the earliest depiction of women golfers. A similar scene at St Andrews in a photograph dating from 1886 (bottom). Both images are reproduced with kind permission of the Royal and Ancient Golf Club of St Andrews.

In Summary

Despite some ambiguity and confusion concerning the relative antiquity of early golf societies, there appears to be no convincing evidence for the existence of organised golf societies prior to the

Figure 14.3 Women's 'long-golf' in the 1880s. By the 1880s, women were increasingly playing on traditional golf courses, rather than only on short putting courses. Illustrated is the author's great-grandmother Annie Johnston (née Shearer; 1861–1934), cowering from her sister Lizzie's backswing (left) and in full swing (right). Possibly at Troon and Machrihanish respectively, and probably in the late 1880s.

mid-eighteenth century. The arrival of the cheaper gutta-percha ball in the mid-nineteenth century helped to make golf a less exclusive and more accessible game and led to the establishment of golf societies for those without the means to afford expensive feather golf balls. Societal changes in the mid-nineteenth century also led to an increasing participation of women in the game of golf, initially in exclusive 'putting clubs' but increasingly in the long game of golf.

Chapter 15

Early Golf in Scotland and the Spread of Golf to Other Countries

There is extensive documentary evidence indicating that the modern game of golf took root in Scotland in the late fifteenth and early sixteenth centuries. It is also apparent that the subsequent appearance of golf in other countries (for example, in the seventeenth, eighteenth and early nineteenth centuries) was largely a consequence of the influence and migration of Scottish golfers. However, while there is a widespread acceptance that golf is historically 'Scotland's Game', it is becoming increasingly common to hear this claim being disputed. Indeed, as was discussed in the opening chapter, one of the most contentious topics in the history of golf concerns its earliest ancestral origins. To an extent, the controversy has arisen as a consequence of the inevitable similarities between golf and other games in which a ball is hit with a club. For example, similarities have been identified with games such as *colf*, *jeu de mail* and *soule à la crosse* (all of which were popular in continental Europe); with the ancient Chinese game of *chui wan*; and with stick-and-ball games that are thought to have been played by the ancient Greeks, Romans and Egyptians.[732] This is a subject that has inflamed the passions of several golf historians and has resulted, most notably, in claims that golf originated from games that were played in areas of continental Europe such as Holland and France.[733] The present chapter will discuss what can be learned about the early history of golf from contemporary documentary evidence.

While it has been argued that early paintings may provide useful insights into the origins of golf,[734] perhaps the most valuable source of reliable historical evidence is to be found in early handwritten and printed documents. Examination of such documents reveals, seemingly without exception, that all identified written references to 'golf' prior to the seventeenth century relate exclusively to Scotland. These early documents are listed below and include references to golf in contemporary handwritten accounts of Scottish Acts of Parliament, treasury expenditure, testaments, burgh records and kirk sessions.

Table 15.1 *References to 'golf' (or a variant spelling of golf) in fifteenth- and sixteenth-century documents. When the date and the location in Scotland of the incident described can be identified, this has been indicated. The context in which the word appears is illustrated by a short extract from each document.*

Date	Location	Reference to 'golf'
1457/8	Scotland	'futbawe ande the golf [. . .] futbaw and the golf'[735]
1471	Scotland	'futbal and golf be abusit in tym cummynge'[736]
1491	Scotland	'fut bawis, gouff, or uthir sic unproffitable sportis'[737]
1503/4	Scotland (St Andrews?)	'the King to play at the golf with the Erle of Bothuile'[738]
1503/4	Scotland (St Andrews?)	'golf clubbes and balles to the King'[739]
1506	Scotland	'golf ballis to the King'[740]
1506	Scotland	'golf clubbes to the King'[741]
1507	Scotland (Brechin)	'*ex subito per ictum baculi viz* golf club'[742]
c. 1530	Scotland	'ane golf staff to driff the ball w^{t}all'[743]
1538	Scotland (Aberdeen)	'at the goiff'[744]
1545	Scotland (Aberdeen)	'thre dossoun and thre goif bawis'[745]
1552/3	Scotland (St Andrews)	'playing at golf futball schuting'[746]
1554	Scotland (Leith)	'Cordiners and Gowf-ball makers of North Leith'[747]
1560/1	Scotland (Stirling)	'straik at hym with ane goiff club'[748]
1565	Scotland (Aberdeen)	'cartis, dyiss, tabillis, goif'[749]
1566	Scotland (Montrose)	'the bow for archerie, the glub for goff'[750]
1568	Scotland (Edinburgh)	'Thre[e] do[zen] of golf ballis'[751]
1568	Scotland (Seton)	'palmall and goif'[752]
1571	Scotland (Leith)	'nyne burgessis of Edinburgh playand at the golf'[753]
1574	Scotland (St Andrews)	'for archerie and goff, I had bow, arrose, glub and bals'[754]
1576	Scotland (Haddington)	'xij Golf Bais'[755]

Date	Location	Reference to 'golf'
c. 1578	Scotland	'2 golf cloubbis'[756]
1581	Scotland	'at the goff, archerie, guid cheir'[757]
1583	Scotland (St Andrews)	'playit in the golf feildis'[758]
1585	Scotland (Kirkwall)	'ane dossen commoun golf ballis'[759]
c. 1585	Scotland	'ane golf staff to driffe the ball witheall'[760]
1587	Scotland (Ayr)	'c[er]tain goff ballis'[761]
1589	Scotland (Glasgow)	'no playing at football, goff, carrict, shynnie'[762]
1591	Scotland (Leith)	'played at the Goffe on the sands at Leithe'[763]
1592	Scotland (Leith)	'upoun the Sabboth day, sic as golf, archerie'[764]
1592/3	Scotland (Leith)	'to pass to Leith to play at the golf'[765]
1593	Scotland (Leith)	'at golf, archerie or other pastymes upon the Lynks'[766]
1596/7	Scotland (Elgin)	'playing at the boulis and golff upoun Sonday'[767]
1597	Scotland	'Golf Ballis the do[zen]'[768]
1598	Scotland (Edinburgh)	'xxxij gouf ballis'[769]
1598	Scotland (St Andrews)	'prophaning of the Saboth day in playing at the gouf'[770]
1599	Scotland (St Andrews)	'goufe and uthir exercise [. . .] goufe or uthir pastymes'[771]
1599	Scotland (Leith?)	'goulff balls [. . .] goulff clubs'[772]
1599	Scotland (Perth)	'playing at the golf in the north inch in time of the preaching'[773]
1590s	Scotland	'ane dussin gouf ballis [. . .] ane klub'[774]

All of these early written references to golf are from handwritten documents, several of which were discussed in previous chapters. In addition, golf is mentioned in some early Scottish printed books. These printed texts have not been included in this chronological list, since they largely repeat material from the manuscript sources. For example, the texts of the 1457/8, 1471 and 1491 Scottish Acts of Parliament were reproduced in books that were published in Scotland in the sixteenth century (for example, in 1566 and 1597).[775]

This list of early manuscripts mentioning golf is not expected or intended to be exhaustive since there are almost certainly additional documents that are still to be examined by historians. Nevertheless, it provides a useful illustration of the extent to which there is clear documentary evidence of golf being played in Scotland prior to the seventeenth century. In all cases, either the original manuscript has been consulted or, when the original document has not survived, a near-contemporary transcript of the original document is available. Excluded from this list are documents that have, on occasion, been suggested to have relevance to early golf but which do not explicitly mention the word 'golf' (such as the purchase of 'clubs' by King James IV from a Scottish bow-maker, as discussed in Chapter 3). Also omitted from the list are claims that have been made about early golf for which no reliable documentary source has been identified (such as claims of golf balls being purchased in 1452, see Chapter 1; or of golf being played in Scotland in 1579 at Bruntsfield Links).[776] Similarly, the list omits claims relating to early golf that can be demonstrated to be factually incorrect (such as the popular myth concerning Catherine of Aragon playing golf in 1513, see Chapter 4).

Where it has been possible to do so, the locations within Scotland of the events that are referred to in these early documentary sources have been indicated. It is notable that many of the identified locations are on the east coast of Scotland (for example, Aberdeen, Edinburgh, Elgin, Haddington, Kirkwall, Leith, Montrose, Perth, St Andrews and Stirling), which is consistent with evidence that, even as late as the mid-nineteenth century, golf was played primarily at seaside locations and predominantly, though not exclusively, on the east coast of Scotland (as will be discussed in the final chapter).

Scottish Golfers and the Spread of Golf in the Seventeenth Century

In addition to the evidence that the earliest written references to golf relate exclusively to Scotland, early references to golf being played *outside* Scotland (the earliest of which dates from 1606) can almost always be attributed to the migration or influence of Scottish golfers. For example, following the union of the Scottish and English Crowns in 1603, King James VI of Scotland relocated his court from Edinburgh to London and, shortly afterwards (in 1606), there is evidence of the Scottish Prince Henry playing golf in England (as is discussed in more detail in Chapter 8). At around the same time (c. 1606), there is evidence of Scottish settlers introducing golf at Newtownards in Ireland during the plantation (colonisation) of Ulster.[777] In contrast, claims that golf was being played in America in the mid-seventeenth century (for example, in 1657 and 1659) appear to lack any documentary evidence and were considered in Chapter 10.

Until recently, the earliest identified evidence of golf being exported from Scotland beyond the British Isles was a reference to golf balls being shipped to British colonial North America in 1739 (discussed later). However, evidence has been identified recently in the Aberdeen Court Records of golf balls and clubs being sent by ship from Aberdeen to Danzig (Gdańsk), Poland in 1657 (Figure 15.1).[778] The records describe the failure of James Andersoun (the captain of an Aberdeen sailing ship) to pay William Mayne (an Aberdeen bow-maker) for 'two dussoun clubs' and 'two du[ssou]n goaf ballis' that had been sold in 'Dansick' (note: because this document does not appear to have been described previously, a full transcription and translation is appended[779]). It is perhaps unsurprising that Poland was among the first countries to which golf balls and clubs were exported, given the extensive trade that occurred at this time between Scotland and Poland (and, notably, between Aberdeen and Danzig).[780] As a consequence of such trade, it has been estimated that, during the seventeenth century, more Scots migrated to areas of the Baltic such as Poland than took part in the extensive plantation and settlement of Ulster.[781] Indeed, it has been estimated that so many Scots travelled by ship to Danzig that there were between 20,000 and 60,000 Scots in Poland at this time.[782]

Scottish Golfers and the Spread of Golf in the Eighteenth Century

There is increasing but sporadic evidence of golf spreading from Scotland to other countries in the early eighteenth century. Surviving records reveal golf balls being sent from Scotland to British colonial North America in 1739 (Figure 15.1)[783] and in the following year there is evidence, from the diary of David, Lord

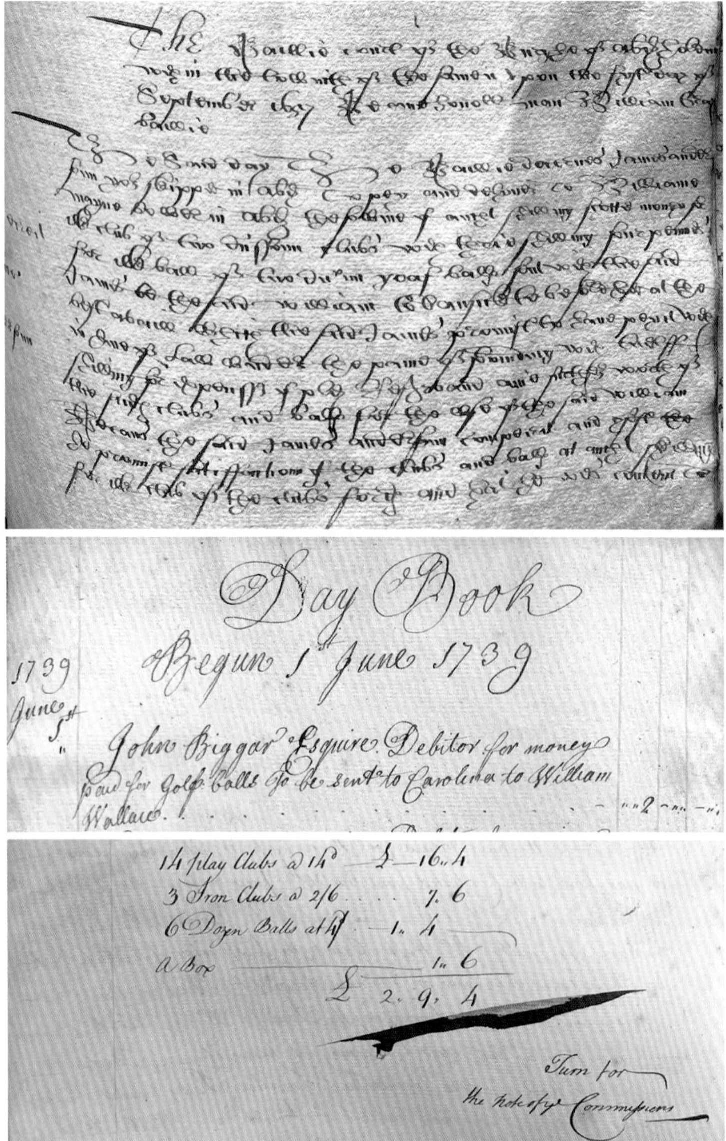

Day Book

Begun 1st June 1739

1739 June 5th

John Biggar Esquire Debitor for money paid for Golf balls to be sent to Carolina to William Wallace. 2

14 play Clubs @ 14d £ — 16.4
3 Iron Clubs @ 2/6 . . . 7.6
6 Dozen Balls at 4/ 1. 4
a Box 1. 6
£ 2. 9. 4

Turn for the Note of ye Commissions

Figure 15.1 The export of golf clubs and balls from Scotland (1657–1748). Illustrated are documents recording golf clubs and balls to be shipped to Danzig (Gdańsk), Poland in 1657 (top), to Carolina, British colonial North America in 1739 (middle) and to Riga, Russia in 1748 (bottom). Top image: Courtesy of Aberdeen City and Aberdeenshire Archives, CA5/1/7. Middle image: National Records of Scotland, GD377/402. Bottom image: Lloyds Banking Group Archives, BLB1/4/71, 28.

Elcho, of golf being played in Rome, Italy by the exiled Scottish prince, Bonnie Prince Charlie (Figure 15.2).[784] Documents from the archives of the British Linen Company record a box of golf clubs and balls being shipped from Scotland to the company's representative in Riga, Russia (now Latvia) in 1748 (Figure 15.1).[785] Evidence has also been uncovered of golf balls and clubs being sent to France 1767[786] and, although they were shipped from London rather than Scotland, it seems likely that, once again, this may reveal the influence of the Scots. The previous year (1766) is the earliest date for which there is documentary evidence of a golf club having been established in England (at Blackheath) and records show that the early members of Blackheath, the only known society of golfers in England at this time, were overwhelmingly Scottish.[787] There are reports of golf being played by British military officers on the sands of Gibraltar in 1773,[788] at a time when it is known that several of the officers serving in Gibraltar were Scottish (Figure 15.3).[789] The influence of the Scots can also be seen in the earliest evidence of golf being played in Africa. The diary of a British botanist who visited Sierra Leone in 1773 describes a two-hole golf course that had been established by Scottish slave traders on the notorious Bunce Island (Figure 15.3).[790] Thus, in all of these cases of early golf being played outside of Scotland, plausible links can be found to Scotland or to the likely influence of Scottish golfers. It should, perhaps, be pointed out that in all of the cases mentioned above of golf being played outside Scotland, these appear to be isolated instances and should not be taken to imply that golf had become established in these countries at such an early date.

Scottish Golfers and the Spread of Golf in the Early Nineteenth Century

In the nineteenth century there is increasing evidence of golf beginning to take hold around the world, particularly within the British Empire. As will be discussed, this includes evidence of golf being played in places such as India (1804), Canada (1826), Australia (1839), Mauritius (1842) and South Africa (1844). Once again, there is strong evidence for the involvement of Scots in the introduction of golf to these countries. For example, Major Hugh Lyon Playfair, who had been educated at St Andrews University, was

Figure 15.2 Prince Charles Edward Stuart. There is evidence that Prince Charles Edward Stuart, 'Bonnie Prince Charlie' (1720–88), played golf while exiled in Rome in 1740. © National Galleries Scotland, PG 1519.

among those involved in establishing the first golf club in India in 1829 (the Dum-Dum Golf Club at Calcutta).[791] There is, however, evidence of golf being played in Calcutta as early as 1804[792] and it may not be a coincidence that this was around the time that Playfair, along with other Scots, arrived in India, having been commissioned into the Bengal Army of the East India Company.

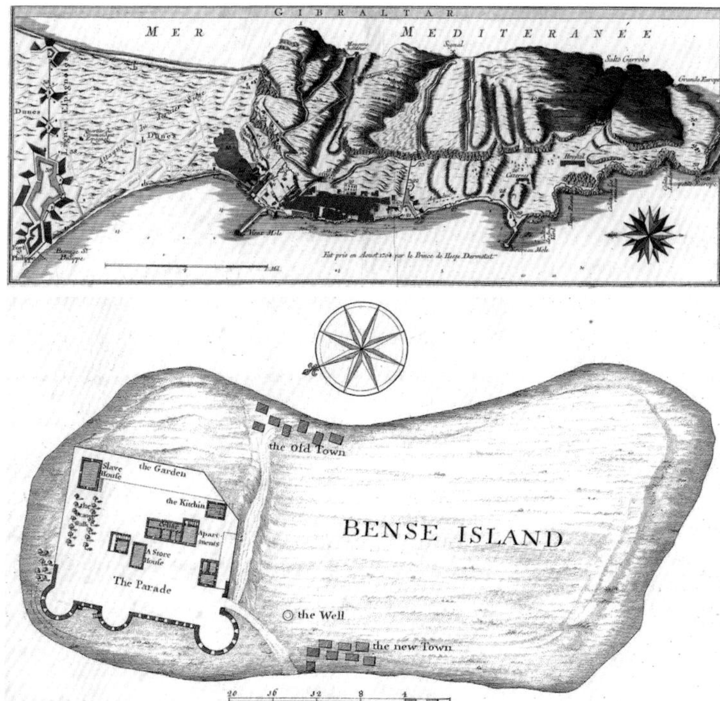

Figure 15.3 Early golf at Gibraltar and Sierra Leone (1773). There is evidence of golf being played by British military officers on the sands of Gibraltar in 1773. This etching (from 1704) shows an area of 'dunes' to the left of the 'rock of Gibraltar' (now the site of Gibraltar's airport) that is likely to have provided a suitable area for golf. The diary of a British botanist who visited Sierra Leone in 1773 describes a two-hole golf course that had been established by Scottish slave traders on the notorious Bunce/Bense Island.

While the oldest golf club in Canada (the Royal Montreal Golf Club) is considered to have been founded in 1873,[793] there is evidence of golf being played in Canada considerably earlier (in 1826) by golfers who were described in the *Montreal Herald* as being 'a few true sons of Scotia'.[794] Similarly, the earliest identified evidence of golf being played in Australia (in 1839) can be found in the diaries of an expatriate Scot, Alexander Brodie Spark.[795]

There is evidence of clubs and balls being shipped from Scotland to Mauritius in 1844.[796] This coincides with separate documentary evidence of a golf club having been established in Mauritius in 1842 that comes from a newspaper report in which these golfers are described as 'Scotia's sons'.[797] The same report that mentions clubs and balls being sent to Mauritius in 1844 also describes them being sent from Scotland to the Cape of Good Hope, providing early evidence of golf being played in South Africa. Some years later (in 1878) there is evidence of a golf club being founded at Cronstad (Kroonstad) in South Africa that had been supplied with 'materials from Edinburgh'.[798]

Thus, there is extensive documentary evidence, spanning some four hundred years (from the mid-fifteenth century to the mid-nineteenth century), that provides a clear picture of golf initially taking root in Scotland and its subsequent arrival in other countries being aided by enthusiastic Scottish golfers.

The Worldwide 'Golf-boom' in the Second Half of the Nineteenth Century

As was discussed in Chapter 12, early golf was played predominantly with expensive leather balls stuffed with feathers. It was not until the development of cheaper gutta-percha balls in the 1840s (see Chapter 12) that golf developed into a more accessible and popular game. For example, prior to the 1840s there were just two golf clubs established in England (at Blackheath in 1766[799] and at Manchester in 1818[800]) but it has been calculated that golf was being played in more than a hundred locations in England by 1887,[801] as well as at several other locations around the world. The mid-Victorian era was a time when golf began to acquire its popular worldwide appeal. Selected examples of locations (other than those mentioned earlier) where there is contemporary documentary evidence of either golf being played or of golf clubs being founded during this period include New Zealand (1863),[802] Indonesia (Dutch East Indies) (1872),[803] Wales (1874),[804] China (1883),[805] Belgium (1888),[806] Egypt (1888),[807] Malta (1888),[808] Sweden (c. 1888),[809] Hong Kong (1889),[810] Singapore (1891),[811] Switzerland (1891),[812] Trinidad (1891),[813] Holland (1893)[814] and Cyprus (1894).[815] While this is not an exhaustive list, it provides an indication of the timescale by which golf spread around the world in the second half of the nineteenth century.

In Summary

It would appear that all of the early (fifteenth- and sixteenth-century) written references to 'golf' are to be found in Scottish manuscripts. While some of these references probably refer to what has been described as 'short golf' (for example, played with inexpensive equipment in places such as churchyards), there is evidence of the emergence of a long form of golf, the forerunner of the modern-day game. It is the 'long game' that appears to have flourished in Scotland in the sixteenth and seventeenth centuries and there is clear evidence that it was the Scots who were largely responsible for spreading the game to other parts of the world. This includes evidence of its export by Scots to England and Ireland in the seventeenth century and to other parts of the world in the eighteenth and early nineteenth centuries. In many cases these early reports of golf beyond Scotland are perhaps just fleeting instances of the game being played by expatriate Scots. It was not until the development of the cheaper gutta-percha ball in the 1840s that there is evidence of a dramatic increase in the affordability and popularity of golf, as well as a proliferation of golf courses and of organised golf. Whether the Scottish game of golf may have had ancestral links to earlier stick-and-ball games played in other countries is a topic that will be discussed in the following chapter.

Chapter 16

The Origin of Golf

The origin of golf is a contentious topic, particularly when considering the question of whether golf may have ancestral links to other early European stick-and-ball games. The first person to speculate upon the possible origins of golf may have been Joseph Strutt who, in 1801, suggested that golf might have links to a game played by the Ancient Romans with a feather-filled ball called a *paganica*.[816] Strutt initiated a debate that has rumbled on for many years and which, for the most part, has taken place with relatively little acrimony. However, it is a topic that in recent years has inflamed the passions of golf historians. For example, the seemingly innocuous question of whether golf originated in Scotland or the Low Countries has resulted in historians accusing one another of 'smugness' and 'conceit'.[817] Statements made concerning this topic have been described as being 'a preposterous hoax' and 'a monumental distortion of golfing history'.[818] So it seems that the quiet world of golf history has become a potentially dangerous place in which to venture.

There has been no shortage of suggestions as to what might have been the origin of golf. For example, there has been speculation that golf has its origins in the English game of bandy-ball,[819] the Flemish game of *chole*,[820] the Chinese game of *chui wan*,[821] the Persian game of *chugán*,[822] the Dutch game of *colf*,[823] the French game of *jeu de mail*,[824] the Palestinian game of *kora*,[825] the Roman game of *paganica*,[826] as well as the Scottish game of shinty.[827] It is common to see conflicting claims, such as golf was 'invented by the Romans'[828] or that the 'Chinese invented golf 1,000 years ago'.[829] Similarly, it is common to see claims such as 'Holland is the cradle of golf'[830] or that golf was 'first played in the Loire region of France'.[831] It is hard not to have some sympathy with a comment made by Garden Smith in 1912 when he wrote, 'The poor Scots are denied the possibility of having a game of their own.'[832]

The 'Origin of Golf' Debate in Perspective

It is clear that very considerable efforts have been made in an attempt to find a plausible location (other than Scotland) for the origin of golf. While several items of evidence have allowed speculation as to possible sites of golf's origin, none appear to be conclusive. It could be argued that, rather than having originated at a specific location, stick-and-ball games such as golf should be considered as being part of an evolving continuum, dating back at least four thousand years. For example, a crude image of a stick-and-ball game is depicted on the Egyptian tomb of Khety at Beni Hassan (tomb BH17), dating from the XI Egyptian Dynasty, c. 2000 BC (Figure 16.1).[833] A similar image is depicted on a Greek marble sculpture that is estimated to date from 510–500 BC (Figure 16.1).[834] Indeed, the use of a club and ball ('*sibi clavam et pilam*') was among a series of outdoor activities listed by the Roman political orator Marcus Tullius Cicero in his *Cato Maior de Senectute* (44 BC).[835] The playing of stick-and-ball games 'club ball' and '*cambuc*' were outlawed in England by an Act of Parliament in the reign of Edward III (in 1363),[836] prior to the Scottish ban on golf of 1457/8. Possible allusions to stick-and-ball games in Britain can be found in Laȝamon's (Layamon's) *Brut*, or Chronicle of Britain (c. 1200), which contains the statement '*sūme heo driūe balles; wide ȝeond þa feldes*' [some they drove balls wide over the fields].[837]

Paganica and Golf: A Popular Misconception

It is extremely common in histories of golf for it to be suggested that golf may have originated from a stick-and-ball game called *paganica*, played by the Ancient Romans. However, while there is evidence that the Latin word *paganica* referred to a feather-filled ball, there appears to be no evidence to suggest that it was a stick-and-ball game. It is a misconception that arose in the early nineteenth century and it is one that has been repeated frequently. The extent to which the story has become all-pervasive can, perhaps, be illustrated by the following comment that appeared in a biography of Tiger Woods:

Figure 16.1 Ancient Egyptian and Greek stick-and-ball games. An image (upper) from the tomb of Khety (BH17) that is thought to date from the XI–XII Egyptian dynasty (c. 2500–2000 BC) and a marble sculpture, estimated to date from 510–500 BC (lower). Upper image: Reproduced with kind permission of Professor Naguib Kanawati. Lower image: National Archaeological Museum of Athens; © Hellenic Ministry of Culture and Sport, Hellenic Organization of Cultural Resources Development, NAM Γ 3477.

> The game of golf was first played by shepherds in Scotland who probably observed Roman soldiers playing a game called *paganica*, which was played with a bent stick hitting a leather ball stuffed with feathers.[838]

The word '*paganica*' appears in two Latin epigrams, both written by the poet Martial (c. AD 100),[839] but they provide little information about the meaning of the word. In fact, all that can be confidently concluded is that *paganica* referred to a ball filled tightly with feathers (*turget paganica pluma*).[840] When Littleton's Latin–English dictionary was published in 1678, the word *paganica* was described as being similar to 'a goff-ball, a stow-ball, stuffed with feathers'.[841] This is, perhaps, not an unreasonable description, given that balls used for the games of golf and stow-ball might have been familiar to readers in the seventeenth century as examples of balls stuffed with feathers. However, *paganica* was probably brought to the attention of golf historians by the publication in 1801 of Joseph Strutt's influential *Sports and Pastimes*. Citing Littleton's Latin dictionary, Strutt concluded that golf 'answers to a rustic pastime of the Romans which they played with a ball of leather stuffed with feathers, called Paganica'.[842] It would appear that Strutt was simply pointing out the similarity between balls such as *paganica* and golf balls (both being stuffed with feathers). However, what appears to have confused matters was a report in *The Golfer's Manual* (1857) that concluded that *paganica* was a game 'played with a crooked stick or bat'.[843] There is certainly no evidence in Martial's epigrams to enable it to be concluded that *paganica* was a stick-and-ball game, yet this appears to have been an extrapolation based on Strutt's more cautious comments. As so often happens, stories such as this tend to evolve and grow. In 1928 Charles Macdonald wrote 'Cæsar came as close as any to modern golf when he played *Paganica*'[844] and in 1969 Billye Ann Cheatum concluded:

> Caesar, utilizing a crooked stick and a leather ball packed with feathers, participated in a game called 'Paganica' over two thousand years ago. During his conquest, Caesar, with his legionnaires, spread the game of 'Paganica' to many countries. As a result, the origin of the modern game of golf is highly controversial.[845]

In 1995 the story was developed yet further with the claim that *paganica* was played with a 'bent stick' that was used to hit a ball 'across open land towards a target like a tree stump or well'.[846] It has even been stated that 'a good paganica player' could drive a ball 'about 150 yards'.[847] Given that *paganica* refers to a feather ball, an unusual variation on the story is that 'The Romans had a game called paganica that involved hitting a stone with a stick.'[848] It is now common to see unsupported conclusions about the influence of *paganica* on the game of golf. For example, it has been stated that *paganica* 'eventually made its way to Scotland, where it became the game we know as golf',[849] and also, the Romans 'might have taken paganica clubs and balls to St Andrews and Carnoustie'.[850] A recent history of golf incorporated several of these misconceptions concerning *paganica* as follows:

> The Romans developed a sport that had a name. It was called 'Paganica' or 'Paganicus.' The game was played with a bent stick and a leather ball, and players were supposed to hit the ball to various targets, whether it was a tree, a rock, or anything in between. Over time, as the Roman Empire expanded, this game spread to countries of Northern Europe and served as a basis for other games that developed.[851]

Of course, it is possible that '*paganica*' may have referred to a ball that was hit with a stick but there appears to be no evidence to support such a conclusion. All we really know is that it is a Latin word that was used in around AD 100 to describe a feather-filled ball.

Golf, *Colf* and *Kolf*

As was discussed in Chapter 1, the earliest written reference to 'golf' is in a Scottish Act of Parliament of 1457/8. In addition, as was discussed in Chapter 15, there are numerous written references to golf being played in Scotland prior to the earliest evidence of golf being played elsewhere (for example, in England and Ireland in the early seventeenth century). However, an idea that has become almost universally accepted is that golf was imported to Scotland from Holland. Indeed, John Kerr wrote in 1869 that 'writers on golf nearly all follow this Dutch importation idea like a flock of sheep'.[852] There are undoubted similarities between the modern game of golf and other stick-and-ball games and when historians have speculated about the origins of golf, the Dutch game of *colf* is mentioned frequently. It may, therefore, be useful to provide a brief description of these games. The outdoor game of *colf* (confusingly, sometimes also spelt '*kolf*', a term now used to describe a short indoor game) was popular in the Low Countries in the sixteenth and early seventeenth centuries but appears to have largely disappeared from historical records by the end of the seventeenth century. It was a game in which a ball was hit towards a predetermined target, for example a wooden post (Figure 16.2), and which, typically, was played with a single club. There are numerous early Dutch paintings depicting the game of *colf*, several of which show it being played on ice.[853] The more recent game of *kolf*, which became popular following the decline of *colf*, is typically played indoors but, as appears to have been common with *colf*, it involves a ball being played towards a post with a single club. It has been estimated that whereas there were once more than a thousand *kolf* courts in the Low Countries, there are now said to be only sixteen.[854]

Colf at Loenen in 1297: A Pervasive Myth

The suggestion that golf may have originated in the Low Countries is a topic that gained considerable prominence with the publication of *Early Golf* (1982) by Steven van Hengel.[855] It is a book that deals primarily with the early history of *colf* in the Low Countries and, as such, the title '*Early Golf*' was seen by some as being controversial. The book attracted particular attention as a result of a claim that *colf* (or 'early golf') was played in 1297 at Loenen aan de Vecht in the Netherlands. Van Hengel used the words 'golf' and '*colf*' somewhat interchangeably; for example, in 1972 he described the game that is said to have been played in 1297 as the 'first game of golf'[856] but elsewhere he described it as the 'first traceable game of colf'.[857] This discrepancy was perhaps a consequence of van Hengel being of the opinion that 'there is absolutely no doubt that colf was an early form of golf'.[858]

Due in part to the publication of van Hengel's *Early Golf*, it is now widely assumed that golf originated in Holland in the late thirteenth century (or, more specifically, in the village of Loenen aan de Vecht). For example, the introductory text on the dust

Figure 16.2 Depictions of the Dutch game of *colf* being played on ice. A watercolour (c. 1620) by Hendrick Avercamp (1585–1634) in which a ball is hit towards a stake as a target (top); a detail from a painting by Adriaen van de Velde (1636–72), thought to be a view of Haarlem in the Low Countries, in which the player who is about to hit the ball is assumed to be wearing a Scottish kilt (bottom); something that may reflect the close trading links between Scotland and the Low Countries in the seventeenth century. Top image: Royal Collection Trust/© Her Majesty Queen Elizabeth, RCIN 906470. Bottom image: © National Gallery, London, NG869.

cover of a popular history of golf (published in 1984) begins with the question, 'How many golfers know that the first recorded game of golf took place in Holland in the year 1296?'[859] The same book goes on to state that 'the beginnings of golf have been traced to the village of Loenen in 1296'.[860] This is a claim that has been repeated frequently in recent years but for which there is no contemporary documentary evidence.

Steven van Hengel's seemingly erroneous interpretation of events at Loenen has been discussed in detail elsewhere[861] and appears to have been based on an account that was first published in a Dutch magazine (in 1870)[862] that described a game of *colf* having been played annually on Boxing Day ['*tweeden Kersdag*'] at Loenen aan de Vecht.[863] It also mentioned that this public entertainment ['*volksvermaak*'] was played for the last time in 1830[864] but, importantly, it made no specific claim about when the annual game had first been played. The following year (1871), Jan ter Gouw expanded on the story by suggesting that the game played at Loenen might date back to the Middle Ages ['*Wel is het mogelijk, dat dit kolfslaan uit de middeleeuwen dagteekent*'] and explained that the annual game in Loenen was thought to have been played as part of annual celebrations commemorating the death in 1296 of Floris V, the Count of Holland.[865] It was probably this that led van Hengel and others to assume (but without any evidence) that the *colf* match had been played every year since 1297. In 1951 the Dutch golf historian J. A. Brongers wrote an article entitled 'Holland – The Cradle of Golf?', in which he stated that 'a game of kolf was played annually up to about 1830' at Loenen and that this had happened for 'nearly five centuries'.[866] It was some years later (in 1982) that van Hengel made the rather more explicit claim that, 'In all probability the first traceable game of colf took place on Boxing Day of the year 1297 at Loenen aan de Vecht.'[867] This is a claim that has subsequently been repeated frequently. For example, the town of Loenen aan de Vecht celebrated '700 Years of Golf' with a two-week exhibition in 1997. The Exhibition catalogue, *700 jaar golf Loenen a/d Vecht 1297–1997*, mentioned that it was absolutely certain ['*onvoorwaardelijk zeker*'] that golf had been played in 1297.[868] However, the event was subsequently reassessed by one of the organisers (J. Ayolt Brongers) in an article published in the Dutch golf magazine *Golf Journaal* (2002), in which he conceded that there is no archival evidence ['*Een archiefstuk* [. . .] *is er niet*'] to show that golf was played in 1297.[869] Others have been rather more outspoken, describing van Hengel's claim as 'a preposterous hoax'[870] and as '*absolute onzin*' [absolute nonsense].[871] A good illustration of how stories such as this can evolve over time is provided by a golf writer who stated (in 2016) that 'the first mention of golf, or something like it, in Scotland was on February 26th 1297'.[872] This claim, concerning early golf in Scotland, is almost certainly a garbled version of van Hengel's unsubstantiated claim that golf was first played in Holland on 26 December 1297.

When van Hengel was interviewed for a golf video, *Legacy of the Links*, in 1985 he was asked where golf originated.[873] In response, he commented that 'the first game that you can trace was played around a village [Loenen ann de Vecht]'. He then continued, 'every year since 1297 the game was played in commemoration of a historic event'. Van Hengel was filmed sitting next to a three-dimensional model of the village that he used to describe how oval balls were hit towards specific targets (the doors of four buildings in the village). Despite the fact that no contemporary evidence has been identified to support the claim that *colf* (or golf) was played at this location in 1297, this has not stopped the story from being repeated. For example, published chronological lists of events in golf history now frequently begin with the date 1297 (or 1296) as being the earliest evidence of golf (or *colf*).[874] In discussing *colf*, one writer has suggested that there is 'proof that it was already popular by 1297',[875] while another has claimed that Dutch stick-and-ball games 'certainly existed by 1296'.[876] It has also been suggested that van Hengel provided an 'unambiguous record of a game being played' and that this was 'at the startlingly early date of 1297'.[877] On occasion, writers appear to have assumed that there is contemporary documentary evidence for golf or *colf* having being played in 1297. For example, this seems to be implied by comments such as 'colf was played in Holland, according to records, from 1297'[878] or that van Hengel 'unearthed documents' concerning *colf* in 1297.[879] Towards the end of his life, van Hengel appears to have become rather more cautious in his claims about the origins of early golf. Whereas he had described the game played at Loenen as 'golf' in 1972,[880] he used the term 'colf' in his later publications (for example, in 1982).[881] Indeed, when he was interviewed shortly before his death in 1985, he was asked about the possibility that golf 'started in Holland' and replied that 'you actually did not hear me say that'.[882]

Early References to *Colf*

In *Early Golf* (1982) van Hengel also identified several documented references to games played in the Netherlands in the fourteenth and fifteenth centuries. However, these tend to be rather vague references to stick-and-ball games, rather than evidence of golf being played. For example, he identifies a document from 1360 that refers to playing with a 'ball and club' ['*wie met colven tsolt*'][883] and another from 1387 that contains a reference 'to play the ball with the club' ['*den bal mitter colven te slaen*'].[884] However, others have argued that these references to '*colven*' concern the confrontational hockey-like game of *soule à la crosse*.[885] The next earliest document identified by van Hengel is a reference from 1390 concerning a 'playing field' in Haarlem.[886] However, it has been suggested that this is more likely to have been a course that was used for playing the popular handball game of *klootschieten*, rather than a game such as *colf*.[887] The phrase '*Mit ener coluen*' [with a club], which is to be found in the medieval poem *Merlijns boec* by Jacob van Maerlant (c. 1261), has been seen by some as early evidence of the game of *colf*,[888] although others have argued that it is a reference to a confrontational game similar to hockey.[889] In fact, the relevant passage in the poem describes the sorcerer Merlin hitting the 'richest boy of the village' on the shin with a club ('*Mit ener coluen vor zine schene*') and it has been argued that this has nothing to do with the description earlier in the poem of the boys in the village playing with a ball ('*Vnde slogan dar eynen bal*').[890]

Golf on the West Coast of Scotland

There is extensive evidence that early golf in Scotland was concentrated largely on the east rather than the west coast. Indeed, this pattern continued into what has been described as the 'Scottish golfing boom' of the late nineteenth century.[891] To an extent, this may simply reflect the higher population density in that region but it has also been suggested that this may be a consequence of close trading links between Scotland's east coast and continental Europe, where stick-and-ball games such as *colf* are known to have been played. In discussing this topic, Henderson and Stirk (1979) state that golf 'remained confined to the East Coast until the nineteenth century'[892] and van Hengel stated (in 1982) that golf 'did not in fact reach the west coast of Scotland before about 1850'[893] but these assertions are not supported by the evidence. There are, for example, several references to golf being played on the west coast of Scotland in the sixteenth, seventeenth and eighteenth centuries. For example, at locations such as Ayr, Ballantrae, Girvan, Glasgow and Maybole.[894] However, perhaps the earliest evidence of golf on the west coast of Scotland can be found in a document from 1587. It concerns the theft of 'goff ballis' by Andro Blakater from a shop in Ayr. As his punishment, Blakater was banished from the town but was also informed that, if he ever returned, he would be 'hangit to the death'.[895] As far as I am aware, this document showing early evidence of golf on the west coast of Scotland has not been discussed previously by golf historians and, for that reason, a full transcription has been provided in the notes section.[896]

The Contributions of Scottish Golf Historians

It seems that Scottish golf historians have often been on the receiving end of criticism from those who favour a continental origin for the game of golf. For example, Andrew Lang, who in 1890 offered his thoughts on the origins of golf,[897] was criticised (over a hundred years later by golf historian Richard Flannery) as being 'appallingly parochial' and was accused of writing 'sheer nonsense'.[898] Heiner Gillmeister has commented (in German) on 'the constant lack of insight on the part of Scottish historians'[899] and it has been suggested (again in German) that 'it is extremely difficult for the Scots to admit the Dutch origin of their national game'.[900] Indeed, when Gillmeister (who argued that golf originated in the Low Countries) was interviewed by a Dutch golf magazine, he described those in Scotland who failed to accept the argument as '*domme golfers*' [dumb/ignorant golfers].[901] This all seems somewhat unreasonable given that it was a Scotsman (James Cunningham) who was the first person (in 1899) to put forward a detailed argument proposing that Scottish golf may have developed from a game played in the Low Countries.[902] Cunningham drew attention to Dutch paintings, to Dutch ceramic tiles and to arguments based on possible etymological links between English and Dutch words relating to golf. Consequently, it seems unreasonable to conclude that the Scots collectively ignored possible links between golf's origins and the Low Countries. In fact, even before James Cunningham published his ideas in 1899, it had been Scottish and British writers and historians who were among the first to draw attention to possible links between golf and other stick-and-ball games. These include suggested links to the Roman game played with a ball called a *paganica* (in 1801),[903] the English game of *cambuca*/bandy-ball (1801),[904] the English game of cricket (1807),[905] the Persian game of *chugán* (1819)[906] and the French game of *jeu de mail* (1857).[907] Similarly, it was the Scots who were among the first to draw attention to the possibility of etymological links between 'golf' and German and Dutch words such as *kolbe* and *kolf* (1824)[908] or to similarities between Scottish golf and paintings by Dutch artists (1899).[909] So it would seem that the Scots have been at the forefront of those who have been open to the idea that the game of golf may have links with other stick-and-ball games.

'Scots as inventors: a popular fallacy'?

It is clear that there are similarities between various stick-and-ball games but it is much harder to establish if one game influenced the development of another. It is notable, however, that in recent years the proponents of a 'Dutch origin' of golf have been emboldened by what is claimed to be new documentary evidence. Indeed, this encouraged Heiner Gillmeister to rewrite the entry for golf in *Encyclopædia Britannica* with the confident headline 'Scots as inventors: a popular fallacy'.[910] The 'new evidence' was summarised in an influential article by Gillmeister in 2002 that stated, 'The purpose of this article is to show that the claim of Scottish origin is unsubstantiated and to bring to the attention of golf historians new source material which proves the continental origin of Scotland's national game.'[911] The 'new source material' identified by Gillmeister was the fifteenth-century Scots poem *The Buik of King Alexander the Conquerour* and Gillmeister's arguments centred around the poet's use of the word 'golf-staff' in an imagined letter written by King Darius III of Persia to King Alexander the Conqueror (c. 332 BC). Gillmeister took the view that the word 'golf' was being used in the poem to describe a confrontational hockey-like game, rather than what we would now understand as golf. However, as was discussed in Chapter 2, it seems likely that the fifteenth-century poet was, in fact, referring to a 'gold staff' rather than 'golf-staff'. As a consequence, it seems highly likely that Gillmeister's interpretation of the Scots poem is erroneous but it also seems inevitable that his conclusions will be perpetuated, particularly since they have been summarised in the *Encyclopædia Britannica* as:

> Proof that golf in Scotland had exactly the same meaning as its Flemish counterpart *kolve* comes in *The Buik of Alexander the Counqueror* [. . .] Such a description leaves hardly any doubt that in 15th-century Scotland the term *golf* primarily referred to a fiercely contended team game, and this accounts for it being banned in the acts of Parliament.[912]

The fifteenth edition of the *Encyclopædia Britannica*, as quoted above, was the last edition to be published in print and includes the section heading 'Scots as inventors: a popular fallacy'. The basis for this claim (as outlined in *Encyclopædia Britannica* but developed in other articles by the same author) centres around four distinct arguments. The first of these concerns the apparent use of the term 'golf-stick' in *The Buik of Alexander the Conquerour*. The remaining three arguments concern 1) a Latin–Dutch school textbook (*Tyrocinium latinæ linguæ*), 2) evidence from medieval paintings and 3) etymological arguments. An important question is whether any of these remaining arguments provide 'proof' that golf originated in continental Europe. Each is discussed briefly below.

Tyrocinium latinæ linguæ

There is extensive evidence that most early continental stick-and-ball games were played to a target above the ground. This has led to the suggestion that playing towards a hole in the ground is one of the elements that makes golf distinct. Consequently, there was some excitement when evidence was found in a Latin–Dutch school textbook, *Tyrocinium latinæ linguæ* (1552),[913] of a game in which a ball was played towards a hole. For example, a section of the text concerning a game played with a leaded club contains the phrase, 'I will go straight for the hole' (in Latin: '*Ego recta petam scrobem*' and in Old Dutch: '*íck salt recht nae den cuyl setten*'),[914] On the basis of this, Gillmeister concluded that 'it seems justified to claim that golf was played on the continent long before any such activity in Scotland'.[915] However, this is a difficult argument to accept, simply on the basis of the evidence that is provided in this Latin–Dutch phrase book. The earliest known edition of *Tyrocinium latinæ linguæ* was published in 1552 (although it may have been written in 1545).[916] In contrast, there is unambiguous evidence of a golf match having been played in Scotland by King James IV earlier than this (in 1503/4), not to mention the references to 'golf' in the Scottish Acts of Parliament of 1457/8, 1471 and 1491. It could be argued therefore that by the time *Tyrocinium latinæ linguæ* was written and published, the established Scottish game of golf would have had a chance to influence those in the Low Countries such as the book's author, Peter van Afferden. There was undoubtedly regular two-way trade between the Scots and continental Europe, in particular with the Flemish[917] (indeed, this is an argument that has been used to support the Dutch games having influenced Scottish golf) and there is clear evidence of an influence from Scotland on Dutch stick-and-ball games. For example, the influence of Scottish golf is suggested by a Dutch poem (1657) that, in describing a Dutch stick-and-ball game played on ice, mentions the use of a '*schotse klik*' [Scottish cleek].[918] Similarly, a Dutch painting from 1668 depicts a kilted Scot playing a stick-and-ball game on ice in Haarlem (Figure 16.2).[919] Certainly, the reference in *Tyrocinium latinæ linguæ* to a game played to a hole, dating from the mid-sixteenth century, cannot be accepted as *proof* of golf having originated in the Low Countries.

Medieval Paintings

Similar arguments concerning the possibility of reciprocal influences between Scotland and the Low Countries could be made about arguments that rely on medieval paintings. Of the paintings discussed in *Encyclopædia Britannica*[920] almost all depict games that do not resemble the 'long game' of golf or images that were painted at a date after which we know that golf was played in Scotland. A frequently cited example is an image from a Flemish Book of Hours dating from c. 1540 and known colloquially as the 'Golf Book' (Figure 16.3).[921] It is hard to know what significance to attribute to this picture, which shows a man kneeling to make a stroke of just a few inches towards a hole. The scene that is depicted occurs in a fenced courtyard, so this is certainly not the 'long game' of golf. In addition, the image dates from the mid-sixteenth century, which is long after the date that we know golf was being played in Scotland.[922]

The arguments concerning medieval paintings are further complicated by them having been used in recent years by different historians to argue that golf originated in two different locations: the Low Countries (an argument favoured by, for example, Steven van Hengel and Heiner Gillmeister)[923] and in the Loire region of France (favoured by Michael Flannery and Richard Leech).[924] An image that features heavily in both arguments is from a manuscript in the *Musée Condé, Chantilly* (*Heures d'Adélaïde de Savoie*, c. 1460–5).[925] In the foreground of the image are two groups of four players playing a stick-and-ball game towards a stake with a third group of four players depicted in the background (Figure 16.4). Flannery and Leech conclude that all three groups are playing the game of *pallemail*.[926] In contrast, Gillmeister argues that the group located in the distance are '*vier Golfspieler*' [four golfers] and that they are playing to a '*loch*' [hole].[927] A close inspection of the image reveals what appear to be marks on the vellum but no clear evidence of a hole. Importantly, the four players in the distance are in a walled area, seemingly on a path leading to where the two groups in the foreground are playing a game resembling *pallemail*. As such, this does not appear to resemble the modern 'long game' of golf. The conclusion that those illustrated in the picture are playing what is described as '*zwar eindeutig um eine Form des heutigen Golfspiels*' [clearly a form of today's golf game][928] seems unconvincing.

Etymological Arguments

Relying on etymological arguments to untangle the origins of a game such as golf is a challenging task. If words in two different languages appear to be similar, it still needs to be established whether one of them influenced the other and, if so, which was derived from which. A further difficulty is that, by necessity, when applying etymological arguments to golf, one is relying on sparse and fragmentary written records. There is an undoubted and obvious similarity between the word 'golf' and the name used for continental games such as *colf*. In addition, there are written references to '*colven*'

Figure 16.3 The Book of Hours, 'The Golf Book' (c. 1540). This image is from a Book of Hours frequently referred to as 'The Golf Book', that was made in Bruges in the mid-sixteenth century. It has been suggested that the image, depicting a ball played towards a hole in an enclosed area, represents an early form of golf. © British Library; Add. MS 24098, f.27r.

Figure 16.4 *Heures d'Adélaïde de Savoie* (c. 1460–5). A French illuminated manuscript that depicts in the foreground a game in which a ball is played towards a stake but which has also been suggested to depict (in the background, right of the main image) a game similar to golf. © *Musée Condé*, Chantilly/*Bibliothèque virtuelle des manuscripts mediévaux*, 0076 (1362), f.2v.

(such as an ordinance issued in Brussels in 1360)[929] that pre-date the earliest written reference to 'golf' in Scotland (1457/8). Of course, the earliest surviving example of a word in a written text should not be assumed to correspond to its first appearance in speech.

James Cunningham drew attention in 1899 to similarities between Dutch words and English words such as 'tee', 'stymie' and 'dormie'.[930] However, it seems that golf historians sometimes search for etymological links where the evidence is rather flimsy. One of the examples provided by Gillmeister in the *Encyclopædia Britannica* but explained in more detail in an article published elsewhere (in German) is the possibility that the Scottish word 'bunker' may be related to the Dutch '*bancaert*'.[931] The basis for this argument is an assumption that the earliest use of a word resembling 'bunker' associated with Scottish golf is 'bunkard club', which appears in a Latin–English textbook *Vocabula* (1685). It has been argued that, because the earliest use of the word in Scotland contained a final 'd', it may derive from the Dutch word '*bancaert*', which is suggested to have a meaning similar to 'bastard' (or '*uneheliches Kind*' in German) and which may have been used as a slang word for 'failure' ('*fehlschlag*').[932] In fact, there *are* earlier uses of the word in Scotland that do not have the final 'd', for example 'bonker clubis' (1629) and 'bonker club' (1633).[933] Another Scottish game that has had its origins debated almost as much as golf is curling. Interestingly, the word 'bunker' is used in curling to describe uneven ice and, perhaps inevitably, an 'origin' for curling beyond Scotland has been sought. In this case the word 'bunker' has been attributed by one source to the Icelandic '*bunga*',[934] meaning swelling (rather than the Dutch '*bancaert*', meaning 'bastard').

The Origin of Golf in France?

A more recent claim is that golf originated in the Loire region of France, rather than in the Low Countries. This argument has been articulated most forcefully by Michael Flannery and Richard Leech in *Golf Through the Ages* (2004),[935] a book they describe as being 'primarily about pictures'. It is a thesis that is based, to a large extent, on an analysis of images of stick-and-ball games and appears to hinge upon an image in a manuscript in the Bodleian Library, Oxford; the *Book of Hours, Use of Paris*

(c. 1400–10).[936] It shows a man swinging a club at a large ball (Figure 16.5) and when Joseph Strutt reproduced the image in 1801 he described it as resembling the English game of *cambuca* or bandy-ball.[937] However, the image is described in *Golf Through the Ages* as being 'the first golf-like swing'.[938] This seems a rather surprising conclusion, given that the depiction of the swing and also the size and the position of the ball are almost indistinguishable from an earlier image (c. 1340), from a stained-glass window in Gloucester Cathedral, that seemingly depicts a very similar stick-and-ball game (Figure 16.5). However, Flannery and Leech describe the English image as depicting the game of *soule à la crosse*, seemingly due to the large size of the ball.[939] It is difficult to see why one image (French, c. 1400–10) depicts a 'golf-like swing' while the other (English, c. 1340) does not. Flannery and Leech also draw attention to what they describe as 'the earliest known depiction of a European ball game'[940] in another English manuscript: the Venerable Bede's *Life of St Cuthbert* (c. 1120). This appears to depict an almost identical club, grip and swing (Figure 16.5) yet, somewhat inexplicably, it is the French image that is considered to be 'the first golf-like swing', rather than either of the two earlier English images (c. 1120 and c. 1340). It seems that the basis upon which Flannery and Leech have claimed that golf originated in France hinges on an image in a French manuscript (c. 1400–10). It is this image that leads the authors on to a discussion concerning 'the myth of Holland as the birthplace of golf'[941] and to assert that golf was 'first played in the Loire region of France'.[942] Flannery and Leech argue that this image is 'essential to a correct interpretation of golf'[943] and that its depiction of an 'unopposed swing with a *crosse* alerts us that six hundred years ago golf was in the making!'.[944] This seems a lot to conclude from a single image.

Chui wan

In 1991 a Chinese academic drew attention to the similarities between modern-day golf and an ancient Chinese game of *chui wan* (捶丸),[945] a game that is thought to have been popular in the Song, Yang and Ming dynasties (960–1500).[946] There would appear to be little doubt that golf and *chui wan* share many similarities. In addition to several images depicting the game, the rules of *chui wan* are recorded in a Chinese text *wan jing* (丸经) dating from 1282.[947]

Figure 16.5 Early depictions of stick-and-ball games. A detail from an illuminated manuscript (c. 1400–10) depicting what has been claimed to be the 'earliest unopposed golf swing' (top). For comparison, a similar but earlier image (c. 1350) from the Great East window of Gloucester Cathedral is shown (bottom left). Also illustrated is an image from a much earlier (c. 1100–50) English manuscript, Bede's *Life of Cuthbert* (bottom right). Top image: © Bodleian Library, MS. Douce 62, f.101v. Bottom left image: Reproduced with kind permission of the Chapter of Gloucester Cathedral. Bottom right image: Reproduced with kind permission of the Master and Fellows of University College, Oxford, MS 165, f.5v.

As is the case with modern-day golf, the description of *chui wan* in *wan jing* reveals that it is a game in which a ball was played towards a hole containing a flag and that it involved playing a ball over varied terrain with multiple clubs.[948] However, it has also been argued that 'the differences between the two games are as profound as the similarities'[949] and it is unclear whether there is likely to have been any influence of *chui wan* upon stick-and-ball games played in Europe before the apparent demise of *chui wan* during the Ming Dynasty. Nevertheless, those searching for evidence of a stick-and-ball game resembling modern-day golf might be hard pressed to find a better example than the Chinese game of *chui wan* despite there being no clear evidence that it had an influence on the development of golf.

In Summary

Perhaps golf historians could be considered a little parochial when squabbling over a possible location within Europe where golf may have originated. It is possible that there was a stick-and-ball game played in continental Europe that had some influence on the development of golf in Scotland (or vice versa) but, if so, these continental European games lost popularity and died out (as did the Chinese game *chui wan*). In contrast, there is evidence that the game of golf took root in Scotland around the beginning of the sixteenth century, where it subsequently flourished, turning into the modern-day game of golf, a sport that is now truly global.[950] While historians will continue to argue that games played in various countries may have played a part in the early pre-history of golf, many will be satisfied that the evidence is sufficient to conclude that, at least in its critical formative years, golf can be considered to have been 'Scotland's game'.[951]

Postscript: Enduring Myths and Popular Misconceptions

The aim of this book has been to separate fact from fiction. Evidence of early golf in Scotland has been re-examined, as has the contentious question of golf's 'origins', and it is clear that some of the claims that have been made on these topics by previous writers are not supported by the evidence. Examples have been identified of errors and of questionable conclusions relating to the history of golf balls, golf clubs and golf societies. However, some of the most enduring myths and popular misconceptions concern the role played by royalty in the history of golf. For example, it has been claimed that several Scottish kings were golfers, despite no evidence having been identified. This is the case with claims relating to King James I of Scotland (b.1394–1436/7), James II (1430–60), James III (1452–88) and James V (1512–42). The frequent claims that Queen Catherine of Aragon (1485–1536) played golf can be dismissed and the numerous similar claims relating to Mary Queen of Scots (1542–86/7) appear to rely on a single document of questionable reliability. There is, however, evidence that golf was played by several Scottish and British monarchs in the sixteenth and seventeenth centuries. This is the case for King James IV of Scotland (1472/3–1513), James VI/I (1566–1625), Charles I (1600–48/9), Charles II (1630–84/5) and James VII/II (1633–1701). Indeed, James IV (and his opponent, the Earl of Bothwell) are the two earliest golfers that can be identified by name (from a record dating from 1503/4). Consequently, the frequent descriptions of golf being a 'Royal and Ancient Game' may have some basis. Of course, the early history of golf is not simply the history of Scottish and British monarchs. That royalty feature so heavily in histories of early golf is, in part, a consequence of the day-to-day activities of the monarchy having been documented in much greater detail than that of their subjects but it probably also reflects a tendency of writers to romanticise golf's early history.

The primary motivation for writing this book was a desire to re-examine and reassess the documentary evidence relevant to the early history of golf and, in the process, several myths and misconceptions have been identified. Highlighting errors or questioning conclusions that have appeared in earlier histories of golf may seem curmudgeonly but the motivation for doing so is simply a hope that this may help us to arrive at a more reliable and accurate account of early golf.

Notes

Chapter 1

1. NRS, PA5/6, f.43v (Scottish Act of Parliament; issued 6 March 1457/8).
2. A wappenshaw was a gathering or a review of troops aimed at ensuring they were properly armed or trained in, for example, archery.
3. Scotland and England had been fighting on a regular basis since the invasion of Scotland by the English King Athelstan in 934. More recently, the two countries had fought the First War of Scottish Independence (1296–1328), noted for the decisive Battle of Bannockburn (1314), and the Second War of Scottish Independence (1332–57). Scotland had also been involved in the Hundred Years War in Western Europe (1337–1453).
4. For a transcription and translation, see RPS, 1458/3/7 (Records of the Parliaments of Scotland to 1707; www.rps.ac.uk).
5. For a transcription and translation, see RPS, 1471/5/6 (Records of the Parliaments of Scotland to 1707; www.rps.ac.uk).
6. For a transcription and translation, see RPS, 1491/4/17 (Records of the Parliaments of Scotland to 1707; www.rps.ac.uk).
7. For a transcription and translation, see RPS, 1424/19 (Records of the Parliaments of Scotland to 1707; www.rps.ac.uk).
8. [Cundell] (1824), 4; Browning (1955), 7; Geddes (1992), 3.
9. Geddes (1992), 3.
10. Maxwell Lyte (1909), 534–5. That golf was not mentioned in the English Act of 1363 is unsurprising, given that golf appears to have been unknown in England at this time.
11. The 'skilled long game' is an expression that has been used by David Hamilton. See, for example, Hamilton (1998), 28.
12. David Hamilton has drawn attention to the likelihood that there were two distinct forms of golf (long and short) during the early history of the game in Scotland; Hamilton (1998), 27–8.
13. For a discussion of 'churchyard golf', with citations to original sources, see Hamilton (1998), 23–7.
14. Hamilton (1998), 23–4.
15. Gillmeister (2002), 3; Flannery and Leech (2004), 241, 249.
16. The possibility of etymological links between the word 'golf' and the Dutch '*kolf*' and the German '*kolbe*' was commented on in 1824; [Cundell] (1824), 2. One of the strongest advocates that *colf* was an early form of golf was Steven van Hengel. See, for example, van Hengel (1972, 1982).
17. For example, see Clark (1875); Ferguson (1908); Hilton and Smith (1912); Browning (1955); Henderson and Stirk (1979).
18. Campbell (1827), 219.
19. Cousins and Pottinger (1974), 8.
20. Henderson (2016), 4. It is unusual to come across claims such as this, where

it has been suggested that King James I of Scotland (b.1394, d.1436/7) played golf, and I am unaware of any evidence indicating that he purchased golf equipment, as is claimed. Although the reign of James I began in 1406, following the death of Robert III, James was not crowned until his release from captivity in England in 1424. So, the period mentioned by the author (1424 to 1437) corresponds to the period from James's coronation in Scotland until his death.

21. Martin (1968), 28.
22. *Santa Cruz Sentinel*, California, USA, Vol. 112, issue 99 (26 April 1968), 13.
23. *Golf Magazine*, New York, USA, Vol. 46, issue 7 (July 2004), 109.
24. *San Francisco Chronicle*, California, USA (15 December 2000), C24.
25. *Golfweek*, Florida, USA, Vol. 37, issue 26 (24 June 2011), 63.
26. *Tampa Bay Singles Golf* (newsletter) (June 2006).
27. [Crosshill] (c. 1974).
28. Donnelly (2010), 5.
29. Thomas (2011), 191.
30. Seltzer (2007), 37.
31. http://tinyurl.com/meh236f (archived 30 May 2016).
32. Temmerman (1993), 30.
33. Scarth (2013), 6.
34. Napier (1848), Vol. 1, 120.
35. https://tinyurl.com/5ydwbjw2 (archived 4 December 2007).
36. For example, see http://tinyurl.com/k6rut8n (archived 28 September 2015); http://tinyurl.com/k6xfhqr (archived 9 September 2015); and http://tinyurl.com/ls66ppx (archived 3 February 2017).
37. For example, see *Newsday*, Long Island, NY, USA (16 June 2004), A40; *The Ottawa Citizen*, Ontario, Canada (3 March 2007), I11.
38. https://tinyurl.com/y7bfrjth (archived 14 December 2012).
39. https://tinyurl.com/yy3yxznh (archived 23 April 2020).
40. https://tinyurl.com/y9dhufav (archived 28 August 2017).
41. Camp (1910), 820.
42. Critchley (1993), 132.
43. Aultman (1969), 8.
44. Jones (1939), 44.
45. Steel and Ryde (1975), 47.
46. Lannon (1983), 86.
47. Ring (1995), Vol. 2, 642.
48. Punia (2008), 97.
49. Butler (2011), 281; Howell (2012), 12; Duncan (2017), 9; McAinsh (2017), back cover.
50. *Guinness World Records* editors (2015), 222 ('600 years since golf was first played at St Andrews Links').
51. Browning (1955).
52. Ibid. 221.
53. Ibid. 12.
54. Ibid. 12.
55. Ibid. 7.

56. Ibid. 12.
57. Ibid. 8.
58. Ibid. 12.
59. Skene (1880), 265–6.
60. Browning (1955), 13.
61. Skene (1877), 354.
62. Hawtree (1996).
63. Ibid. 62.
64. Ibid. 66.
65. Ibid. 63.
66. Mackenzie (1946), 232.
67. Skene (1877), 354.
68. BLO, MS Fairfax 8, f.182r (*Liber Pluscardensis*, Chronicle of Scotland to 1435); GUL, MS Gen 333, f.282r (*Liber Pluscardensis*).
69. In both of these fifteenth-century manuscript versions of *Liber Pluscardensis*, rather than '*palmam*', the word used is '*palma*' (a word that can mean the 'palm' of the hand). This could be seen as bringing us closer to Fred Hawtree's interpretation of the Latin text as 'playing at palm' (or *jeu de paume*), rather than the interpretation of his 'Oxford don', which was 'playing for a prize'. However, I am reliably informed (by a professor of Latin at my own institution, University College London) that the preposition *ad* is always followed by an accusative (and the accusative of *palma* is *palmam*). Furthermore, the ending *-m* was often not written in medieval and early modern Latin manuscripts. So, it seems that we are back with the Latin phrase '*Scotus ad palma[m] ludentibus*' ('Scots playing for victory'). There would seem to be no clear reason for assuming that what is being described is either a stick-and-ball game or a handball game.
70. Miller and Hill (2016), 339.
71. Lennox (2008), 12.
72. Macintosh (2010), 13.
73. Hanna (1993), 15.
74. Hanna (2009/2010), 6.
75. McGimpsey and Neech (1999), 9.
76. https://tinyurl.com/ynnpvkjr (archived 26 January 2021).
77. https://tinyurl.com/bfse9hts (archived 1 June 2021).
78. Keay and Keay (2000), 329.
79. For example, see Lennox (2008), 15.
80. Laird (2017), 159.
81. Ibid. 159.
82. Aitchison and Lorimer (1902), [xvi].
83. It appears that Robert Cameron had been employed a few years earlier to design the clubhouse for the Edinburgh Burgess Golfing Society. See Laird (2017), 159.
84. The pseudo-archaic use of the letter y in 'ye' is an attempt to recreate the Old English letter 'thorn' (þ) in the word 'þe', an early form of 'the'.
85. For further details, see Laird (2017), 159; Robbie (1936), Part I, 74.
86. https://tinyurl.com/pdky6bda (archived 21 May 2016).

87. https://tinyurl.com/5a7r66yn (archived 21 May 2016).
88. Taneja (2009), Vol. II, 145.
89. For example, see Smeaton (1904), 377; Smeaton (1905), 364; Birrell (1980), 96.
90. Steel and Ryde (1975), 329; Sidorsky (2008), 4.
91. ECA, SL1/1/35, 225 (Edinburgh Town Council minutes, 25 December 1695); Johnston and Johnston (1993), 150–1.

Chapter 2

92. NRS, PA2/1, f.67r (Scottish Acts of Parliament, 1466–1474); RPS, 1471/5/6.
93. Li (2014), 385.
94. Ewell (2006), 223.
95. *Golf Illustrated* (31 December 1909), 32.
96. There are numerous references to William Dunbar during the reign of James IV in the Accounts of the Lord High Treasurer and in the Privy Seal Register; Small (1983), Vol. I, cliv–clvi.
97. Small (1893), Vol. I, xiv.
98. Small (1893), Vol. II, 310–11.
99. *The Bookman*, London (April 1895), 26–7.
100. *St Andrews Citizen* (8 January 1910), 3; Johnston and Johnston (1993), 27; Hawtree (1996), 102.
101. Wingfield (2013).
102. *Encyclopædia Britannica* editors (2010), Vol. 28, 150.
103. Gillmeister (2002), 1–2.
104. *Encyclopædia Britannica* editors (2010), Vol. 28, 151.
105. BL, Add MS 40732 ('*The Buike off King Allexander the Conqueroure*'); Cartwright (1986), ix; Mapstone (1994), 1.
106. NRS, GD112/71/9 ('*Buik of King Alexande the Conqueror*'). It is believed that the later manuscript was copied from the earlier one that, in turn, was copied either from Hay's original manuscript (c. 1460) or from a revised version of it. Cartwright (1986), xiii, xv; Mapstone (1994).
107. Cartwright (1986), 110, lines 4330–1. 'And sulk ane quhile apoun þai moderis kne/Quhill bettir starkyn for the were þou be' [And suck a while on your mother's knee/Until better stiffened for the war thou be].
108. Ibid. lines 4326–7.
109. Herrmann (1898), 10–11.
110. Cartwright transcribes the line as 'That was to say a gol[f]°-staff and ane ball'; Cartwright (1986), 109, line 4288. The letter 'f' was placed in square brackets to indicate an emendation and the symbol '°' was used to indicate that a hyphen had been inserted.
111. Cartwright (1986), 109, line 4288; 110, line 4326.
112. Wingfield (2013).
113. Pritchard (1992), 5.
114. Haight (1955), 44.

115. Budge (1889), 46.
116. Wolohojian (1969), 58.
117. Pritchard (1992), 32.
118. Cartwright (1986), xvi.
119. See Hilka (1920), 75 (note: Hilka used as his source the Berlin *Kupferstichkabinett* manuscript 78.C.1). The following manuscript copies of *Roman d'Alexandre* (all of which are held in the British Library) also refer to '*une crosse d'or*' [a golf staff]: Harley MS 4979, f.30v; Royal MS 15 E VI, f.10v; Royal MS 19 D I, f.13r; Royal MS 20 A V, f.23v.
120. Gillmeister (2002), 1–30.
121. Ibid. 12.
122. Gowland (2013), 25.
123. Nijs and Nijs (2014), 19.
124. Gillmeister (2008), 9.
125. Ibid. 9.
126. Paul (1900), 418.
127. *Encyclopædia Britannica* editors (2010), Vol. 28, 151.

Chapter 3

128. Paul (1900), 418 (3 February 1503/4).
129. Ibid. 418 (6 February 1503/4).
130. Paul (1901), 187 (29 March 1506).
131. Ibid. 206 (23 July 1506).
132. Concannon (1995), 22.
133. *Korea JoonAng Daily*, Seoul (12 March 2006).
134. Scott (1975), 11.
135. Pinner (1988), 30.
136. Paul (1900), 341 ('Item, the xxj day of September, to the bowar of Sanct Johnestoun for clubbes, xiiijs', 21 September 1502).
137. Paul (1900), cviii.
138. For example, see Paul (1900); Paul (1901); Paul (1902); Paul (1903).
139. For example, see Paul (1900), 376.
140. Paul (1900), c.
141. Paul (1901), 206.
142. Paul (1900), 376.
143. Ibid. 159, 341, 470; Paul (1901), 358.
144. Paul (1900), cviii.
145. The accounts record that 'golf clubbes and ballis' were purchased simultaneously on 6 February 1503/4. In addition, 'golf ballis' were purchased on 29 March 1506 and 'golf clubbes' on 23 July 1506.
146. Mackie (1849), 57; Dunbar (1999), 201.
147. Paul (1900), xcix.
148. Dickson (1877), ccli–cclii.
149. Ibid. ccxlix, 95 (the accounts indicate that James IV paid £180 for a hawk in 1488).

150. Baxter (1899), 31.
151. Ibid. 32.
152. Browning (1955), 143.
153. Ibid. 143.
154. Nijs and Nijs (2011), 199.
155. Paul (1900), 341. In addition, three days later (on 25 September 1502), the king is recorded as having made a payment to 'the bedell of Sanctandrois' (an official of the University of St Andrews); Paul (1900), 342.
156. In addition to entries in the exchequer accounts indicating that the king was at Falkland the day after the purchase of 'clubbes' from the Perth bow-maker, he appears to have been in Stirling several days earlier. Consequently, it is possible that he made a detour to Perth when travelling between his official residences in Stirling and Falkland but there is no evidence to indicate that this happened, just as there is no evidence that the 'clubbes' were golf clubs.
157. For example, see Scott (1972), 33.
158. Stirk (1987), 29.
159. Barrett (2000), 10.
160. Lennox (2008), 22.
161. Stott (1957), 15.
162. Matuz (1997), 583; Macintyre (2005), 18.
163. Williamson (2018), 211.
164. NRS, E21/6, 287 (Exchequer Records; Accounts of the Treasurer, 1502–1505; 3 February 1503/4); Paul (1900), 418.
165. Smith (1890), 221.
166. Paul (1900), 418.
167. Geddes (1992), 9.
168. Flannery and Leech (2004), 254–5.
169. Harris (2007b), 30.
170. Durie (2003), 190.
171. Nijs and Nijs (2014), 78, 134.
172. Macdougal (1989), 189; Hamilton (1998), 28.
173. Story (1902), 323.
174. https://tinyurl.com/y7dnp9cm (archived 22 February 2021).
175. Concannon (1995), 22.
176. *Edinburgh Evening News* (9 June 1939), 18.
177. McHugh (2008), 462.
178. Millar (2017c), 22–5.
179. Ibid. 22–5.
180. Paul (1900), 417.
181. Ibid. 417.
182. Ibid. 418.
183. NRS, E21/6, 288 (Exchequer Records; Accounts of the Treasurer, 1502–1505; 6 February 1503/4). 'Item, for golf clubbes and balles to the King that he playit with, . . . ix s' [Item, for golf clubs and balls to the King that he played with, . . . 9 shillings].
184. Clark (1875), vii.

185. For example, see Compton (1882), 388; Ferguson (1908), 15; Hilton and Smith (1912), 6; Browning (1955), 1; van Hengel (1972), 9; Cotton (1975), 12.
186. Paul (1900), 418.
187. One of the arguments that has been used to support the possibility that James IV's golf match took place in Edinburgh is an entry in *Registrum Magni Sigilli Regum Scotorum* (The Register of the Great Seal of Scotland) indicating that a proclamation was issued in Edinburgh on 5 February (two days after the golf match and the day before the purchase of golf clubs and balls); Paul (1882), 588. However, as has been discussed elsewhere (Dickinson (1958), 54–5), it appears that the date and location recorded in *Registrum Secreti Sigilli Regum Scotorum* does not necessarily reflect the date and location that a document was signed and there are several examples confirming this in both the Great Seal and Privy Seal accounts in the reign of James IV; see, for example, Paul (1882), 611, nos. 2877 and 2878; Livingston (1908), 160–1, nos. 1101 and 1102. Another argument that has been used to suggest that James IV's golf match took place in Edinburgh is an entry in the king's accounts on the same day that he played golf. The entry records a payment to 'the gysaris [masqueraders] of Edinburgh that daunsit [danced] in the Abbay'; Paul (1900), 418. However, that same day further payments are made to the 'priestis of Dunblane'; Paul (1900), 418; and to 'Johne Barbour with the Beschop of Sanctandrois'; Paul (1900), 418. This highlights that when payments to individuals are recorded in the accounts, it does not necessarily indicate the presence of the king at that location. An established feature of funerals from this period was the funeral feast. Just as a modern-day funeral might end in a wake, there was a tradition of feasting, music and dancing after funerals in the medieval period. The *Oxford Companion to Scottish History* explains that 'food and drink were always available' at funerals and goes on to say that dancing was believed to counteract evil; Lynch (2001), 165. It is likely that many of the Scottish nobility would have attended the funeral of the king's brother in St Andrews and it is equally likely that feasting and entertainment would have followed the funeral and may have continued for several days.
188. Paul (1901), 187, 206. On the basis of the king's accounts that were transcribed by Paul, the date of King James IV's purchase of golf clubs is often cited as being 23 July 1506. However, the more extensive handwritten accounts (NRS, E21/7, f.141v) suggest a date of 22 July.
189. Clark (1875), 123* (note: some page numbers were duplicated in this edition and were identified with asterisks).
190. For example, see Compton (1882), 388; Ferguson (1908), 15; Hilton and Smith (1912), 6; Campbell (1952), 47; van Hengel (1972), 9.
191. Macdougal (1989), 195; Geddes (2007), 14; Eunson (2012).
192. Johnston and Johnston (1993), 29; Hamilton (1998), 32.
193. Paul (1901), 187, 206.
194. There are several references in the accounts to 'Sanctandrois' in the period 12–19 March 1505/6; see Paul (1901), 185–6. There is also evidence that James IV wrote a letter from St Andrews on 14 March 1505/6; Mackie (1953), 21.

195. James IV's golf match against the Earl of Bothwell is discussed in Chapter 3.
196. *The Scotsman* (10 March 2006).
197. https://tinyurl.com/5exop956 (archived 18 February 2021).
198. https://tinyurl.com/19x6owsy (archived 5 April 2006).
199. Adams (2008), 35; https://tinyurl.com/2voh7fyb (archived 15 August 2016).
200. Anonymous (1969).
201. Anonymous (c. 2010), 27.
202. Pitcairn (1833), Vol. 1, Part I, 108.
203. Livingstone (1908), 224.
204. NRS, PS1/3, f.160r (Privy Seal; Latin and English Register, Old Series, 1490–1509; 16 September 1507).
205. SCA, SBC/37/1/4 (Stirling Burgh Records, 'straik at hym with ane goiff club', 7 March 1560/1); https://tinyurl.com/yht7nby3 (archived 6 September 2016); Anonymous (1887), 78.
206. Anonymous (1887), 133 ('struckin him thairwith, als also with ane golf club'; 25 January 1613).
207. Wood (1931), 150 ('streking him with ane golff clube', 20 November 1616).
208. NRS SC67/67/1, f.4v (Court Book of the Regality of Falkirk and Barony of Callander); Hunter (1991), 10 ('stryking of him with ane stalfe or golfeclub', 2 February 1639).
209. SCA, SBC/37/1/4 (Stirling Burgh Records, 7 March 1560/1); https://tinyurl.com/yht7nby3 (archived 6 September 2016); Anonymous (1887), 78.
210. Burnett (2000), 16.
211. Anonymous (1887), 133.

Chapter 4

212. BL, Cotton MS Caligula D VI, 93 (Records and Correspondence [. . .] Concerning England and France, 1475–1517).
213. Benger (1821), Vol. I, 73–5.
214. Ibid. Vol. I, 74.
215. *The London Literary Gazette*, London (17 February 1821), 1.
216. Anonymous (c. 1821), 3–4.
217. Kerr (1896), 21.
218. Pascoe (1898), 279–80.
219. Hilton and Smith (1912), 6.
220. Campbell (1952), 47.
221. Darwin (1954), 153.
222. Browning (1955), 2.
223. Ellis (1824), Vol. 1, 83.
224. Turner (1826), 100.
225. Strickland (1842), Vol. IV, 102.
226. For example, see Hilton and Smith (1912), 6; Johnston and Johnston (1993), 32–3.
227. Brewer (1862), Vol. I, 657.
228. Brewer (1920), Vol. I, Part 2, 974.

229. See, for example, Turner (1826), 100; Strickland (1842), 102; Finch (1883), Vol. I, 279; Childe-Pemberton (1913), 54; Claremont (1939), 149; Starkey (2003), 142.
230. For example, see https://tinyurl.com/18cm7ssh (archived 11 November 2020).
231. Richardson (2010).
232. To demonstrate (literally) that the erroneous link between Catherine of Aragon and golf has been retold in 'dozens of golf books', twenty-four examples are listed: Scott (1972), 33; Cotton (1975), 12; Menzies (1982), 16; Nickerson (1987), 8; McCrone (1988), 166; Allen (1989), 12; Glenn (1991), 6; Wiren (1991), 338; Geddes (1992), 10; Celsi (1992), 16; Green (1994), 12; Rice (1995), 46; Sommers (1995), 13; Concannon (1995), 23; Burnett (1997), 108; Stirk (1998), 273; Druzin (2001), 8; McDonnell (2002), 114; Sherman (2002), 9; Martin (2005), 114; Hudson (2008), 2; Beard (2009), 18; Arscott (2011), 16; Steen (2014), 80.
233. Stott (1957), 15.
234. Browning (1955), 2.
235. *Linlithgowshire Gazette* (18 August 1939), 4.
236. Temmerman (1993), 31.
237. Browning (1955), 3.
238. Mallon and Jerris (2011), xiii.
239. Young (1969), 121.
240. Jenchura (2010), 50.
241. Isaac (1998), 25.
242. Hart (2012).
243. Druzin (2001), 8.
244. Sommers (1995), 13.
245. Martin (2005), 114.
246. Pinner (1988), 30.
247. Macintosh (2010), 72.
248. Concannon (1995), 63.

Chapter 5

249. Roy (1792), Vol. 1, 517–18.
250. Miller (1824), 231; Miller (1844), 60.
251. Kerr (1896), 34.
252. *Pall Mall Gazette*, London (5 November 1896), 9.
253. Hilton and Smith (1912), 6.
254. Campbell (1952), 50.
255. Kerr (1896), 375.
256. Ellis (2007), Vol. I, 312.
257. Kerr (1896), 250.
258. Grimsley (1966), 7.
259. Cotton (1975), 12; Concannon (1995), 23; Machat and Dennis (2000), 20; Bohn (2007), 18; Macpherson (2014), 26.

260. Concannon (1995), 23.
261. Pinner (1988), 30.
262. *The Gaberlunzie-man* was included in an anthology of songs published in 1731 (Anonymous (1731), Vol. 5, 140). It states: 'the Words and Tune compos'd by King James V of Scotland, on occasion of an Adventure of his in Disguise after a Country Girl'. Gaberlunzie is an early Scots word for a beggar.
263. Cromeck (1808), 94. The handwritten comments concerning *The Gaberlunzie-Man* appear on p. 270. They are taken from the original 'interleaved copy' of *The Scots Musical Museum* that forms part of the collection of the Robert Burns Birthplace Museum, Alloway, South Ayrshire, Scotland.
264. Lockhart (1835), 142; Cunningham (1842), 566; Anonymous (1844), Vol. II, 369.
265. Dick (1908). Dick's transcription of the handwritten annotation to *The Gaberlunzie-man* (p. 63) indicates that it is signed 'R.R.'. Dick also mentions (on p. 118) that in Cromek's text 'the initials of Robert Riddell are suppressed'.
266. *Encyclopædia Britannica* editors (1910), Vol. XII, 219.
267. Lenaghan (1996), 14.
268. Manchester (1980), 244.
269. Osterhoudt (2006), Vol. 1, 174.
270. Barrett (2000), 11.
271. Concannon (1995), 23.
272. Halsey (1980), Vol. 8, 126.
273. Scott (1972), 34.
274. Stirk (1998), 172.
275. Stuart (1874), Vol. I, xxx–xxxii.
276. NRS, GD45/26/52 (Papers of the Maule family; a history of the family of Panmure).
277. NRS, GD45/26/52, 140.
278. Kerr (1896), 89.
279. Browning (1955), 30–1.
280. For example, see Dobereiner (1981), 63; Beard (2009), 19.
281. Steel and Ryde (1975), 150; Steel (1980), 7; Mallon and Jerris (2011), xiii.
282. Harris (2007a), 9.
283. Van Dam (2016), Chapter 8.

Chapter 6

284. La Bella (2013), 13.
285. http://tinyurl.com/l8qyfhm (archived 1 August 2014).
286. Eunson (2012), 51.
287. Hutchinson (1899), 5
288. Loeffelbein (1998), 194.
289. http://tinyurl.com/k94lsk8 (archived 22 October 2014).
290. Cossey (1984), 12.

291. Wesson (2009), 223.
292. Hudson (2008), 2.
293. Lynch (2001), 273.
294. Gordin (1967), 2.
295. Hilton and Smith (1912), 6.
296. https://tinyurl.com/h4uk3e3r (archived 21 September 2020).
297. *The Rotarian* (December 1996), 29.
298. Skae (1912), 72.
299. Ruskin and Renfrew (2010), 140.
300. Harris (1953), 36.
301. *Illustrated London News* (23 September 1905), 441.
302. *The Falkirk Herald*, online edition (15 November 2014), http://tinyurl.com/oez8gak (archived 14 May 2015).
303. *The Rotarian* (December 1996), 29.
304. Guy (2005), 146.
305. Story (1902), 324.
306. Brown (1952), 113.
307. Elliott and May (1994), 26.
308. Finegan (1996), 27.
309. *The Courier & Advertiser*, Fife Edition (11 September 2015), 30.
310. Cairns (2014), 56.
311. Fabian-Baddiel (1994), 6.
312. Elliott (1991), 3.
313. As will be discussed later, this is the only location for which there is evidence, from a contemporary source, that Mary Queen of Scots may have played golf.
314. *The Landmark* magazine, Vol. XIII (June 1931), 382.
315. Fife Golfing Association (c. 1988), 150.
316. BL, Add MS 33531 (State Papers and Correspondence Relating to England and Scotland 1449–c. 1594, containing the 'Hopetoun manuscript/Book of Articles').
317. Mahon (1923), 28.
318. Ibid. 21. This is a conclusion that appears to be generally accepted. For example, see Gatherer (1958); Weir (2008), 175. However, it is thought that Lennox may have also contributed; Mahon (1923), 21.
319. Gatherer (1958), ix.
320. BL, Add MS 33531, f.60r (The 'Hopetoun manuscript/Book of Articles'); Hosack (1869), 541.
321. Courtney (1983), 170; Nijs and Nijs (2011), 9, 27, 125.
322. BL, Cotton MS Caligula C IV, f.322; Boyd (1907), 66 (Letter from the Bishop of Ross to Mary Queen of Scots, 26 November 1574); Boyd (1907), 66.
323. Drury's letter to Cecil is reproduced in Tytler (1864), Vol. III, 412–13.
324. McInnes (1970), 47.
325. Letter, dated 25 April 1562, from Thomas Randolph, the English ambassador of Elizabeth I, to William Cecil, Elizabeth's chief advisor; Bain (1898), 619.

326. It is thought that the *Oration* may have been written, at least in part, by Thomas Wilson, an English diplomat and a member of Elizabeth I's government.
327. Buchanan (1571b).
328. Buchanan (1571a).
329. Anonymous (1572).
330. Buchanano (1582), 531. The Latin text is: '*ipsa quotidie in campum propinquum ad lusus consuetos, nec eos plane muliebres prodibat*' [in the neighbouring fields she daily amused herself with sports that were clearly unsuited to women].
331. Furgol (1987).
332. Fleming (1897), 59–60.
333. Furgol (1987), 225–6.
334. For example, see Anonymous (1863), lxix–lxxi.
335. Bain (1900), 142.
336. Mackern (1897), 69.
337. Lang (1901), 175.
338. Mumby (1922), 202.
339. Lang (1890), 11.
340. *Illustrated London News* (23 September 1905), 441.
341. Leach (1907), 98.
342. Leach (1914), 24.
343. Baxter (1899), 7.
344. Porter and Prince (2008), 880.
345. George (1993), 197 (Mary is described as gazing into her diamond ring 'as she stood on the links of St Andrews, playing golf').
346. Eunson (2012), 52.
347. Fabian-Baddiel (1994), 6.
348. *The Times* magazine supplement, London (28 March 1992), 30.
349. Anonymous (c. 2011), 13.
350. Howell (2012), 16.
351. *The American Golfer*, New York (8 April 1922), 22.
352. Richardson (2010).
353. http://tinyurl.com/la7nqqt (archived 11 October 2014).
354. Kaye (1996), 5.
355. Adams (2008), 36.
356. Cotton (1975), 12.
357. White (2014), 94.
358. Lennox (2009), 311.
359. It has been suggested that 'the word caddie is the Scottish spelling of the French *cadet*, meaning a little chief, a title originally given to the younger sons of the French nobility who came to Edinburgh as pages in the train of Mary Queen of Scots'; Browning (1955), 64. That this may have relevance to the origin of the golfing term 'caddie' has been suggested frequently but is hard to either confirm or refute. There is, however, a more plausible explanation, namely that the word, as applied to golf, is derived from the term 'caddies' that was used to describe the young porters and messengers in eighteenth-century Edinburgh; Hamilton (1998), 94.

360. Nickerson (1987), 9.
361. Sherman (2002), 54.
362. *Antiques Roadshow* (BBC TV), Series 35, Episode 4. Recorded at St Andrews University and presented by Fiona Bruce. Originally broadcast on BBC ONE at 20:00 on Sunday 28 October 2012. A transcript is available at https://tinyurl.com/2p8f54ma (archived 20 March 2019).
363. *The Teenagers' Weekly*, supplement to *The Australian Women's Weekly* (20 July 1960), 15.
364. Concannon (2009), 18.
365. Weir (2008), 56.
366. Anonymous (1894), 10.
367. *Golf*, London (2 March 1894), 391.
368. Kerr (1896), 472.
369. Stirk (1998), 24.
370. http://tinyurl.com/qjqfoxx (archived 6 November 2014).
371. *Scotland Now* (the online edition of the *Daily Record*, Glasgow) (6 April 2014): http://tinyurl.com/po6z6o7 (archived 14 May 2015).
372. Eunson (2012), 52–3.

Chapter 7

373. Galbraith (1950), 146; Browning (1955), 208; Scott (1972), 34; Ferguson (c. 1987), 9; Geddes (1992), 12; Menzies (1982), 16; Barrett (2000), 12; Campbell (2001), 174.
374. Browning (1955), 208.
375. Miller (1935), 11.
376. Behrend and Lewis (1998), 92–5.
377. Baxter (1899), 116.
378. https://tinyurl.com/4ih7gnsd (archived 23 February 2013).
379. As will be discussed in Chapter 8, Royal Blackheath Golf Club adopted the slogan 'Instituted in 1608' based on a separate tradition that is linked with James VI/I.
380. Hutchinson (1897), 936.
381. Browning (1955), 208.
382. Scott (1972), 34.
383. Pinner (1988), 30.
384. Miller (1906), 12.
385. NRS, PS1/73, 234 (Privy Seal: Latin and English Register, Old Series, 1595–1603).
386. NRS, CC8/8/58 (Testament dative of Beatrix Richardsone, Edinburgh Commissary Court; Register of Testaments, 11 August 1636 to 13 August 1638; 16 January 1637); Whitelaw (1977), 298.
387. Hamilton (1996), 13.
388. Johnston and Johnston (1993), 58.
389. Paul (1900), 418.

390. NRS, E21/76, April 1603 (Exchequer Records; Accounts of the Treasurer 1601–1604). An abbreviated transcript is provided in Walker (1835), Appendix, lxxxvi.
391. The text from the original manuscript (BL, Add MS 34275, f.18v) is transcribed by Warner (1893), lxx.
392. NRS, E21/74, September 1600 (Exchequer Records; Accounts of the Treasurer 1600–1601); Walker (1835), Appendix, lxxvii.
393. NRS, E21/76, December 1601 (Exchequer Records; Accounts of the Treasurer 1601–1604); Walker (1835), Appendix, lxxx.
394. Anonymous (c. 1935), 304.
395. Hutchinson (1897), 936.
396. A Scots pound was equivalent to one-twelfth of an English pound Sterling in 1603.
397. Paton (1905), 448.
398. Grant (1906), 41, 65, 91, 107, 124.
399. NRS, CC8/8/47 (Testament dative of William Mayne, Edinburgh Commissary Court; Register of Testaments, 11 January 1612 to 29 December 1613; 10 July 1612). In contrast to some other bowers, the details of William Mayne's testament dative were not described by Whitelaw (1977).
400. Craigie (1951), 677.
401. *OED Online* (www.oed.com), see entry for *flock, n.2.*, Oxford University Press, Oxford.
402. Bargmann (2010), 18.

Chapter 8

403. There have been claims from as early as the 1830s (but unsupported by documentary evidence) that golf had been played at Blackheath during the reign of King James VI/I. See, for example, *The Times*, London (8 June 1835), 2. However, the first appearance in print of the claim that the Royal Blackheath Golf Club was 'instituted in 1608' may have been in *The Field* (18 April 1863), 371. The claim reappeared in *The Golfer's Year Book for 1866*; Smith (1867), 2. Although no justification or explanation was provided in these sources for a date of 1608, it is a claim that has been repeated frequently. Prior to the appearance of the claim 'instituted in 1608', it had been suggested (for example, in 1830) that Blackheath Golf Club had been founded 'prior to 1745' (see Chapter 14 for more details).
404. An assessment of the claim that Blackheath Golf Club was 'instituted in 1608' is provided in Scaife (2009), 20. The author comments: 'despite the fact that the author is firmly of the belief that the absence of evidence is not evidence of absence, 1608 is destined, one fears, to remain a largely traditional, rather than factual, date of institution'.
405. Johnston (1985), 374–81.
406. Browning (1955), 4.
407. Cousins (1975), 13.

408. BL, Harley MS 6391 (A Relation of Prince Henryes noble and vertuous Disposition).
409. BNdF, *Français* 7108, f.180v–183v (*XXXVII Ambassade en Angleterre de M. DE LA BODERIE, 1606–1609*).
410. D'Israeli (1835), Vol. II, 162.
411. BL, Harley MS 6391, f.5r (A Relation of Prince Henryes noble and vertuous Disposition).
412. Copies of the French ambassador's letters are preserved in the *Bibliothèque Nationale de France* (*Français* 7108 and 7109). For a transcript of the relevant letter, see Anonymous (1750), *Tome I*, 398–403.
413. At the trial of one of the conspirators in 1606, the indictment stated that the aim had been to 'blow up and utterly destroy with gunpowder the King, Prince Henry, and the Lords and Commons, when assembled in the Parliament-House'; Jardine (1835), Vol. II, 240.
414. Cloake (1995), Vol. I, 180; Cloake (2000), 24.
415. For example, see the sources cited in Birch (1760), 74–5.
416. Anonymous (1750), *Tome I*.
417. Ibid. *Tome I*, 392–403.
418. Cloake (2000).
419. Henderson and Stirk (1981), 3.
420. Tipping (1929), 330.
421. LMA, E/MW/C/0014 (Indenture of Feoffment) and E/MW/C/0016 (Indenture of Sale).
422. Story (1902), 324.
423. McComb (2004), 42.
424. Macgregor (1881), 27
425. NA, E 351/2794 and AO 1/2021/2 (Exchequer accounts; Privy Purse, Sir D. Murray, Keeper of the Privy Purse to Henry, Prince of Wales). The accounts describe 'Clubbes xxxvj, balles to them xiiij dozen. Arrowes headed wth silver xlij and a velvett quyver richelie laced wth golde'.
426. BL, Add MS 12528 (Sir Sackville Crowe's Book of Accompts, Containing the Receipts and Disbursements on Behalf of the Duke of Buckingham [George Villiers], 1622–1628).
427. Millar (2016), 17–18.
428. *Cambridgeshire Live* (27 November 2018; www.cambridge-news.co.uk). https://tinyurl.com/232863ds (archived 25 February 2021).

Chapter 9

429. Browning (1955), 4.
430. Allen (1989), 13.
431. Giuseppi (1933), 163.
432. Cunningham (1899b), 137.
433. *Greenock Telegraph and Clyde Shipping Gazette* (14 June 1900), 4.
434. Ferguson (c. 1987), 9.

435. Haig (1824), Vol. IV, 366, 380. For details of the king's Scottish coronation journey, see Brydon and Brydon (1993).
436. NRS, PC2/11, f.213v (Privy Council: Register of Decreta 1627–1630); Brown (1901), 174.
437. Tytler (1792), 503–4.
438. There is evidence that Charles knew of the Rebellion by 28 October when he attended Parliament in Edinburgh, although he did not depart for London until 18 November. See Cundell (1824), 23.
439. NLS, Acc.4277 (Wodrow manuscripts). The relevant passage is transcribed in Wodrow (1842), Vol. II, 209.
440. NRS, PA (Records of the Scottish Parliament). Also available online: www.rps.ac.uk.
441. NRS, PA6/5 (Letter from Edward Chichester to King Charles I concerning the Irish Rebellion: Belfast, 24 October 1641).
442. Lang (1890), 16.
443. Rice (1995), 47.
444. Pinner (1988), 30.
445. Eunson (2012), 55.
446. *Papers from the Scots Quarters* (14 October 1646), 2 (BL, Thomason 57:E.357[10]).
447. *A Letter from New-Castle* (14 September 1646), 2 (BL, Thomason 57:E.354[3]).
448. *A Letter from Newcastle* (1 February 1646/7), 2 (BL, Thomason 58:E.373[5]).
449. *A Continuation of Papers from the Scotts Quarters* (5 November 1646), 4 (BL, Thomason 58:E.360[10]).
450. *Papers of Some Passages between the King* (1646), 4 (BL, Thomason 56:E.349[6]).
451. *Mercurius Diutinus* (3 February 1646/7), 79 (BL, Thomason 59:E.373[11]).
452. *The Scots Treacherous Designes Discovered* (1647), 5 (HL, Wing 822:35).
453. Ritchie (1883), 62–4.
454. Kerr (1896), 38.
455. Pascoe (1898), 280.
456. Ibid. 280.
457. [Sharpe] (c. 1815), 30.
458. Ibid. 23.
459. Ibid. 41.
460. Ibid. 24.

Chapter 10

461. Story (1902), 325.
462. Nijs and Nijs (2011), 203.
463. Ferguson (1908), 16.
464. Chapman (1964), 165.
465. Ashley (1971), 146.
466. Allen (1989), 13.

467. Chapman (1964), 184. A reference is cited by Chapman (Lyon (1851)) but this appears to provide nothing of relevance.
468. Tyler (1976), 10.
469. Kerr (1902), 229.
470. Grierson (1910), 72; Matuz (1997), 584; Straus (2006), xii.
471. The ninth edition of the *Encyclopædia Britannica* states 'nothing whatever is ascertained'; *Encyclopædia Britannica* editors (1879), Vol. X, 766. The fourteenth edition states 'nothing whatever is known'; *Encyclopædia Britannica* editors (1929), Vol. 10, 499.
472. Lang (1875), Vol. II, 330–2.
473. NRS, GD40/2/4/73 (Memorandum by the Earl of Lothian, 9 January 1651).
474. Fraser (1892), Vol. I, 283.
475. NLS, Dep.313/497 (Papers of the Kerr Family, Marquises of Lothian; Correspondence and Legal Papers, Lothian papers, Vol. IV).
476. WAL, WAM 25188 (Letter from Thomas Harbottle, Fieldkeeper of Tothill Fields, 9 February 1658).
477. Scott (1901), 434.
478. Laing (1863), 240.
479. Ibid. 332–3. These diary entries concerning golf at the 'well of Riuus' date from 1672 and, from other information provided in the diaries, the location is likely to be in the vicinity of Burgie House near Forres on the Moray coast of Scotland.
480. The date has been given here as 1661/2 because Brodie (a Scotsman) recorded the date in his diary as 7 February 1662 (using the modern dating system adopted in Scotland in 1660, in which the year began on 1 January) but in England (until 1752) the year began on 25 March.
481. Hamilton (1998), 250.
482. Transcribed extracts from Brodie's diaries were published in a series of articles between 1845 and 1849 in the *Forres, Elgin and Nairn Gazette.* The passage concerning 'Goulf in Totl Fields' was published on 6 February 1847, p. 4.
483. Laing (1863), xii.
484. [Chamberlayne] (1669), 269.
485. [Chamberlayne] (1669a), 280; Chamberlayne (1669b), 268; Chamberlayne (1669c), 269; Chamberlayne (1670), 280; Chamberlayne (1671), Part I, 187; Chamberlayne (1672), Part I, 193; Chamberlayne (1673), Part I, 197.
486. Chamberlayne (1674), Part I, 195.
487. Chamberlayne (1676), Part I, 170.
488. Chamberlayne (1677), Part I, 170; Chamberlayne (1679), Part I, 175.
489. Chamberlayne (1682), Part I, 183; Chamberlayne (1684), Part II, 183.
490. De-Laune (1681), 114; De-Laune (1690), 107; Besant (1895), 302; Besant (1903), 367.
491. Chamberlayne (1682), Part 1, 183; Chamberlayne (1684), Part II, 183.
492. NA, LC 3/25, 170 and LC 3/73, 194 (Records of the Lord Chamberlain and other officers of the Royal Household; Lord Chamberlain's Department: Various Registers). In both documents, James Carstairs is identified as a 'Goff Clubmaker' (26 August 1663).

493. Armet (1951), 15.
494. Wilcock (1903), 262.
495. Madan and Craster (1924), Vol. VI, 70.
496. BLO, MS Malone 44, f101v and f108r ('Copy, by Edmund Malone, of Money Paid by Baptist May on Account of the Privy Purse of Charles II, 1665/6–1669').
497. Ashley (1971), 147.
498. Hore (1886), Vol. II, 249.
499. For example, see Martin (1936), 44; Durant and Bettmann (1965), 8; Carruth (1993), 23.
500. For example, see Matuz (1997), 584; Macintyre (2005), 4; Janke (2007), 12–13; Lonnstrom and Riso (2018), 54.
501. I am grateful to Charles Gehring for providing this transcription of the Dutch manuscript. The 1657 document is a court action against three Dutchmen (Claes Hendericksen, Meeuwes Hoogenboom and Gijsbert van Loenen) for playing '*gekolft*' on ice on a day of prayer. The original document is preserved in the New York State Archives (NYA, A1876–78, V16, pt2, 0051) and is dated 20 March 1657. Perhaps because the document describes a game being played on ice, it has also been assumed to be referring to the game of hockey. See translation in van Laer (1923), Vol. II, 23.
502. The 1659 document is an ordinance against '*het kolven*' being played in the streets due to it causing damage to windows or injuring people. For a translation, see O'Callaghan (1868), 367; van Laer (1923), 235. O'Callaghan cites the document as 'Book A, Mortgage No. 1, in Co. Clerk's Office, Albany, 209'. A facsimile and transcription of the original document (9–10 December 1659) can be found in a letter by Steven van Hengel dated 22 March 1983 that is held in the archives of the Netherlands Golf Federation.
503. van Hengel (1985), 66. Note: the topic of early *colf* or 'golf' being played in America was not discussed in the earlier (1982) edition of van Hengel's *Early Golf*.

Chapter 11

504. The first person to use the expression 'the first international golf match' in this context may have been John Kerr in 1896; Kerr (1896), 39. It is a phrase that has been repeated frequently and is still being used more than a hundred years later. For example, see Matuz (1997), 584; Lennox (2008), 17; Eunsen (2012), 55.
505. MacQueen and MacQueen (2009), 177.
506. Chambers (1824), Part II, 197–200.
507. Ibid. Part II, 198.
508. [Cundell] (1824), 23–9.
509. Ibid. 26–7.
510. Chambers (1825) Vol. I, 199.
511. Chambers (1847), 296.

512. Strickland (1846), Vol. IX, 124.
513. Ibid. 124.
514. [Dalrymple] (1774), 235–8.
515. MacQueen and MacQueen (2009), 387.
516. Ibid. 387.
517. Pitcarnii (1727), 50; MacQueen and MacQueen (2009), 184–5.
518. Pitcarnii (1727), 76; MacQueen and MacQueen (2009), 196–7.
519. Pitcarnii (1727), 52; MacQueen and MacQueen (2009), 208–9.
520. Paul (1875).
521. Burnett and Urquhart (1998), 9.
522. Ker (1891), 326.
523. Armet (1951), 51.
524. The Burgh Records indicate that John Paterson was a maker of golf clubs, rather than a maker of leather 'feathery' golf balls, a trade that might require the skills of a shoemaker. John Paterson is recorded as being required to pay an annual duty of 'five merks Scottis money or ane sett of clubs yearly for the Lord provost'. See Wood and Armet (1954), 184. The Edinburgh Burgh Records also describe John Paterson as having recently built a house on the Links of Leith, rather than in Canongate.
525. This conclusion is based on a comparison of people identified in Pitcairne's poems (for example, by MacQueen and MacQueen (2009)) and members of the Royal Company of Archers, for example, as identified in Paul (1875).
526. Anonymous (1710). See the British Library's copy (shelfmark G.9767), which lists as subscribers 'Archibald Pitcairn M.D.', 'The Most Reverend Father in God JOHN Lord Arch-Bishop of Glasgow' and also 'John Paterson Eldest Son to the Arch-Bishop of Glasgow'.
527. Pitcarnii (1727), 63–5; MacQueen and MacQueen (2009), 126–9.
528. MacQueen and MacQueen (2009), 345.
529. BL, Sloane MS 3198, f.15 (Robert Freebairn's notes to his edition of *Selecta Poemata*).
530. MacQueen and MacQueen (2009), 302.
531. ECA, Moses, Bundle 93, No. 3997 (Disposition by Roderirk Bayne to The Bishop of Glasgow and his sone, 18 August 1692).
532. MacQueen and MacQueen (2009), 44–5.
533. Anonymous (1760), Vol. V, 3365.
534. Robbie (1936), Part II, 10.
535. Henderson and Stirk (1979), 17.
536. Wilson (1848), Vol. II, 82.
537. Ibid. 82.
538. For example, see Johnston and Johnston (1993), 126–30.
539. Anonymous (1877), 346.
540. Eunson (2012), 55.
541. Kerr (1896), 39.
542. Donnelley (2010).
543. Grimsley (1966), 8.
544. Williamson (2018), 12.

545. Riach (2018), 83. This story is particularly bizarre, given that King Charles I died in 1649 and could not have had any involvement in a golf match that the author states took place in 'the early 1680s'.
546. McPherson (1891), 70.
547. Lang (1903), 30.
548. Arthur (1902), 164. The original letter is currently held in a private collection; Johnston and Johnston (1993), 126; McDonough and Georgiady (2013), 108.
549. NLS, Acc.13144 ('Pocketbook of Sir John Werden, diplomat and politician'; 4 February 1679).
550. Feinstein (2004), viii–ix.
551. Young (2002), 1, 93. Young identifies the source of the story as: 'August and September 1935 issues of the Farmingdale Post of Farmingdale, New York'.

Chapter 12

552. An early account (Strutt (1801), 81) mentions that, whereas golf balls were typically 'a ball of leather stuffed with feathers', they were also 'sometimes, though rarely, stuffed with cotton'. As was described in Chapter 7, there is a reference to 'flok goiff ballis' in 1612. The term 'flok' (or flock) was used to describe materials such as wool or cotton for stuffing quilting or bedding.
553. Gutta-percha is a latex-like material extracted from trees of the genus *Palaquium* that becomes flexible and malleable when warmed in hot water but hardens when cooled.
554. Further details of the history of the golf ball can be found in McGimpsey (2003).
555. Grierson (1807), 233.
556. [Mathison] (1743), 10–11.
557. Simson (1744), 654–65.
558. Seltzer (2007), 37.
559. Rowe (1996), 7.
560. Corbett (2007), 151.
561. Rhoads (1995), 179.
562. Stirk (1998), 110.
563. Hutchinson (1893), 4.
564. *Dundee Evening Telegraph* (11 March 1898), 3. This was part of an eight-part series of articles on golf by Horace Hutchinson that was published in several newspapers in 1898.
565. Mortimer (2004), 4.
566. Cotton (1965), 16.
567. Grout (1982), 13.
568. Robertson (c. 1967), 30.
569. Martin (1968), 30.
570. *Popular Science*, New York (June 1992), Vol. 240, 29.
571. Simpson (1887), 13.
572. *Popular Mechanics*, Chicago, IL (June 1924), Vol. 41, 839.

573. Rhoads (1995), 179.
574. Martin (2005), 22.
575. www.tinyurl.com/2oqykjy6 (archived 4 July 2019).
576. Nijs and Nijs (2011), 139–61.
577. Williams (1844), 25.
578. Martin (1698), 122–3.
579. Lang (1902), Vol. II, 555.
580. NLS, Adv.MS.33.1.1 [v], 74 (State Papers Collected by Sir James Balfour of Denmilne, Volume 5: Letters and Papers, 1610–1622).
581. *Sunday Post*, Glasgow (25 June 1944), 4.
582. *Nottingham Evening Post* (1 February 1944), 3.
583. *Somerset Guardian and Radstock Observer* (5 March 1943), 5.
584. Sherman (2002), 12.
585. *Nepali Times*, Kathmandu, No. 253 (24–30 June 2005).
586. Handley et al. (2012), 439.
587. https://tinyurl.com/klmwqisn (archived 13 February 2021).
588. Hoofts (1642).
589. ECA, McLeod Bundle 0007, item 0002. (Copy Act of the Deacon Convenor of the United Trades of the Canongate re Differences Between the Cordwainers of the Canongate and the Cordwainers and Golfball Makers of North Leith, 24 August 1554); Robbie (1936), Part II, 30.
590. NRS, GD1/14/1 (Minute book; Incorporation of Cordiners of the Canongate, Edinburgh, 1584–1773). See also Hallen (1886), 102–3.
591. Vans Agnew (1887), Part II, 341.
592. Hamilton (1986); Dickinson (1952).
593. Hamilton (1986), 20.
594. Maxtone-Graham (2018b), 10–13.
595. NRS, CC8/8/93, 447–52 (Testament Dative of John Dickson, Clubmaker of Leith; 16 April 1731).
596. It has been suggested that the differing qualities of golf ball may have arisen from 'variations in the firmness, toughness and the thickness of the leather, its stitching and stuffing' and perhaps due to 'variations in the stuffing material from straw and hair to feathers'; Maxtone-Graham (2018b), 13. Possible ancestral links have been identified to 'Dicksons' who are listed as golf-ball makers and shoemakers; Maxtone-Graham (2018a), 28–31.
597. NRS, CC8/8/93, 451 (Testament Dative of John Dickson, Clubmaker of Leith; 16 April 1731).
598. NRS, PS1/87, ff.169–70 (Privy Seal: Latin and English Register, Old Series, 1614–1620); Geddes (2007), 19, 96–8; Maxtone-Graham (2018b), 10–13.
599. NRS, PC2/11, f.213v (Privy Council: Register of Decreta 1627–1630); Brown (1901), 174.
600. Browning (1955), 136.
601. van Hengel (1982), 51.
602. Unger (1939), 359, 373, 426, 442, 485, 487, 489, 492, 495. The exported goods are generally referred to simply as *ballen*, although there is one instance of *vlas ende ballen* (p. 426), which may be a reference to flax-filled

balls. In addition, there is a reference to export duty imposed on *caetsballen* in 1519 (p. 85), used for the tennis-like game of *caets*.

603. Rorke (2001).
604. Watson (2003).
605. NRS, E4/3, f.5v (Exchequer Records: Exchequer Act Books or Register, 1597–1600).
606. NRS, E76/2 (Exchequer Records: Books of Rates, 1611); Anonymous (1611).
607. NRS, E76/3 (Exchequer Records: Books of Rates, 1612).
608. Vans Agnew (1887), Part II, 341.
609. For example, see Anonymous (1604), 'Balls vocat.'; Anonymous (1657b), 'Balls voc.'.
610. Anonymous (1604), 'Balls vocat.'; Anonymous (1657b), 'Balls voc.'; Watson (2003), Appendices 1b, 2b, 3b.
611. Anonymous (1657a), 20.
612. Corbett (2007), 151.
613. White (2011), Section 10.2.1, 187.
614. Sherman (2002), 12.
615. Handley et al. (2012), 439.
616. Robertson (c. 1967), 8.
617. Macintyre (2005), 7.
618. Matuz (1997), 584; Barton (2009), 75.
619. Hoggard (2006), 144.
620. McCord and Harney (2006), 18.
621. Campbell (2001), 17.
622. Concannon (1989), 15.
623. Plans (1994), 221.
624. Grimsley (1966), 12.
625. Machat and Dennis (2000), 21.
626. McGimpsey (2003), 1.
627. Cooke (2008), 2 (from an article that was originally published in the *New York Times*, 1973).
628. Balfour (1887), 16.

Chapter 13

629. NRS, E21/6, 288 (Exchequer Records: Accounts of the Treasurer, 6 February 1503/4); Paul (1900), 418. It is frequently assumed that an earlier reference to 'clubbes' being purchased by King James IV from a Perth bow-maker in September 1502 may have been golf clubs. However, as is discussed in Chapter 3, this is uncertain.
630. Temmerman (1993).
631. Flannery and Leech (2004).
632. Bargmann (2010).
633. Hamilton (1998), 27–8; Hamilton (2021), 34–7.
634. Pinner (1988), 18; Cousins (1975), 3.

635. NRS, E21/6, 288 (Exchequer Records: Accounts of the Treasurer, 6 February 1503/4); Paul (1900), 418.
636. BL, Add MS 12528 (Sir Sackville Crowe's Book of Accompts, Containing the Receipts and Disbursements on Behalf of the Duke of Buckingham [George Villiers], 1622–1628); Millar (2016), 17–18.
637. NLS, MS.1393, 77 (letter from Alexander Monro, regent at St Andrews, dated 27 April 1691). Transcribed in Dickinson (1952), xxxix; Geddes (2007), 62.
638. NRS, GD248/557/17, item 21 (Papers of the Ogilvy family, Earls of Seafield; Seafield Correspondence; 2 September 1690). Transcribed in Tayler and Tayler (1933), 43–4.
639. NLS, Acc.11208/2. The earliest known rules of golf (1744), from the minute book of the Gentlemen Golfers of Edinburgh, subsequently the Honourable Company of Edinburgh Golfers; Chapman (1997), 14.
640. Grace (1875), 4; Clapcott (1935), 95.
641. The account books of Sir John Foulis (8 February 1703), transcribed in Hallen (1894), 315.
642. This reference to golf clubs from 1629 is from a notebook that was discovered in an Edinburgh bookshop and is thought to have belonged to the son of a William Law of Stirling. The notebook and its contents are described in two articles published in *The Scotsman* in 1896 and 1907. See *The Scotsman* (5 May 1896), 7 and (7 September 1907), 8.
643. A transcript of Montrose's financial accounts during his studies at St Andrews (1628–9), as recorded by his assistant John Lambye, is provided in Napier (1848).
644. Napier (1848), 127.
645. The accounts of James Graham, Earl of Montrose (15, 22 and 24 November 1628, respectively), transcribed in Napier (1848), 173–4.
646. A 'history timeline' on the website of the Royal Montrose Golf Club suggests that these payments to caddies by the Earl of Montrose occurred in Montrose. However, the three payments to boys for carrying golf clubs, as documented in John Lambye's written accounts, occurred between November and December 1628 and other entries in the accounts confirm that Montrose was lodging 'in the College' at St Andrews during this time. Later entries in Lambye's accounts do indicate that Montrose also played golf in 'Montrois' (Montrose) but this was a year later. The three entries that record golf being played in 'Montrois' are dated as either November or December 1629.
647. Extracts from the account books of Sir John Foulis of Ravelston were transcribed and published in Hallen (1894). Hallen states that two of the original volumes were missing when he transcribed the diaries in 1894. Whereas the original accounts transcribed by Hallen are now lost, the two volumes that were unavailable to Hallen in 1894 were acquired by the National Library of Scotland in 1936: MS.6153 (Account Book 2; 1684–1686) and MS.6154 (Account Book 3; 1686–1689). See Geddes (1992), 33.
648. The account books of Sir John Foulis (13 April 1672), transcribed in Hallen (1894), 4.

649. The account books of Sir John Foulis (17 December 1692), transcribed in Hallen (1894), 151.
650. NLS, Adv.MS.32.7.7 (Diary of Thomas Kincaid), transcribed in Meikle (1949).
651. NLS, Adv.MS.32.7.7 (Diary of Thomas Kincaid), transcribed in Meikle (1949), 150.
652. Stirk (1989), 45–6.
653. Tytler (1792), 504.
654. *Caledonian Mercury* (26 April 1792), 3; *The Scots Magazine* (1 May 1792), 223.
655. NLS, Acc.11208/1 ('Records of the Gentlemen Golfers', the first Minute Book (1744–1781) of the Honourable Company of Edinburgh Golfers); Johnston (1985), 67.
656. RNA, GM002/RNA 70 012 ('No. II Minute Book [of the St Andrews Golf Club], Commencing 4 May 1766'), 27 June 1771.
657. Clapcott (1935), 24; Robbie (1936), Part II, 68.
658. *Caledonian Mercury* (28 April 1787), 1.
659. [Smollett] (1771), Vol. II, 68.
660. Johnston (1985), 103.
661. For example, see Hamilton (1988), 29–30.
662. NLS, Adv.MS.32.7.7. (Diary of Thomas Kincaid), transcribed in Meikle (1949), 133.
663. NRS, GD220/6/2006, item 1 (Papers of the Graham Family, Dukes of Montrose; Accounts of the Duke of Lennox, 2 April 1599).
664. The accounts of James Graham, Earl of Montrose (16 November 1629), transcribed in Napier (1848), 199.
665. NLS, MSS.6153–4. Account books of Sir John Foulis (30 January 1686), transcribed in Geddes (1992), 34.
666. From accounts in the 'Delvine papers' (3/4 March 1713), transcribed in Dickinson (1952), 77.
667. NLS, MSS.6153–4. Account books of Sir John Foulis (22 December 1686), transcribed in Geddes (1992), 34.
668. References to horn being attached to clubs can be found in accounts from 1713–14 in the 'Delvine papers', as transcribed in Dickinson (1952), 75, 76, 79, 81, 88.
669. [Smollett] (1771), Vol. II, 67.
670. A letter from Alexander Monro, regent at St Andrews (dated 27 April 1691), is transcribed in Dickinson (1952), xxxix.
671. The account books of Sir John Foulis (5 January 1691), transcribed in Hallen (1894), 131.
672. NRS, GD220/6/2006, item 1 (Papers of the Graham Family, Dukes of Montrose; Accounts of the Duke of Lennox, 2 April 1599).
673. Gowland (2011), 42.
674. See references to 'tynning' cited in *Dictionaries of the Scots Language* (http://dsl.ac.uk).
675. *Encyclopædia Britannica* editors (1797), Vol. VIII, 12.
676. Jones (1790), 288.

677. The letter is reproduced in Henderson and Stirk (1979), 93. I have not been able to locate the original letter but it seems reasonable to assume that the transcript provided by Henderson and Stirk is accurate.
678. NLS, MSS.6153–4. Account books of Sir John Foulis (30 January 1686), transcribed in Geddes (1992), 34.
679. It has been suggested that 'scrapers' were wooden clubs used for approach shots; Stirk (1998), 75.

Chapter 14

680. ECA, SL1/1/64 (Minutes of the Town Council of Edinburgh, 7 March 1774).
681. NLS, Acc.11208/1 ('Records of the Gentlemen Golfers', the first Minute Book [1744–81] of the Honourable Company of Edinburgh Golfers); Johnston and Johnston (1993), 208–18.
682. Robertson (1784), 51; Anonymous (1786), 73. For further details concerning the appearance of early golf societies in the *Edinburgh Almanack*, see Laird (2017), 144–7.
683. Anonymous (1812), 125. I am informed that the date '1744' also appears in the preceding edition of *The Edinburgh Almanack* (1811) but I have been unable to locate copies of the 1809–11 editions to verify this. However, the claimed foundation date of 1744 does not appear in editions of either *The Edinburgh Almanack* or *The Universal Scots Almanack* published prior to 1809.
684. Evidence that the entry in *The Edinburgh Almanack* was a request from the Blackheath Golf Club can be found in an entry from 1830 in the accounts from the 1830/31 season of the Blackheath Winter Golf Club. It states: 'to ensure the insertion of the Blackheath Golf Clubs in the Edinburgh Almanack, 12 [copies] are ordered annually'.
685. Anonymous (1830), 511.
686. Anonymous (1832), 370.
687. Anonymous (1837), 500.
688. The earliest minute book of the Musselburgh Golf Club dates from 1784 but 1774 is the date of a silver cup in the club's possession; Ironside and Douglas (c. 1999), 2–3. The foundation date of 1761 that is claimed by the Bruntsfield Links Golfing Society is based on an entry in their minutes dated 30 July 1790, stating 'this Golfing Society had subsisted above thirty years'; Colledge (2011), 12–14.
689. Anonymous (1834), 357.
690. Anonymous (1835), 468.
691. Robbie (1936), Part I, 8.
692. Ibid. Part II, 46.
693. The first two volumes of *The Chronicles of the Royal Burgess Golfing Society* (Robbie (1936); [Borthwick] (1987)) were published to commemorate its bicentenary celebrations in 1936 and 250th anniversary celebrations in 1987.
694. Johnston (1985), 167–99.
695. Charles Clapcott examined the various titles of the society and concluded that whereas the earliest title was 'The Gentlemen Golfers' (from 1744 to 1768),

the title 'The Honourable Company of Edinburgh Golfers' had been in use since 1784; see Johnston (1985), 355–65. This is despite the society being referred to in *The Edinburgh Almanack* as the 'Edinburgh Company of Golfers' until 1833; Anonymous (1833b), 350.

696. Anonymous (1839), 550.
697. Behrend and Lewis (1998), 92–6.
698. *Fifeshire Journal* (5 July 1855), 5. In the published list of golf clubs identified, both 'The Edinburgh Company of Golfers' and 'The Leith Golf Club' were listed as having foundation dates of 1744 but these are both names that have been used to describe the same golf society (now known as The Honourable Company of Edinburgh Golfers).
699. There have been claims from as early as the 1830s (but always lacking documentary evidence) that golf had been played at Blackheath during the reign of King James VI/I; see, for example, *The Times*, London (8 June 1835), 2. The first appearance in print of the claim that the Royal Blackheath Golf Club was instituted in 1608 may have been in *The Field* (18 April 1863), 371. No justification or explanation was provided for a date of 1608 but the claim has been repeated frequently and is discussed in more detail in Chapter 8.
700. See, for example, on the Club's website; https://tinyurl.com/mse6f5yw (archived 10 March 2021).
701. Whitney (1895), 374.
702. A biography of Charles Clapcott and details of his extensive golf library can be found in Johnston and Murdoch (1989).
703. *The Scotsman* (3 May 1938), 13. Clapcott's letter (reproduced in Johnston (1985), 371) was in response to an article in the newspaper that had described a forthcoming match between Royal Blackheath and Royal Burgess as being 'the two oldest golf clubs in the world' (*The Scotsman* (28 April 1938), 18). Following the publication of Clapcott's letter, the same golf match was subsequently described by the newspaper as involving 'two of the oldest golf clubs in the world' (*The Scotsman* (14 June 1939), 20).
704. Johnston (1985), 374–81.
705. Clapcott's suggested foundation date of 1760 for the Bruntsfield Links Golfing Society was based on a comment in a minute book that is now lost but which was transcribed and published in 1875; Clark (1875), 95. Although the earliest entry in the lost minute book dates from 1787, an entry from 1790 states: 'This Golfing Society had subsisted above thirty years' (hence the suggested foundation date of 1760). Clapcott's suggested date of 'previous 1760' as the foundation date of the Royal Burgess Golfing Society relies additionally on an entry in a minute book dating from 1818 that claimed the Burgess Society was 'senior' to the Bruntsfield Society. Therefore, it was on the basis of these two claims (dating from 1790 and 1818) that led Clapcott to conclude, 'The Burgess must have been anterior to 1760'. See Johnston (1985), 379.
706. Scottish Golf History website, https://tinyurl.com/yv5ta576 (archived 10 October 2021).
707. Scaife (2009), 21. Charles Dickens's character Thomas Gradgrind (who stated 'what I want is Facts [. . .] nothing but Facts. Facts alone are wanted in life') has become a metaphor for inflexible devotion to facts.

708. The earliest written records of the Blackheath Golf Club are in a cash book dated 1787. However, the club has an engraved silver trophy with the names of its captains dating back to 1766. The club also has a seal and brass coat button with the date 1745 but these are thought to date from the nineteenth century; Scaife (2009), 24. Earlier dates that have been suggested as being the foundation date of the society (for example, 1608 and 'prior to 1744') are discussed elsewhere in this chapter.
709. The earliest surviving records of the Royal Burgess Golfing Society are in a minute book dating from 1773; Robbie (1936), Part I, 8. Earlier dates that have been suggested as being the foundation date of the society (for example, 1735 and 'previous 1760') are discussed elsewhere in this chapter.
710. *Faulkners Dublin Journal* (23 October 1762), 'The Goff Club meet to dine at the house of Mr. Charles Moran at Bray on Thursday the 28th October'; Gibson (1988), 9; Gibson (2012), 21.
711. NLS, Acc.4796, item 124 (Minute book of Fraserburgh Golf Club, 1777–1786).
712. *Caledonian Mercury* (26 April 1787), 3.
713. A ballot box has survived with an inscription dated 1780, as has a set of 'Regulations' and 'Laws' dating from 1783, but no other records of this society have survived. The modern-day golf club was founded in 1818. Smith (1909), 13–14; Edwards (2005), 1–7.
714. Crampsey (c. 1987), 1–11.
715. For a discussion of this topic, see Johnston (1985), 167–8.
716. Mair (1994), 22.
717. Johnston (1985), 372.
718. *Caledonian Mercury* (24 April 1738), 18571. For a more detailed discussion, see Millar and Hamilton (2015).
719. Carlyle (1795), 1–49.
720. Ibid. 19.
721. Ibid. 19.
722. Ibid. 19.
723. Fea (1787), 21.
724. Wemyss (1791), 424.
725. McAinsh (2017).
726. Morrison (2021), 52.
727. *The Graphic: An Illustrated Weekly Newspaper* (7 June 1873), 530.
728. Bauchope (1889), 292; Duncan (1892), 258, 296.
729. Duncan (1892), 296.
730. Duncan (1890), 126.
731. Morrison (2021), 53.

Chapter 15

732. Possible links between golf and other stick-and-ball games will be discussed in Chapter 16.

733. For example, see van Hengel (1982); Gillmeister (2002); Flannery and Leach (2004).
734. For example, see Flannery and Leach (2004).
735. NRS, PA5/6, f.43v (Scottish Act of Parliament, 6 March 1457/8).
736. NRS, PA2/1, f.67r (Scottish Act of Parliament, 6 May 1471).
737. NRS, PA2/5, f.150r (Scottish Act of Parliament, 18 May 1491).
738. NRS, E21/6, 287 (Exchequer Records; Accounts of the Treasurer, 3 February 1503/4).
739. NRS, E21/6, 288 (Exchequer Records; Accounts of the Treasurer, 6 February 1503/4).
740. NRS, E21/7, f.192v (Exchequer Records; Accounts of the Treasurer, 29 March 1506).
741. NRS, E21/7, f.141v (Exchequer Records; Accounts of the Treasurer, 22 July 1506).
742. NRS, PS1/3, f.160r (Privy Seal: Latin and English Register, Old Series, 1490–1509, 16 September 1507); Pitcairn (1833), 108.
743. BL, Add MS 40732, f.60v ('The Buik of King Alexander the Conquer-oure'); Cartwright (1986), 109 and 244.
744. ACA, Aberdeen Burgh Records, Vol. 16 (1538); Jamieson (1825), 498.
745. ACA, Aberdeen Burgh Records, Vol. 19 (1545); Jamieson (1825), 498.
746. UStA, msdep106/1 (25 January 1552/3; Licence granted by the burgh of St Andrews to the Archbishop of St Andrews to farm rabbits on the Links, St Andrews).
747. ECA, McLeod Bundle 0007, item 0002 (Copy Act of the Deacon Convenor of the United Trades of the Canongate re Differences Between the Cordwainers of the Canongate and the Cordwainers and Golfball Makers of North Leith, 24 August 1554); Robbie (1936), Part II, 30.
748. SCA, SBC/37/1/47 (Stirling Burgh Records, 7 March 1560/1).
749. ACA, Aberdeen Burgh Records, Vol. 26 (1565); Jamieson (1825), 86.
750. NLS, Adv.MS.34.4.15, 16. (Diary of James Melville); Pitcairn (1842), 17.
751. NRS, CC8/8/1, 305 (Testament dative of Jonet Faythnay, spouse of John Miller); Edinburgh Testaments, Vol. I, f153.
752. BL, Add MS 33531, f60r (The 'Hopetoun manuscript/Book of Articles').
753. Transcribed in Anonymous (1833a), 285.
754. NLS, Adv.MS.34.4.15, 25 (Diary of James Melville); Pitcairn (1842), 29.
755. ELA, HAD/4/2/3/4, 22 (Haddington Burgh Court Book); Kerr (1896), 286.
756. BL, Add MS 34275, f.18v (Catalogue of the library of King James VI of Scotland, 1573–1583); Warner (1893), lxx. Warner (p. xx) suggests a date of c. 1578.
757. NLS, Adv.MS.34.4.15, 94 (Diary of James Melville); Pitcairn (1842), 126.
758. UStA, CH2/316/1/1, 325 (St Andrews Kirk Sessions, 18 December 1583); Fleming (1890), 515.
759. Letter sent from Kirkwall, Orkney, 23 November 1585. Transcribed in Vans Agnew (1887), Part II, 341.
760. NRS, GD112/71/9, 108 ('Buik of King Alexander the Conqueroure'); Cartwright (1986), 109, 244.

761. AYA, B6/11/1/3, f.453r (Ayr Burgh Court and Council Records, Ayrshire Archives under Charge and Superintendence from the National Records of Scotland; 2 December 1587). For a full transcription of this text, see note 896.
762. GCA, CH2/550/1, 239 [f.120r] (Glasgow Kirk Sessions); Wodrow (1845), Vol. II, Part I, 14.
763. NA, SP 52/47, f.105r (State Papers Scotland Series I); Boyd and Meikle (1936), 578.
764. Edinburgh Burgh Records, 19 April 1592; Anonymous (1927), 63.
765. BL, Cotton MS Caligula D II, f.59v–61r (Records and Papers Concerning England and Scotland, 1590–1603); Cameron (1936), 48–50.
766. Edinburgh Burgh Records, 20 April 1593; Anonymous (1927), 86.
767. NRS, CH2/145/1, f.97r (Elgin Kirk Sessions, 19 January 1596–7); Cramond (1897), 31.
768. NRS, E4/3, f.5v (Exchequer records; 'Table of customs').
769. NRS, CC8/8/31, 631 (Testament dative of Thomas MacClellane); Edinburgh Testaments, Vol. XXXI, f322.
770. UStA, CH2/316/1/1, 538 (St Andrews Kirk Sessions, 29 March 1598); Fleming (1890), 846.
771. UStA, CH2/316/1/1, 583 (St Andrews Kirk Sessions, 29 December 1599); Fleming (1890), 913.
772. NRS, GD220/6/2006, item 1 (Papers of the Graham Family, Dukes of Montrose; Accounts of the Duke of Lennox, 2 April 1599). Contains several references to 'golf'.
773. NRS, CH2/521/3, 120 (Perth Kirk Sessions, 19 November 1599); Clark (1875), 120.
774. NRS, GD112/35/1, #4 (Papers of the Campbell Family; accounts of the Laird of Glenorchy, c. 1590–1599).
775. Anonymous (1566); Anonymous (1597).
776. Smeaton (1904), 337; Birrell (1980), 30.
777. A first-hand account of the introduction of golf by Scottish settlers at Newtownards in the north of Ireland is described in the 'Montgomery Manuscripts'. Extracts from these documents were published as a series of articles in the *Belfast Newsletter*. The manuscripts describe the establishment of a school at Newtownards containing a 'green' that was used by 'the schollars' for 'recreation at goff, foot ball and archery' (*Belfast Newsletter* (5 September 1786), 4). Further detail can be found in Hill (1869), 126; Gibson (1988), 5–6.
778. ACA, CA5/1/7 (Aberdeen City, Baillie Court Book, 1st series; 5 September 1657). This information from the Aberdeen archives, which was initially identified by Dr Thomas Brochard, was brought to my attention by Czeslaw Kruk.
779. The following is a full transcription (and also a translation into modern English) of the Aberdeen Court Record of 5 September 1657 (ACA, CA5/1/7) relating to the shipment of golf balls and clubs to Danzig (Gdańsk), Poland: 'The Baillie court of the Burghe of Ab[er]d[een] holdene within the tolbuith of the samen upon the fyfth day of September 1657 Be ane hon[orabi]ll man William Gray. The said day The Baillie

decernes James Andersoun yo[unge]r skipper in Ab[er]d[een] To pey and delyver to William Mayne bower in Ab[er]d[een] the sowme of aucht shilling Scots money for ilk club of two dussoun clubs with thrie shilling four pennies for ilk ball of two du[ssou]n goaf ballis sent with the said James be the said William to Dansick to be sold ther at the best availl which the said James promist to have peyit within the t[er]me of Law under the paine of poinding with tuelff shilling for expensis of pley Reservand anie further worth of the saidis clubs and ballis for the use for the said William. Becaus the said James Andersoun compeirit and confest that he promist satisfactioun of the clubs and balls at aucht shilling for ilk club of the clubs fors[ai]ds and that he wes content to that what more suld be gottin for the s[ai]ds clubs & ballis the (*sa*)men suld be furthcumand for the said William Inro[lli]t wherupon the baillie decernit in maner fors[ai]ds.'

The following translation is an attempt to convey the meaning of the Aberdeen Court Record of 5 September 1657, rather than a literal translation: The bailie court of the burgh of Aberdeen which was held in the tolbooth of the burgh of Aberdeen on the 5 September 1657 before an honourable man, William Gray. On this same day, the bailie ordered James Andersoun younger, skipper in Aberdeen to pay William Mayne, bow-maker in Aberdeen the sum of eight shillings Scots money for each of two dozen clubs and three shillings four pence for each of two dozen golf balls which William Mayne had sent with him to Danzig to sell at the best price he could obtain. James Andersoun had promised to pay this at the legal term or else to have his goods confiscated to the value of the debt and to pay twelve shillings costs. He had been summoned to appear and confessed that he had agreed on eight shillings per club and that if he got more for the clubs and balls, he would be ready to give to William when he required it. This was entered in the roll as the bailie had determined above.

780. Ditchburn (1990), 12–22.
781. Kay (2006), 41.
782. Ibid. 43.
783. NRS, GD377/402, 1 and 4 (Accounts recording debts incurred for sending 'golf balls' and 'golf clubs' to Carolina; on 1 and 29 June 1739, respectively).
784. The journal of David, Lord Elcho (1721–87), which is written in French, survives in the Wemyss family archive at Wemyss Castle, Fife. The relevant passage, concerning Lord Elcho's encounter with Bonnie Prince Charlie in Rome, has been translated as '[he] would spend all his time shooting blackbirds and thrushes, or playing the Scottish game of golf'; Wemyss (2003), 27.
785. LBA, BLB1/4/7/1 [NRAS945/6/24/1] (28 June 1748); Malcolm (1950), 18.
786. An entry (dated 30 June 1767) in the account books of the London wine merchant Chalié and Dolignon describes 'goff balls and clubs' being sent to the firm's representative in Bordeaux, France. See *The Tatler* (14 August 1901), 345.
787. It has been suggested that, of the fifty-five members of Blackheath Golf Club recorded in the *Goff Club Cash Book* (from the archives of the Royal Blackheath Golf Club), almost all were Scottish; Scaife (2009), 26.

788. Twiss (1775), 272.
789. Millar et al. (2013), 30–3.
790. A description of golf being played on a two-hole course at Bunce Island (Bense Island) in Sierra Leone was recorded in the diary of the botanist Henry Smeathman in 1773 (Uppsala University MS D 26). A transcript of the relevant passage can be found in Fyfe (1964), 70–1. Evidence that the course had been established by the Scottish owners of Bunce Island is described in Coleman (2018), 148–9.
791. Playfair and Gibson (2017), 44–7.
792. *Calcutta Gazette* (12 January 1804), 2 ('The Lovers of this Amusement may be accommodated with CLUBS and BALLS – by application to R. BEARD, Calcutta Hotel; who will send proper people to point out the Ground for Play.').
793. Macpherson (2014), 320–5.
794. *Montreal Herald* (23 December 1826), 3.
795. Richardson and Sheret (2014), 40–9.
796. *Perthshire Advertiser* (1 August 1844), 3.
797. *Bells' Life in London and Sporting Chronicle* (18 February 1844), 3. This report from 1844 describes golf having been 'introduced two years ago'; Fletcher and Williams (2019), 34.
798. Gibson (2019), 36.
799. See Chapters 8 and 14.
800. Russell (1988).
801. Cameron (2010).
802. *Otago Daily Times* (19 September 1863), 6 (an advertisement seeking 'Gentlemen desirous of forming a golf club'); *Otago Daily Times* (22 September 1863), 4 ('steps are being taken here to establish the old Scotch national game of Golf').
803. *Fifeshire Journal* (5 September 1872), 6. Batavia Golf Club was established with 'clubs and gutties' from Bombay. Batavia, capital of the Dutch East Indies, is now the Indonesian capital of Jakarta.
804. *The Field* (31 July 1875), 143 (a report of golf having been introduced to Conway, North Wales 'last summer', i.e. 1874).
805. *North-China Herald*, Shanghai (10 October 1883), 405 (a report of 'The September meeting of Hankow Golf Club'). It has also been claimed that the Club was founded in 1878 and that informal golf has played at Hankow since 1870; *Dundee Courier* (1899), 4; Xing and Meister (2021), 42–7.
806. *The Field* (31 March 1888), 455 ('a golf club has recently been formed in Antwerp').
807. *The Field* (8 September 1888), 365 (mentions 'Cairo Golf Club' and describes golf 'on the links of Gezireh').
808. Bauchope (1889), 248 (Royal Malta Golf Club 'instituted Autumn of 1888').
809. There is evidence from surviving minute books of a golf club founded at Gothenburg, Sweden in 1891; Kittel (2018), 7. In addition, there is evidence that provides strong support for a private golf course at Ryfors, Sweden (c. 1888); Kittel (2018), 76.

810. *Overland China Mail*, Hong Kong (25 September 1889), 265 ('Golf is now in full swing at Wong-nei-cheong'). This is the area of Hong Kong that is also referred to as 'Happy Valley'.
811. *The Straits Times*, Singapore (1891), 3; Duncan (1892), 282.
812. *The Globe and Traveller*, London (8 August 1891), 2 ('A golf club has been established at St. Moritz').
813. Duncan (1894), 411 ('St Andrews Golf Club, Trinidad, instituted 12th October 1891').
814. *Inverness Courier* (26 December 1893), 6 (report of a Golf Club having been established at the Hague, Holland).
815. Duncan (1894), 18.

Chapter 16

816. Strutt (1801), 81.
817. Flannery (2009a), 109.
818. Ibid. 109.
819. Sinclair (1807), 601.
820. Green (1987), 8. Green suggests that 'the ancient Flemish game of *chole* [. . .] could be a genuine forerunner of golf'.
821. Ling (1991).
822. Ouseley (1819), 346.
823. van Hengel (1982). Van Hengel states (on p. 11), 'There is absolutely no doubt that colf was an early form of golf.'
824. [Farnie] (1857), 5. *Jeu de Mail* is described as being 'exactly our golf, but played under different circumstances'.
825. Rosen (1930), 3. In his memoirs, Rosen describes playing *kora* in Hebron as a boy (c. 1860) and describes it as 'no more nor less than golf, a marble serving as ball and bent sticks as golf clubs [. . .] I have often wondered whether the game so popular among our wealthy classes had not its origin in the game of these Arab boys.'
826. Forgan (1881), 1.
827. [Robb] (1863), 2.
828. Penner et al. (2013), 136.
829. *The Independent* (12 January 2006), 8.
830. Lang (1899), 138.
831. Flannery and Leech (2004), 364.
832. Smith (1912), 2.
833. Tomb of Khety at Beni Hassan, Egypt (Tomb BH17; XI Egyptian Dynasty). The image depicting a stick-and-ball game (or perhaps a stick-and-hoop game) is the fourth scene from the top, on the eastern pilaster of the south wall of the tomb; Newberry (1893), Part II, 51–77 and plate XVI; Kanawati and Evans (2020), 45, plate 60 and plate 110.
834. National Archaeological Museum, Athens, Greece; a carved image on a marble base of a funerary kouros, found in Athens 510–500 BC (inventory number *NAM Γ 3477*).

835. Powell (1988), 79.
836. Maxwell Lyte (1909), 534–5.
837. BL, MS Cotton Caligula A.IX, f.146v (Layamon's Brut); Madden (1847), Vol. II, 616.
838. Londino (2006), 40.
839. Ker (1919), 444; Ker (1920), 456.
840. Ker (1920), 456.
841. Littleton (1678), see entry for '*Pāgānica*'.
842. Strutt (1801), 81–2.
843. [Farnie] (1857), 1.
844. Macdonald (1928), 8.
845. Cheatum (1969), 2–3.
846. Concannon (1995), 11.
847. Barrett and Mingo (2000), 51.
848. Morris (2013), 1.
849. Krause (2002), 8.
850. Alliss and Ferrier (1989), 27.
851. Lonnstrom and Riso (2018), 2.
852. Kerr (1896), 24.
853. Bargmann (2010).
854. Eijkman et al. (2016), 46.
855. van Hengel (1982).
856. van Hengel (1972), 1.
857. van Hengel (1982), 17.
858. Ibid. 1.
859. Henderson and Stirk (1984), dust cover, front flap.
860. Ibid. 12.
861. Nijs and Nijs (2014), 141–60.
862. Breuninghoff (1870), 225–7.
863. Ibid. 226.
864. Ibid. 227.
865. ter Gouw (1871), 693.
866. Brongers (1951), 31.
867. van Hengel (1982), 17.
868. Brongers (1997), 3.
869. Brongers (2002), 48.
870. Flannery (2009a), 109.
871. Houdijk [interview with Heiner Gillmeister] (2005), 25.
872. Henderson (2016), 2.
873. Schwab (1985), 30 minutes 5 seconds.
874. Temmerman (1987), 15; Mallon and Jerris (2011), xiii.
875. Green (1987), 9.
876. Pilley (1988), 10.
877. Burnett (2000), 15.
878. Stirk (1987), 18.
879. Glanville (2010), 5.
880. van Hengel (1972), 1.

881. van Hengel (1982), 17.
882. Schwab (1985), 31 minutes 52 seconds.
883. van Hengel (1982), 19.
884. Ibid. 19.
885. Gillmeister (1996), 24–5.
886. van Hengel (1982), 19–21.
887. van den Boom (2007), 25.
888. Eijkman et al. (2016), 12.
889. Gillmeister (1996), 24–5.
890. Discussed in more detail by Nijs and Nijs (2011), 63–77.
891. Morrison (2020), 26–30.
892. Henderson and Stirk (1979), 20.
893. van Hengel (1982), 12.
894. Mitchell (1907), lxix, 17; Hamilton (1985), 1–15; Crampsey (c. 1987); Johnston and Johnston (1993), 49, 52, 55, 92, 279; Hamilton et al. (2008), 4–12.
895. AYA, B6/11/1/3, f.453r (Ayr Burgh Court and Council Records, Ayrshire Archives under Charge and Superintendence from the National Records of Scotland; 2 December 1587).
896. The passage from the Ayr Burgh Court and Council Records (AYA, B6/11/1/3, f.453r) is dated 'Se[cun]do Decembris 1587' and states 'Andro Blakater borne In Angus within the parochin of Brechin being recentlie apprehendit Reidhand w[i]th reseling of ane gad of Irn fra David Ingrames buyth duir & c[er]tane goff ballis furth of Adam Donnaldis buyth w[i]thin this burgh/ And being accusit th[air]anent confessit the sami[n] And th[air]foir is ordanit to be scurgit & baneist this toun for evir upoun his awin cönfessioun gif ever he salhappin to be apprehendit w[i]thin this toun or Jurisdictioun th[ai]rof in ony tyme heireftir Consentis to be hangit to the deyth but ane assys su[m]marlie'.
897. Lang (1890).
898. Flannery (2009b), 127.
899. Gillmeister (2008), 12.
900. Gillmeister (2015).
901. Houdijk [interview with Heiner Gillmeister] (2005), 23.
902. Cunningham (1899a), 378–9.
903. Strutt (1801), 81.
904. Ibid. 81.
905. Hall (1807), Vol. I, 123.
906. Ouseley (1819), 346.
907. [Farnie] (1857), 5.
908. [Cundell] (1824), 2.
909. Cunningham (1899a), 378–9.
910. *Encyclopædia Britannica* editors (2010), Vol. 28, 150.
911. Gillmeister (2002), 1–2.
912. *Encyclopædia Britannica* editors (2010), Vol. 28, 151.
913. Apherdiano (1552), 45–6.
914. Bargmann (2021), 40.

915. Gilmeister (2002), 17.
916. The introduction to *Tyrocinium linguæ Latinæ* is dated 'Anno 1545'; Apherdiano (1552), 3.
917. Fleming and Mason (2019).
918. van Chandelier (1657), 63.
919. The painting *Golfers on the Ice near Haarlem* (1668) by Adriaen van de Velde is part of the collection of the National Gallery, London (inventory number NG869).
920. *Encyclopædia Britannica* editors (2010), Vol. 28, 150–1.
921. BL, Add MS 24098 (Book of Hours, the 'Golf Book', c. 1540).
922. See Chapters 1 and 15.
923. van Hengel (1982); Gillmeister (2002), (2008) and (2015). See also Houdijk, Angela [interview with Heiner Gillmeister] (2005).
924. Flannery and Leech (2004). See, for example, p. 364, in which the authors state that golf was 'first played in the Loire region of France'.
925. *Musée Condé, Chantilly*, 0076 1362 (*Heures d'Adélaïde de Savoie*).
926. Flannery and Leech (2004), 122.
927. Gillmeister (2008), 12–13.
928. Ibid. 13.
929. van Hengel (1982), 18. The phrase '*wie met colven tsolt*' [he who plays at *colf*] can be found in *Gemeente Archief Brussel, ordonnantie van* 1360; Inv. Nr. A.V.B., A.A., Cartularium II, f.215v.
930. Cunningham (1899a), 379.
931. Gillmeister (2008), 15.
932. Ibid. 15.
933. References to 'bonker clubis' and a 'bonker club' appear in a notebook that was discovered in an Edinburgh bookshop and is thought to have belonged to a young man in Edinburgh who was the son of a William Law of Stirling. The notebook and its contents are described in two articles published in *The Scotsman* in 1896 and 1907. The notebook records the purchase (on 28 October 1629) of '2 bonker clubis, a iyrone club, and twa play clubis' and a payment (in 1633) 'for mending bonker club'. See *The Scotsman* (5 May 1896), 7 and (7 September 1907), 8.
934. [Macnair] (1882), 73.
935. Flannery and Leech (2004). See, for example, p. 364, in which the authors state that golf was 'first played in the Loire region of France'.
936. BLO, MS Douce 62, f.101v (Book of Hours, Use of Paris, c. 1400–10).
937. Strutt (1801), 81.
938. Flannery and Leach (2004), 58.
939. Ibid. 15–23.
940. Ibid. xi.
941. Ibid. 43.
942. Ibid. 364.
943. Ibid. 56.
944. Ibid. 51.
945. Ling (1991).
946. Butler et al. (2017), 9.

947. Several manuscript copies of *wan jing* survive. For example, CUL, manuscript FB.55:28.33.
948. For a detailed discussion of *chui wan* and golf, see Butler et al. (2017).
949. Butler et al. (2017), 70.
950. In 2021 there were believed to be more than 38,000 golf courses, spread across 206 of the world's 251 countries; Anonymous (2021), 4–5. It has also been estimated that there are 60 million golfers worldwide; Anonymous (2018), 5.
951. This is a phrase that has been used widely, notably as the title to the influential history of golf, *Golf: Scotland's Game*; Hamilton (1998).

Bibliography

Adams, Matthew E. (2008) *In the Spirt of the Game: Golf's Greatest Stories*, The Lyons Press, Guilford, CT.

Aitchison, Thomas S. and George Lorimer (1902) *Reminiscences of the Old Bruntsfield Links Golf Club 1866–1874*, published privately.

Allen, Peter (1989) *The Sunley Book of Royal Golf*, Stanley Paul, London.

Alliss, Peter and Bob Ferrier (1989) *The Best of Golf*, Partridge Press, London.

Anonymous (1566) *The Actis and Constitutiounis of the Realme of Scotland* [. . .], Edinburgh.

Anonymous (1572) *Histoire de Marie Royne d'Escosse* [. . .], Edinburgh.

Anonymous (1597) *The Lavves and Actes of Parliament, Maid be King James the First, and his Svccessovrs Kinges of Scotland*, Robert Walde-graue, Edinburgh.

Anonymous (1604) *The Rates of the Marchandizes as they are Set Downe in the Booke of Rates* [. . .], London.

Anonymous (1611) *The Rates of the Marchandizes as they are Set Downe in the Booke of Rates* [. . .], Edinburgh.

Anonymous (1657a) *A Book of Values of Merchandize Imported; According to which, Excise is to be Paid by the First Buyer*, Edinburgh.

Anonymous (1657b) *The Rates of the Merchandizes that is to Say, the Subsidy of Tonnage* [. . .], London.

Anonymous (1710) *Virgil's Æneis, Translated into Scottish Verse*, Edinburgh.

Anonymous (1731) *The Musical Miscellany; Being a Collection of Choice Songs and Lyrick Poems*, John Watts, London.

Anonymous (1750) *Ambassades de Monsieur de la Boderie, en Angleterre. Sous le regne d'Henri IV. & la minorité de Louis XIII. depuis les années 1606. jusqu'en 1611.*

Anonymous (1760) *Biographia Britannica: or, the Lives of the Most Eminent Persons who have flourished in Great Britain and Ireland*, Vol. V, London.

Anonymous (1786), *The Edinburgh Almanack and Scots Register for the Year 1786*, Edinburgh.

Anonymous (1812) *The Edinburgh Almanack and Imperial Register for 1812, Being Leap Year*, Edinburgh.

Anonymous (c. 1821) *Manchester Golf Club*, J. Aston, Manchester.

Anonymous (1830) *The Edinburgh Almanack or Universal Scots and Imperial Register for 1830*, Oliver & Boyd, Edinburgh.

Anonymous (1832) *The Edinburgh Almanack or Universal Scots and Imperial Register for 1832, Being Leap Year*, Oliver & Boyd, Edinburgh.

Anonymous (1833a) *A Dirurnal of Remarkable Occurrents That Have Passed Within the Country of Scotland Since the Death of King James the Fourth till the Year M.D.LXXV*, Bannatyne Club, Edinburgh.

Anonymous (1833b) *The Edinburgh Almanack or Universal Scots and Imperial Register, for 1833, Being the First After Leap Year*, Oliver & Boyd, Edinburgh.

Anonymous (1834) *The Edinburgh Almanack or Universal Scots and Imperial Register, for 1834, Being the Second After Leap Year*, Oliver & Boyd, Edinburgh.

Anonymous (1835) *The Edinburgh Almanac or Universal Scots and Imperial Register, for 1835, Being the Third After Leap Year*, Oliver & Boyd, Edinburgh.

Anonymous (1837) *Oliver & Boyd's New Edinburgh Almanac and National Repository for the Year 1837*, Oliver & Boyd, Edinburgh.

Anonymous (1839) *Oliver & Boyd's New Edinburgh Almanac and National Repository for the Year 1839*, Oliver & Boyd, Edinburgh.

Anonymous (1844) *The Works of Robert Burns*, Blackie & Son, Glasgow.

Anonymous (1863) *Inuentaires de la Royne Descosse Douairiere de France: Catalogues of the Jewels, Dresses, Furniture, Books, and Paintings of Mary Queen of Scots 1556–1569*, Edinburgh.

Anonymous (1877) *Belgravia an Illustrated London Magazine*, Vol. XXXII, Chatto & Windus, London.

Anonymous (1887) *Extracts from the Records of the Royal Burgh of Stirling AD. 1519–1666*, Glasgow Stirlingshire and Sons of the Rock Society, Glasgow.

Anonymous (1894) *Catalogue of the Eglinton Family Jewels* [auction date: 22 February 1984], Christie, Manson & Woods, London.

Anonymous (1924) 'Golfer' Skill Improved by Science', in *Popular Mechanics*, Vol. 41, No. 6, June 1924, 839–41.

Anonymous (1927) *Extracts from The Records of The Burgh of Edinburgh AD. 1589 to 1603*, Oliver & Boyd, Edinburgh.

Anonymous (c. 1935) *Encyclopedia of Sports Games and Pastimes*, Fleetway House, London.

Anonymous (1969) *Stirling Golf Club Centenary 1869–1969*, Stirling Golf Club, Stirling.

Anonymous (c. 2010) *Stirling Golf Club Yearbook 2010/11*, Stirling Golf Club, Stirling.

Anonymous (c. 2011) *Mary Queen of Scots (linked to Falkland Palace): The National Trust for Scotland Teachers' Pack*, National Trust for Scotland, Edinburgh.

Anonymous (2013) *Longniddry Golf Club Official Brochure* (2013), Longniddry Golf Club, Longniddry.

Anonymous (2018) *The Truth About Golf*, The R&A and the International Golf Federation, St Andrews and Lausanne.

Anonymous (2021) *Golf Around the World 2021*, Fourth Edition, The R&A, St Andrews.

Apherdiano, M. Petro [Peter van Affenden] (1552) *Tyrocinium Linguæ Latinæ*, Antwerp.

Armet, Helen (ed.) (1951) *Register of the Burgesses of the Burgh of the Canongate from 27th Jume 1622 to 25th September 1733*, Scottish Record Society, Edinburgh.

Arscott, David (2011) *Golf: A Very Peculiar History*, Book House, Brighton.

Arthur, Harold (1902) 'Some Familiar Letters of Charles II. and James Duke of York Addressed to their Daughter and Niece, the Countess of Litchfield', in *Archaeologia*, or, *Miscellaneous Tracts Relating to Antiquity*, Vol. 58, 153–88, Society of Antiquaries, London.

Ashley, Maurice (1971) *Charles II: The Man and the Statesman*, Weidenfeld & Nicolson, London.

Aultman, Dick (1969) *Learn to Play Golf*, Rand McNally, Chicago, IL.

Bain, Joseph (ed.) (1898) *Calendar of the State Papers Relating to Scotland and Mary, Queen of Scots 1547–1603*, Vol. I, HMSO, Edinburgh.

Bain, Joseph (ed.) (1900) *Calendar of the State Papers Relating to Scotland and Mary, Queen of Scots 1547–1603*, Vol. II, HMSO, Edinburgh.

Balfour, James (1887) *Reminiscences of Golf on St Andrews Links*, David Douglas, Edinburgh.

Bargmann, Robin K. (2010) *Serendipity of Early Golf*, published privately, Netherlands.

Bargmann, Robin K. (2021) 'More than a Textbook', in *Through the Green*, March 2021, 38–41.

Barrett, Ted (2000) *The Daily Telegraph Golf Chronicle*, Carlton Books, London.

Barrett, Erin and Jack Mingo (2000) *Al Capone Was a Golfer: Hundreds of Fascinating Facts from the World of Golf*, Conari Press, San Francisco.

Barton, John (2009) *The Golf Guru: Answers to Golf's Most Perplexing Questions*, Quirk Books, Philadelphia.

Bauchope, John (1889) *The Golfing Annual 1888–89*, Vol. II, Horace Cox, London.

Baxter, Peter (1899) *Golf in Perth and Perthshire*, Thomas Hunter, Perth.

Beard, Henry (2009) *Golf: An Unofficial and Unauthorized History of the World's Most Preposterous Sport*, Simon & Schuster, New York.

Behrend, John and Peter N. Lewis (1998) *Challenges & Champions: The Royal and Ancient Golf Club 1754–1883*, The Royal & Ancient Golf Club of St Andrews, St Andrews.

Benger, [Elizabeth] (1821) *Memoirs of the Life of Anne Boleyn, Queen of Henry VIII*, Longman, London.

Besant, Walter (1895) *Westminster*, Chatto & Windus, London.

Besant, Walter (1903) *London in the Time of the Stuarts*, Adam & Charles Black, London.

Birch, Thomas (1760) *The Life of Henry Prince of Wales, Eldest Son of King James I. Compiled Chiefly from His Own Papers, and Other Manuscripts, Never Before Published*, A. Miller, London.

Birrell, J. F. (1980) *An Edinburgh Alphabet*, The Mercat Press, Edinburgh.

Bohn, Michael K. (2007) *Money Golf*, Potomac Books, Washington, DC.

[Borthwick, Shearer] (1987) *The Chronicle of the Royal Burgess Golfing Society of Edinburgh 1936–1985*, Vol. II, Alna Press, Broxburn.

Boyd, William K. (ed.) (1907) *Calendar of the State Papers Relating to Scotland and Mary, Queen of Scots 1547–1603*, Vol. V, HMSO, Edinburgh.

Boyd, William K. and Henry W. Meikle (eds) (1936) *Calendar of the State Papers Relating to Scotland and Mary, Queen of Scots 1547–1603*, Vol. X, HMSO, Edinburgh.

Breuninghoff, H. (1870) 'Het kolfslaan bij het slot Kronenburg te Loenen, door den Hoofdonderwijzer', in *Nieuwe Bijdragen, ter Bevordering van het Onderwijs en de Opvoeding, Voornamelijk met Betrekking tot de Lagere Scholen in het Koningrijk der Nederlanden*, De Gebroeders van Cleef, 's Gravenhage (The Hague).

Brewer J. S. (ed.) (1862) *Letters and Papers, Foreign and Domestic, of the Reign of Henry VIII*, Vol. I, Longman, Green, Longman & Roberts, London.

Brewer, J. S. (ed.) (1920) *Letters and Papers, Foreign and Domestic, of the Reign of Henry VIII*, Second Revised Edition, Vol. I, Part 2, HMSO, London.

Brongers, J. A. (1951) 'Holland – The Cradle of Golf?', in *The Golfers' Year*, Tom Scott (ed.), Vol. II, 29–38, Nicholas Kaye, London.

Brongers, J. Ayolt (1997) *700 Jaar Golf Lonen a/d Vecht 1297–1997*, Catalogue from an exhibition held in the Townhall at Loen aan de Vecht, 6–20 September 1997.

Brongers, J. Ayolt (2002) '*Begon golf in 1297 wel in Loenen?*', in *GolfJournaal*, 10, December/January 2002/3, 48–9.

Brown, P. Hume (ed.) (1901) *The Register of the Privy Council of Scotland*, Second Series, Vol. III, HMSO, Edinburgh.

Brown, Marjorie (1952) *In the Steps of Mary Queen of Scots*, Rich & Cowan, London.

Browning, Robert (1955) *A History of Golf: The Royal and Ancient Game from its Beginnings to the Present Day*, J. M. Dent & Son, London.

Brydon, Robert and Lindsay Brydon (1993) *The Scottish Coronation Journey of King Charles I*, Sporting Partnership, Kirkcaldy.

Buchanan, George (1571a) *Ane Detectioun of the duinges of Marie Quene of Scottes, touchand the murder of hir husband, and hir conspiracie, adulterie, and pretensed marriage with the Erle Bothwell. And ane defence of the trew Lordis, mainteineris of the Kingis graces action and authoritie.*

Buchanan, George (1571b) *De Maria Scotorum Regina, totaque eius contra Regem coniuratione, foedo cum Bothuelio adulterio, nefaria in maritum crudelitate & rabie, horrendo insuper & deterrimo eiusdem parricidio: plena, & tragica plane Historia.*

Buchanano, Georgio (1582) *Rerum Scoticarum Historia.*

Budge, Ernest A. Wallis (1889) *The History of Alexander the Great Being a Syriac Version of the Pseudo-Callisthenes*, Cambridge University Press, Cambridge.

Burnett, James (1997) *Tee Times: On the Road with the Ladies Professional Golf Tour*, Scribner, New York.

Burnett, John and Robert H. J. Urquhart (1998) 'Early Papingo Shooting in Scotland', in *Review of Scottish Culture*, Vol. 11, 4–12.

Burnett, John (2000) *Riot, Revelry, and Rout: Sport in Lowland Scotland Before 1860*, Tuckwell Press, East Linton.

Butler, Richard (2011) 'The Influence of Sport on Destination Development: The Case of Golf at St Andrews, Scotland', in James Higham (ed.), *Sport Tourism Destinations: Issues, Opportunities and Analysis*, Routledge, Abingdon.

Butler, Anthony, David Hamilton and John Moffett (2017) *Chui Wan: An Ancient Chinese Golf-Like Game*, The Partick Press, St Andrews.

Cairns, I. H. (2014) *Golf Over Two Inches*, published privately, Perth.

Cameron, Annie I. (ed.) (1936) *Calendar of the State Papers Relating to Scotland and Mary, Queen of Scots 1547–1603*, Vol. XI, HMSO, Edinburgh.

Cameron, Donald, M. (2010) *Social Links: The Golf Boom in Victorian England*, Social Links Publishing, Cambridge.

Camp, Walter (1910) 'Golf, the Game of Courtesy', in *The Century Magazine*, Vol. LXXX, New York, October 1910, 820–32.

Campbell, Alex (1827) *The History of Leith from the Earliest Accounts to the Present Period*, William Reid & Son, Leith.

Campbell, Guy (1952) 'The Early History of British Golf', in Bernard Darwin et al., *A History of Golf in Britain*, Chapter III, Cassell & Company Ltd, London.

Campbell, Malcolm (2001) *The Scottish Golf Book*, Lomond Books, Edinburgh.

Carlyle, Alexander (1795) 'Parish of Inveresk', in John Sinclair (ed.), *The Statistical Account of Scotland*, Vol. 16, 1–44, William Creech, Edinburgh.

Cartwright, John (1986) *The Buik of Alexander the Conquerour by Sir Gilbert Hay*, Scottish Text Society, Edinburgh.

Carruth, Gordon (1993) *The Encyclopedia of American Facts and Dates*, Ninth Edition, HarperCollins, New York.

Celsi, Teresa (1992) *Golf: The Lore of the Links*, Andrews & McMeel, Kansas City.

[Chamberlayne, Edward] (1669a) *Angliæ Notitia, or The Present State of England: Together with Divers Reflections upon the Ancient State Thereof*, First Edition, London.

Chamberlayne, Edward (1669b) *Angliæ Notitia; or, The Present State of England: Together with Divers Reflections upon the Ancient State Thereof*, Second Edition, London.

Chamberlayne, Edward (1669c) *Angliæ Notitia; or, The Present State of England Together with Divers Reflections upon the Ancient State Thereof*, Third Edition, London.

Chamberlayne, Edward (1670) *Angliæ Notitia; or, The Present State of England: Together with Divers Reflections upon the Ancient State Thereof*, Fourth Edition, London.

Chamberlayne, Edward (1671) *Angliæ Notitia; or, The Present State of England: Together with Divers Reflections upon the Ancient State Thereof*, Fifth Edition, London.

Chamberlayne, Edward (1672) *Angliæ Notitia; or, The Present State of England: Together with Divers Reflections upon the Ancient State Thereof*, Sixth Edition, London.

Chamberlayne, Edward (1673) *Angliæ Notitia; or, The Present State of England: Together with Divers Reflections upon the Ancient State Thereof*, Seventh Edition, London.

Chamberlayne, Edward (1674) *Angliæ Notitia; or, The Present State of England: Together with Divers Reflections upon the Ancient State Thereof*, Eighth Edition, London.

Chamberlayne, Edward (1676) *Angliæ Notitia: or, The Present State of England: Together with Divers Reflections upon the Ancient State Thereof*, Ninth Edition, London.

Chamberlayne, Edward (1677) *Angliæ Notitia: or, The Present State of England: Together with Divers Reflections upon the Ancient State Thereof*, Tenth Edition, London.

Chamberlayne, Edward (1679) *Angliæ Notitia: or, The Present State of England: Together with Divers Reflections upon the Ancient State Thereof*, Twelfth Edition, London.

Chamberlayne, Edw. (1682) *Angliæ Notitia: or, The Present State of England: Together with Divers Reflections upon the Ancient State Thereof*, Fourteenth Edition, London.

Chamberlayne, Edw. (1684) *Angliæ Notitia: or, The Present State of England: Together with Divers Reflections upon the Ancient State Thereof*, Fifteenth Edition, London.

Chambers, Robert (1824) *Traditions of Edinburgh or Sketches & Anecdotes of the City in Former Times*, First Edition, William Chambers, Edinburgh.

Chambers, Robert (1825) *Traditions of Edinburgh*, Second Edition, W. & C. Tait, Edinburgh.

Chambers, Robert (1847) *Select Writings of Robert Chambers Volume VI. Traditions of Edinburgh*, W. & R. Chambers, Edinburgh.

Chapman, Hester W. (1964) *The Tragedy of Charles II in the Years 1630–1660*, Little Brown & Co., Boston.

Chapman, Kenneth G. (1997) *The Rules of the Green: A History of the Rules of Golf*, Virgin Books, London.

Cheatum, Billye Ann (1969) *Golf*, W. B. Saunders Co., Philadelphia.

Childe-Pemberton, William S. (1913) *Elizabeth Blount and Henry the Eighth*, Eveleigh Nash, London.

Clapcott, C. B. (1935) *The Rules of the Ten Oldest Golf Clubs from 1754 to 1848 Together with the Rules of the Royal & Ancient Golf Club of St Andrews for the Years 1858, 1875, 1888*, Golf Monthly, Edinburgh.

Claremont, Francesca (1939) *Catherine of Aragon*, R. Hale Ltd, London.

Clark, Robert (ed.) (1875) *Golf a Royal and Ancient Game*, R. & R. Clark, Edinburgh.

Cloake, John (1995) *Palaces and Parks of Richmond and Kew: The Palaces of Shene and Richmond*, Phillimore, Chichester.

Cloake, John (2000) *Richmond Palace its History and its Plan*, Richmond Local History Society, Richmond.

Coleman, Deirdre (2018) *Henry Smeathman, the Flycatcher: Natural History, Slavery, and Empire in the Late Eighteenth Century*, Liverpool University Press, Liverpool.

Colledge, Pat (2011) *The Bruntsfield Links Golfing Society 1761–2011*, The Bruntsfield Links Golfing Society Ltd, Edinburgh.

Compton, C. H. (1882) 'Golf', in *The Journal of the British Archaeological Association*, 38, 371–81.

Concannon, Dale (1989) *Golfing Bygones*, Shire Publications, Aylesbury.

Concannon, Dale (1995) *Golf: The Early Days*, Salamander Books, London.

Concannon, Dale (2009) *The Original Rules of Golf*, Bodleian Library, Oxford.

Cooke, Alistair (2008) 'History of the Scottish Torture', in *The Marvellous Mania: Alistair Cooke on Golf*, Penguin Books, London.

Corbett, Jim (2007) *The Pocket Idiot's Guide to Golf Rules & Etiquette*, Alpha Books, New York.

Cossey, Rosalynde (1984) *Golfing Ladies*, Orbis, London.

Cotton, Henry (1965) *Golf: The Picture Story of the Golf Game*, World Distributors, London.

Cotton, Henry (1975) *Golf: A Pictorial History*, William Collins Sons & Co., London.

Courtney, Nicholas (1983) *Sporting Royals: Past and Present*, Hutchinson/Stanley Paul, London.

Cousins, Geoffrey and Don Pottinger (1974) *An Atlas of Golf*, Thomas Nelson & Sons, London.

Cousins, Geoffrey (1975) *Golf in Britain: A Social History from the Beginnings to the Present Day* (1975), Routledge & Kegan Paul, London.

Craigie, William A. (1951) *A Dictionary of the Older Scottish Tongue*, Part XIII, Oxford University Press, London.

Cramond, Wm (1897) *Records of the Kirk Session of Elgin 1584–1779*, Elgin Courant and Courier, Elgin.

Crampsey, Robert A. (c. 1987) *St. Mungo's Gowfers. The History of Glasgow Golf Club 1787–1987*, published privately, Glasgow.

Critchley, Bruce (with Bob Ferrier) (1993) *Golf and All its Glory: a Modern Look at an Ancient Game*, BBC Books, London.

Cromeck, R. H. (1808) *Reliques of Robert Burns; Consisting Chiefly of Original Letters, Poems and Critical Observations on Scottish Songs*, T. Cadell & W. Davies, London.

[Crosshill] (c. 1974) *An Anthology of the Golf Ball* (a leaflet, included in a boxed set of replica golf balls, issued by the Worthington Ball Co.).

[Cundell, John] (1824) *Rules of the Thistle Golf Club with some Historical Notices Relative to the Progress of the Game of Golf in Scotland*, James Ballantyne & Co., Edinburgh.

Cunningham, Allan (1842) *The Works of Robert Burns*, Henry G. Bohn, London.

Cunningham, James (1899a) 'Concerning Golf in Holland', in *Harper's Weekly*, Vol. XLIII (15 April 1899), 378–9, New York.

Cunningham, Andrew S. (ed.) (1899b) *Inverkeithing, North Queensferry, Limekilns, Charlestown, The Ferry Hills, their Antiquities and Recreative Resources. History of Dunfermline Golf Club and Plan of Course*, W. Clarke & Son, Dunfermline.

[Dalrymple, David (Lord Hailes)] (1744) 'Of the Latin Poems of Dr Pitcairn', in *The Edinburgh Magazine and Review by a Society of Gentlemen*, Vol. I (February 1774), Edinburgh.

Darwin, Bernard (1954) *Golf*, Burke, London.

De-Laune, Tho. (1681) *The Present State of London: or, Memorials Comprehending a Full and Succinct Account of the Ancient and Modern State Thereof*, London.

De-Laune, Tho. (1690) *Angliæ Metropolis: or, The Present State of London with Memorials Comprehending a Full and Succinct Account of the Ancient and Modern State Thereof*, London.

Dick, James C. (ed.) (1908) *Notes on Scottish Song by Robert Burns Written in an Interleaved Copy of The Scots Musical Museum with Additions by Robert Riddell and Others*, Henry Frowde, London.

Dickinson, William Croft (1952) *Two Students at St. Andrews 1711–1716*, Oliver & Boyd, Edinburgh.

Dickinson, W. Croft (1958) 'The Register of the Privy Seal', in *The Scottish Historical Review*, 35, 54–61.

Dickson, Thomas (ed.) (1877) *Comopta Thesaurariorum Regum Scotorum: Accounts of the Lord High Treasurer of Scotland, Vol. II,* A.D. *1473–1498*, HMSO, Edinburgh.

D'Israeli, I. (1835) *Curiosities of Literature*, Baudry's European Library, Paris.

Ditchburn, David (1990) 'Cargoes and Commodities. Aberdeen's Trade with Scandinavia and the Baltic, c.1302–c.1542', in *Northern Studies*, Vol. 27, 12–22.

Dobereiner, Peter (1981) *For the Love of Golf: The Best of Peter Dobereiner*, Stanley Paul, London.

Donald, Colin Dunlop (1889) 'The Glasgow Golf Club', in *The Regalty Club*, First Series, 147–56, James Maclehose & Sons, Glasgow.

Donnelley, Paul (2010) *Firsts, Lasts & Onlys: Paul Donnelley Presents the Most Amazing Golf Facts from the Last 600 Years*, Hamlyn, London.

Donnelly, Kevin (2010) *Reduction of Ship Resistance Through Induced Turbulent Boundary Layers*, MSc thesis, Florida Institute of Technology.

Druzin, Randi (2001) *The Complete Idiot's Guide to Women in Sport*, Alpha Books.

Dunbar, John G. (1999) *Scottish Royal Palaces: The Architecture of the Royal Residences during the Late Medieval and Early Renaissance Periods*, Tuckwell Press, East Linton.

Duncan, David Scott (ed.) (1890) *The Golfing Annual 1889–90*, Vol. III, Horace Cox, London.

Duncan, David Scott (ed.) (1892) *The Golfing Annual 1891–92*, Vol. V, Horace Cox, London.

Duncan, David Scott (ed.) (1894) *The Golfing Annual 1893–94*, Vol. VII, Horace Cox, London.

Duncan, Ishbel MacDonald (2017) *The St Andrews Walking Tour Guide*, Lulu Enterprises, Raleigh, NC.

Durant, John and Otto Bettmann (c. 1965) *Pictorial History of American Sports: from Colonial Times to the Present*, Revised Edition, A. S. Barnes, New York.

Durie, Bruce (2003) *The Murder of Young Tom Morris*, Gath-Askelon Publishing, Edinburgh.

Edwards, Ian (2005) *The Royal Aberdeen Golfers: 225 Years on the Links*, Grant Books, Droitwich.

Eijkman, Michiel et al. (eds) (2016) *Colf, Kolf, Golf*, The Dutch Golf Archive Foundation Early Golf.

Elliott, Alan (1991) *Lundin Ladies Golf Club 1891*, Artigraf Printing Co., Buckhaven.

Elliott, Alan and John Allan May (1994) *A History of Golf*, Chancellor Press, London.

Ellis, Henry (1824) *Original Letters Illustrative of English History*, Harding, Triphook & Lepard, London.

Ellis, Jeffery B. (2007) *The Clubmaker's Art: Antique Golf Clubs and their History*, Second Edition, Zephyr Productions, Oak Harbor, WA.

Encyclopædia Britannica editors (1788–97) *Encyclopædia Britannica; or A Dictionary of Arts, Sciences and Miscellaneous Literature*, Third Edition, A. Bell & C. Macfarquhar, Edinburgh.

Encyclopædia Britannica editors (1875–89) *The Encyclopædia Britannica: A Dictionary of Arts, Sciences, Literature and General Information*, Ninth Edition, Little Brown & Co., Boston, MA.

Encyclopædia Britannica editors (1910–11) *The Encyclopædia Britannica: A Dictionary of Arts, Sciences, Literature and general Information*, Eleventh Edition, Cambridge University Press, Cambridge.

Encyclopædia Britannica editors (1929–73) *The Encyclopædia Britannica: A New Survey of Universal Knowledge*, Fourteenth Edition, Encyclopædia Britannica Co., London.

Encyclopædia Britannica editors (1974–2010) *The New Encyclopædia Britannica*, Fifteenth Edition, Encyclopædia Britannica Inc., Chicago, IL.

Eunson, John K. V. (2012) *Sporting Scots: How Scotland Brought Sport to the World (and the World Wouldn't Let Us Win!)*, Black & White, Edinburgh.

Ewell, Ken (2006) *Travelling with Philosophies*, iUniverse Inc., Lincoln, NE.

Fabian-Baddiel, Sarah (1994) *Miller's Golf Memorabilia*, Miller's, London.

[Farnie, H. B. (using the pseudonym 'A Keen Hand')] (1857) *The Golfer's Manual: Being an Historical and Descriptive Account of the National Game of Scotland*, Whitehead & Orr, Cupar.

Fea, James (1787) *Considerations of the Fisheries in the Scotch Islands*, London.

Feinstein, John (2004) *Open: Inside the Ropes at Bethpage Black*, Back Bay Books, New York.

Ferguson, J. C. (1908) *The Royal and Ancient Game of Golf from its Earliest Days Till Now*, Dumfries and Galloway Courier and Herald, Dumfries.

Ferguson, Douglas M. (c. 1987) *Dunfermline Golf Club 1887–1987*, Dunfermline Golf Club, Dunfermline.

Fife Golfing Association (c. 1988) *A History of Golf Clubs in Fife*, Levenmouth Printers, Leven.

Finch, Barbara Clay (1883) *Lives of the Princesses of Wales*, Remington & Co., London.

Finegan, James W. (1996) *Blasted Heaths and Blessed Green: A Golfer's Pilgrimage to the Courses of Scotland*, Simon & Schuster, New York.

Flannery, Michael and Richard Leech (2004) *Golf Through the Ages: Six Hundred Years of Golfing Art*, Golf Links Press, Fairfield, IA.

Flannery, Michael (2009a) 'Golf: The True History', in *Golf International Magazine*, Issue 87, March/April 2009, 108–14.

Flannery, Michael (2009b) 'Golf: The True History: Part IV', in *Golf International Magazine*, Issue 90, August/September 2009, 126–30.

Fleming, David Hay (1890) *Register of the Minister Elders and Deacons of the Christian Congregation of St. Andrews* [. . .], *Part Second: 1582–1600*, Edinburgh University Press, Edinburgh.

Fleming, David Hay (1897) *Mary Queen of Scots from Her Birth to Her Flight into England*, Hodder & Stoughton, London.

Fleming, Alexander and Roger Mason (eds) (2019) *Scotland and the Flemish People*, Birlinn, Edinburgh.

Fletcher, Bob and Richard Williams (2019) 'The Oldest Club in the Southern Hemisphere', in *Through the Green*, September 2019, 34–7.

Forgan, Robert (1881) *The Golfer's Handbook*, John Innes, Cupar.

Fraser, William (1892) *The Sutherland Book*, Edinburgh.

Furgol, Edward M. (1987) 'The Scottish Itinerary of Mary Queen of Scots, 1542–8 and 1561–8, in *Proceedings of the Society of Antiquaries of Scotland*, 117, 219–31 and fiche 1, C1-D6.

Fyfe, Christopher (1964) *Sierra Leone Inheritance*, Oxford University Press, Oxford.

Galbraith, William (1950) *Prestwick St. Nicholas Golf Club*, Prestwick St. Nicholas Golf Club, Prestwick.

Gatherer, W. A. (1958) *The Tyrannous Reign of Mary Stewart*, Edinburgh University Press, Edinburgh.

Geddes, Olive M. (1992) *A Swing Through Time: Golf in Scotland 1457–1743*, HMSO, Edinburgh.

Geddes, Olive M. (2007) *A Swing Through Time: Golf in Scotland 1457–1744*, National Library of Scotland, Edinburgh.

George, Margaret (1993) *Mary Queen of Scotland and the Isles*, Pan Books, London.

Gibson, William H. (1988) *Early Irish Golf: The First Courses, Clubs and Pioneers*, Oakleaf Publications, Naas.

Gibson, William H. (2012) 'The First Golf Club in Ireland', in *Through the Green*, September 2012, 21–3.

Gibson, William H. (2019) 'Early South Africa Golf', in *Through the Green*, December 2019, 36–41.

Gillmeister, Heiner (1996) 'A Tee for Two: On the Origins of Golf', in *Homo Ludens VI, Ball- und Kugelspiele*, 17–37, Verlag Emil Katzbichler.

Gillmeister, Heiner (2002) 'Golf on the Rhine: On the Origins of Golf, with Sidelights on Polo', in *International Journal of the History of Sport*, 19, 1–30.

Gillmeister, Heiner (2008) 'Die Schotten und das Golfspiel, oder: You Can't Teach an Old Dog New Tricks', in *Golf – Facetten einer Leidenschaft* [*1st Drossapharm Golf Symposium*], 9–15, Drossapharm, Basle/Arlesheim.

Gillmeister, Heiner (2015) *Über den Ursprung des Golfspiels*, https://tinyurl.com/4dj95cts (archived 20 September 2021).

Giuseppi, M. S. (ed.) (1933) *Calendar of the Manuscripts of the Most Hon. the Marquess of Salisbury*, Part. XVI, HMSO, London.

Glanville, Bob (2010) *Golf: The Game of Lessening Failures*, Trafford Publishing.

Glenn, Rhonda (1991) *The Illustrated History of Women's Golf*, Taylor Publishing, Dallas, TX.

Gordin, Richard D. (1967) *Robert Tyre Jones, Jr. His Life and Contributions to Golf*, PhD thesis, Ohio State University.

Gowland, Robert G. (2011) *The Oldest Clubs 1650–1850*, Robert Gowland & Associates.

Gowland, Bob (2013) 'Concerning the c.1460 Golf Reference', *Through the Green*, June 2013, 25–7.

Grace, Stuart [Hon. Sec.] (1875) *Rules for the Game of Golf as it is Played by the Royal and Ancient Golf Club of St Andrews Over Their Links*, Fife Herald, Cupar.

Grant Francis J. (ed.) (1906) *The Register of Apprentices of the City of Edinburgh 1583–1666*, Scottish Record Society, Edinburgh.

Green, Robert (1987) *Golf: An Illustrated History of the Game*, Willow Books, London.

Green, Robert (1994) *The Illustrated Encyclopedia of Golf*, Ted Smart, London.

Grierson, James (1807) *Delineations of St Andrews; Being a Particular Account of Every Thing Remarkable in the History and Present State of the City* [. . .], Edinburgh.

Grierson, Elizabeth (1910) *Peeps at Many Lands: Scotland*, Adam & Charles Black, London.

Grimsley, Will (1966) *Golf: its History, People & Events*, Prentice-Hall, Englewood Cliffs, NJ.

Grout, Jack (1982) *On the Lesson Tee: Basic Golf Fundamentals*, Sterling Publishing Co., New York.

Guinness World Records editors (2015) *Guinness World Records 2016*, Hoffman und Campe, Hamburg.

Guy, John (2005) *Queen of Scots: The True Life of Mary Stuart*, First Mariner Books, New York.

Haig, James (ed.) (1824) *The Historical Works of Sir James Balfour*, Hurst Robinson & Co., London.

Hall, James (1807) *Travels in Scotland, by an Unusual Route*, Vol. I, J. Johnson, London.

Hallen, A. W. Cornelius (ed.) (1894) *The Account Book of Sir John Foulis of Ravelston 1671–1707*, Scottish History Society, Edinburgh.

Hallen, A. W. Cornelius (ed.) (1896) *The Scottish Antiquary or Northern Notes & Queries*, Vol. X (1886), Edinburgh.

Halsey, William D. (1980) *Merit Students Encyclopedia*, Macmillan Educational Corporation, New York.

Hamilton, David (1985) *Early Golf in Glasgow 1589–1787*, The Partick Press, Oxford.

Hamilton, David (1986) *Early Golf at St Andrews*, The Partick Press, Glasgow.

Hamilton, David (1988) *Early Golf at Edinburgh & Leith: The Account Books of Sir John Foulis of Ravelston*, The Partick Press, Glasgow.

Hamilton, David (1996) 'Bowmakers Did Make Early Clubs', in *Through the Green*, June 1996, 12–13.

Hamilton, David (1998) *Golf: Scotland's Game*, The Partick Press, Kilmacolm.

Hamilton, David, David B. Smith, David McClure and Robert Close (2008) 'The Girvan Clique: Ayrshire golf in 1751', in *Ayrshire Notes*, Vol. 36, Autumn 2008, 4–12.

Hamilton, David (2021) 'Scottish Shinty and the Origins of Modern Golf', in *Through the Green*, March 2021, 34–7.

Handley, Brett. A., David M. Marshall and Craig Coon (2012) *Principles of Engineering*, Delmar Cengage Learning, New York.

Hanna, John (1993) 'Small is Beautiful', in *Through the Green*, September 1993, 15–16.

Hanna, John (2009/2010) 'Early Ulster Golf Clubs and the Founding of the Golfing Union of Ireland', in: *Golfika*, 5, Winter 2009/2010, 6–14.

Harris, Robert (1953) *Sixty Years of Golf*, The Batchworth Press, London.

Harris, Ed (2007a) *Golf Facts, Figures & Fun*, Facts, Figures & Fun, Wisley.

Harris, Tim (2007b) *Sport: Almost Everything You Ever Wanted to Know*, Yellow Jersey Press, London.

Hart, John (2012) *The National CV of Britain*, The National CV Group, Tadley.

Hawtree, Fred (1996) *Triple Baugé: Promenades in Medieval Golf*, Cambuc Archive, Oxford.

Hazelton Haight, Elizabeth (1955) *The Life of Alexander of Macedon by Pseudo-Callisthenes*, Longmans, Green & Co., New York.

Henderson, Ian T. and David I. Stirk (1979) *Golf in the Making*, Henderson & Stirk Ltd, Crawley.

Henderson, Ian T. and David I. Stirk (1981) *Royal Blackheath*, Henderson & Stirk Ltd, London.

Henderson, Ian T. and David I. Stirk (1984) *The Compleat Golfer: An Illustrated History of the Royal and Ancient Game*, Victor Gollancz Ltd, London.

Henderson, James (2016) *Golf on Arran*, Voice for Arran, Isle of Arran.

Herrmann, Albert (1898) *The Taymouth Castle Manuscript of Sir Gilbert Hay's 'Buik of King Alexander the Conquerour'*, R. Gaertners Verlagsbuchhandlung, Berlin.

Hilka, Alfons (1920) *Der Altfranzösische Prosa-Alexanderroman*, Halle.

Hill, George (ed.) (1869) *The Montgomery Manuscripts (1603–1706): Compiled from Family Papers*, James Cleeland, Belfast.

Hilton, Harold H. and Garden G. Smith (ed.) (1912) *The Royal & Ancient Game of Golf*, Golf Illustrated Ltd, London.

Hoofts, P. C. (1642) *Neederlansche Histoorien sedert de Ooverdraght der Heerschappye van Kaizar Karel den Vysden, op Kooning Philips Zynen Zoon*, Louys Elzevier, Amsterdam.

Hoggard, Rex (2006) *The Golf Geek's Bible: All the Facts and Stats You'll Ever Need*, MQ Publications, London.

Homer, Trevor (2006) *The Book of Origins*, Hachette, London.

Hore, J. P. (1886) *History of Newmarket and the Annals of the Turf*, A. H. Baily & Co., London.

Hosack, John (1869) *Mary Queen of Scots and Her Accusers*, William Blackwood & Sons, Edinburgh.

Houdijk, Angela [interview with Heiner Gillmeister] (2005) 'Hólland is the Home of Golf', in *GolfJournaal*, 3, April/May 2005, 20–7.

Howell, Brian (2012) *Golf*, ABDO Publishing, Minneapolis, MN.

Hudson, David L. (2008) *Women in Golf: The Players, the History and the Future of the Sport*, Greenwood Publishing Group, Westport, CT.

Hunter, Doreen M. (ed.) (1991) *The Court Book of the Barony and Regality of Falkirk and Callendar, Vol. 1 1638–1656*, The Stair Society, Edinburgh.

Hutchinson, Horace G. (1897) 'The Boom in Golf', in *Harper's Weekly*, XLI, 18 September 1897, 936–7, New York.

Hutchinson, Horace (1893) *Golfing, The 'Oval' Series of Games*, George Routledge & Sons, London.

Hutchinson, Horace G. (1899) *The Book of Golf and Golfers*, Longmans, Green & Co., London.

Ironside, Robert and Harry Douglas (c. 1999) *A History of Royal Musselburgh Golf Club 1774–1999*, Royal Musselburgh Golf Club, Musselburgh.

Isaac, Candy (1998) 'Take a Swing at Golf', in *The Rotarian* magazine, August 1998, 25.

Jamieson, John (1825) *Supplement to the Etymological Dictionary of the Scottish Language*, Edinburgh University Press, Edinburgh.

Janke, Ken (2007) *Firsts, Facts, Feats, & Failures in the World of Golf*, Wiley, Hoboken, NJ.

Jardine, David (1835) *Criminal Trials*, Charles Knight, London.

Jenchura, John R. (2010) *Golf – A Good Walk & Then Some*, Mountain Lion, Merion, PA.

Johnston, Alastair J. (ed.) (1985) *The Clapcott Papers* (1985), published privately, Edinburgh.

Johnston, Alastair J. and Joseph S. F. Murdoch (1989) *C. B. Clapcott and His Golf Library*, Grant Books, Droitwich.

Johnston, Alastair J. and James F. Johnston (1993) *The Chronicles of Golf: 1457 to 1857*, published privately, Cleveland, OH.

Jones, Charles (ed.) (1790) *Hoyle's Games Improved*, London.

Jones, Robert Trent (1939) 'The Old Course, St Andrews', in *Town & Country*, Vol. 94, June 1939, 44–9, New York.

Kanawati, Naguib and Linda Evans (2020) *Beni Hassan, Volume VI, The Tomb of Khety*, The Australian Centre for Egyptology: Reports 44, Abercromby Press, Wallasey.

Kay, Billy (2006) *The Scottish World: A Journey into the Scottish Diaspora*, Mainstream Publishing, Edinburgh.

Kaye, Brian H. (1996) *Golf Balls, Boomerangs and Asteroids: The Impact of Missiles on Society*, VCH Publishers Inc., New York.

Keay, John and Julia Keay (2000) *Collins Encyclopaedia of Scotland*, HarperCollins, London.

Ker, William Lee (1891) 'The Papingo', in *Transactions of the Glasgow Archaeological Society*, New Series, Vol. II, Part I, 324–39.

Ker, Walter C. A. (1919) *Martial Epigrams*, Vol. I, William Heinemann, London.

Ker, Walter C. A. (1920) *Martial Epigrams*, Vol. II, William Heinemann, London.

Kerr, John (1896) *The Golf-Book of East Lothian*, T. & A. Constable, Edinburgh.

Kerr, John (1902) 'Archery, Golf and Curling', in James Paton (ed.), *Scottish History & Life*, James Maclehose & Sons, Glasgow, 226–33.

Kittel, Georg (2018) *När Golfen Var Ung: Sveriges Första Golfklubbar Och Banor*, Swedish Golf History Society/*Svenska Golfhistoriska Sällskapet*.

Krause, Peter (2002) *Play by Play Golf*, Lerner Publications Company, Minneapolis, MN.

La Bella, Laura (2013) *Women and Sports*, Rosen Publishing Group, New York.

Laing, David (ed.) (1863) *The Diary of Alexander Brodie of Brodie, MDCLII–MDCLXXX. and of His Son James Brodie of Brodie, MDCLXXX–MDCLXXXV*, The Spalding Club, Aberdeen.

Laird, Neil (2017) *Bruntsfield Links Home of Club Golf*, Golfiania Caledonia, Edinburgh.

Lang, David (ed.) (1875) *Correspondence of Sir Robert Kerr, First Earl of Ancram and His Son William, Third Earl of Lothian*, R. & R. Clark, Edinburgh.

Lang, Andrew (1890) 'The History of Golf', in Horace G. Hutchison (ed.), *Golf: The Badminton Library of Sports and Pastimes*, Longmans, Green & Co., London.

Lang, Andrew (1899) 'Golf from a St Andrews Point of View', in *The North American Review*, July 1899, Vol. 169, 138–44.

Lang, Andrew (1901) *The Mystery of Mary Stuart*, Longmans Green, London.

Lang, Andrew (1902) *A History of Scotland from The Roman Occupation* (1902), William Blackwood & Sons, Edinburgh.

Lang, Andrew (1903) *Prince Charles Edward Stuart: The Young Chevalier*, Longmans, Green & Co., London.

Lannon, Tom (1983) *The Making of Modern Stirling*, Forth Naturalist and Historian, Stirling.

Leach, Henry (1907) *The Spirit of the Links*, Methuen & Co., London.

Leach, Henry (1914) *The Happy Golfer*, Macmillan, London.

Lenaghan, Kim (1996) *A Little History of Golf*, Appletree Press, Belfast.

Lennox, Doug (2008) *Now You Know Golf*, Dundurn Press, Toronto.

Lennox, Doug (2009) *Now You Know Big Book of Sports*, Dundurn Press, Toronto.

Li, Wanhu (2014) 'Historical Research into China as the Birthplace of Golf', in *2014 International Conference on Social Science and Management*, DEStech Publications, Lancaster, PA, 385–9.

Ling, Hongling (1991) 'Verification of the Fact that Golf Originated from Chuiwan', in *Australian Society for Sports History Bulletin*, No. 14, July 1991, 12–23.

Littleton, Adami (1678) *Linguæ Latinæ Liber Dictionarius Quadripartitius. A Latine Dictionary*, London.

Livingstone, M. (1908) *Registrum Secreti Sigilli Regum Scotorum: The Register of the Privy Seal of Scotland, Vol. 1, A.D. 1488–1529*, HMSO, Edinburgh.

Lockhart, John (1836) *The Works of Robert Burns*, Judd Loomis & Co., Hartford, CT.

Loeffelbein, Bob (1998) *Offbeat Golf: A Swingin' Guide to a Worldwide Obsession*, Santa Monica Press, Santa Monica, CA.

Londino, Lawrence J. (2006) *Tiger Woods: A Biography*, Greenwood Press, Westport, CT.

Lonnstrom, Douglas and Sara Riso (2018) *The Handbook of Golf History*, Dorrance Publishing Co., Pittsburgh, PA.

Lynch, Michael (ed.) (2001) *The Oxford Companion to Scottish History*, Oxford University Press, Oxford.

Lyon, C. J. (1851) *Personal History of Charles the Second*, Thomas George Stevenson, Edinburgh.

Macdonald, Charles Blair (1928) *Scotland's Gift: Golf*, Charles Scribner's Sons, New York.

Macdougal, Norman (1989) *James IV*, John Donald, Edinburgh.

Macgregor, Robert (1881) *Pastimes and Players*, Chatto & Windus, London.

Machat, Udo and Larry Dennis (2000) *The Golf Ball Book*, Sport Images, Oakland, CA.

Macintosh, Iain (2010) *Everything You Ever Wanted to Know About Golf but Were Too Afraid to Ask*, A. & C. Black, London.

Macintyre, John (2005) *The Whole Golf Book*, Sourcebooks Inc., Naperville, IL.

Mackenzie, Agnes Mure (1946) *Scottish Pageant*, Oliver & Boyd, Edinburgh.

Mackern, Louie (1897) 'Ladies' Golf', in Garden G. Smith, *Golf*, Lawrence & Bullen Ltd, London.

Mackie, Charles (1849) *The Castles, Palaces and Prisons of Mary Queen of Scots*, C. Cox, London.

Mackie, R. L. (ed.) (1953) *The Letters of James the Fourth 1505–1513 Calendared by Robert Kerr Hannay, LL.D.*, Scottish History Society, Edinburgh.

[Macnair, John] (1882) *An Account of the Game of Curling with Songs for the Canon-Mills Curling Club*, Edinburgh.

Macpherson, Scott (2014) *Golf's Royal Club's Honoured by The British Royal Family 1833–2013*, The Royal and Ancient Golf Club of St Andrews, St Andrews.

MacQueen, John and Winifred MacQueen (eds) (2009) *Archibald Pitcairne: The Latin Poems*, Medieval and Renaissance Texts and Studies, Vol. 359, Royal Van Gorcum, Tempe.

Madan, Falconer and H. H. E. Craster (1924) *A Summary Catalogue of Western Manuscripts in the Bodleian Library at Oxford, Vol. VI*, Clarendon Press, Oxford.

Madden, Frederic (1847) *Laȝamons Brut, or Chronicle of Britain; a Poetical Semi-Saxon Paraphrase of The Brut of Wace*, The Society of Antiquaries of London, London.

Mahon, R. H. (1923) *The Indictment of Mary Queen of Scots as Derived from a Manuscript in the University Library at Cambridge, Hitherto Unpublished*, Cambridge University Press, Cambridge.

Mair, Norman (1994) *Muirfield: Home of the Honourable Company (1744–1994)*, Mainstream Publishing, Edinburgh.

Malcolm, Charles A. (1950) *The History of the British Linen Bank*, T. & A. Constable, Edinburgh.

Mallon, Bill and Randon Jerris (2011) *Historical Dictionary of Golf*, Scarecrow Press, Lanham, MD.

Manchester, Richard B. (1980) *Mammoth Book of Fascinating Information*, A. & W. Visual Library, New York.

Mapstone, Sally (1994) 'The Scots *Buke of Phisnomy* and Sir Gilbert Hay', in A. A. MacDonald, Michael Lynch and Ian B. Cowen (eds), *The Renaissance in Scotland: Studies in Literature, Religion, History and Culture*, E. J. Brill, Leiden, 1–44.

Martin, M. (1698) *A Late Voyage to St Kilda, the Remotest of all the Hebrides*, D. Brown & T. Goodwin, London.

Martin, H. B. (1936) *Fifty Years of American Golf*, Dodd, Mead & Co., New York.

Martin, John Stuart (1968) *The Curious History of the Golf Ball: Mankind's Most Fascinating Sphere*, Horizon Press, New York.

Martin, Chris (2005) *The Golfer's Companion*, Robson Books, London.

[Mathison, Thomas] (1743) *The Goff. An Heroi-Comical Poem. In Three Cantos*. J. Cochran & Co., Edinburgh.

Matuz, Roger (1997) *Inside Sports: Golf*, Visible Ink Press, Detroit, MI.

Maxtone-Graham, Rob (2018a) 'Dickson Dynasties Part 1 The Early Ballmakers', in *Through the Green*, March 2018, 28–31.

Maxtone-Graham, Rob (2018b) 'Dickson Dynasties Part 2 Ballmakers and Clubmakers', in *Through the Green*, December 2018, 10–13.

Maxwell Lyte, H. C. (ed.) (1909) *Calendar of the Close Rolls, Preserved in the Public Record Office, Edward III, Vol. XI., A.D. 1360–1364*, HMSO, London.

McAinsh, Seonaid (2017) *St Andrews Ladies' Golf Club 1867–2017*, St Andrews Golf Press, St Andrews.

McComb, David G. (2004) *Sports in World History*, Taylor & Francis, New York.

McCord, Gary and Alicia Harney (2006) *Golf for Dummies*, UK Edition, John Wiley & Sons, Chichester.

McCrone, Kathleen E. (1988) *Playing the Game: Sport and the Physical Emancipation of English Women 1870–1914*, University Press of Kentucky, Lexington, KY.

McDonough, Dick and Peter Georgiady (2013) *Great Golf Collections of the World*, Seaton Press, Ridgeland, SC.

McDonnell, Michael (2002) *Classic Golf Quotes: Golfing History in the Words of Those Who Made It*, Robson Books, London.

McGimpsey, Kevin and David Neech (1999) *Golf Implements and Memorabilia*, Philip Wilson, London.

McGimpsey, K. W. (2003) *The Story of the Golf Ball*, McGimpsey/Philip Wilson, London.

McHugh, Erin (2008) *Who? What? When? Where? Why? A Substantial Gathering of Intriguing & Delightful Knowledge*, Reader's Digest Association, Pleasantville, NY.

McInnes, Charles Thorpe (ed.) (1970) *Accounts of the Treasurer of Scotland Vol. XII 1566–1574*, HMSO, Edinburgh.

McPherson, J. Gordon (1891) *Golf and Golfers Past and Present*, William Blackwood & Sons, Edinburgh.

Meikle, Henry W. (1949) 'An Edinburgh Diary 1687–1688', in *The Book of the Old Edinburgh Club*, Vol. 27, 111–54, The Old Edinburgh Club, Edinburgh.

Menzies, Gordon (ed.) (1982) *The World of Golf*, British Broadcasting Corporation, London.

Millar, Neil S. and David Hamilton (2012) 'A 1725 Postmortem and the Manufacture of Feather Golf Balls', in *Through the Green*, June 2012, 42–5.

Millar, Neil. S. (2013) 'Golf Caddies in the 17th to 19th Centuries', in *Through the Green*, March 2013, 36–40.

Millar, Neil, William Gibson and David Hamilton (2013) 'Evidence of Golf in Gibraltar', in *Through the Green*, June 2013, 30–3.

Millar, Neil. S. (2015a) 'Catherine of Aragon and an Enduring Golf Myth', in *Through the Green*, March 2015, 13–16.

Millar, Neil. S. (2015b) 'Mary Queen of Scots, Golf and the Seton Necklace', in *Through the Green*, June 2015, 11–16.

Millar, Neil S. and David Hamilton (2015) 'Women Golfers on Bruntsfield Links in 1738', in *Through the Green*, March 2015, 17–19.

Millar, Neil. S. (2016) 'Early Golf in England (1606–1659)', in *Through the Green*, September 2016, 14–20.

Millar, Neil. S. (2017a) 'William Mayne: Clubmaker to King James VI', in *Through the Green*, March 2017, 10–15.

Millar, Neil. S. (2017b) 'King James V and the Gosford Golf Myth', in *Through the Green*, June 2017, 40–3.

Millar, Neil. S. (2017c) 'King James IV and Early Golf in St Andrews', in *Through the Green*, December 2017, 22–5.

Millar, Neil. S. (2018) 'A Sixteenth Century Golf Match at Leith', in *Through the Green*, December 2018, 38–9.

Millar, Neil. S. (2019) 'King Charles I and Early Golf in Scotland and England', in *Through the Green*, March 2019, 6–9.

Millar, Neil. S. (2020) 'The Origin and Evolution of a Golf Myth', in *Through the Green*, June 2020, 10–11.

Miller, James (1824) *St Baldred of the Bass. A Pictish Legend*, Oliver & Boyd, Edinburgh.

Miller, James (1844) *The Lamp of Lothian; or the History of Haddington*, James Allan, Haddington.

Miller, Judith and Mark Hill (2016) *Miller's Collectables Handbook & Price Guide 2016–2017*, Hachette, London.

Miller, T. D. (1906) 'An Inland Island Links', in David Scott Duncan (ed.), *The Golfing Annual 1905–1906*, Vol. XIX, 12–16, Horace Cox, London.

Miller, T. D. (1935) *The History of the Royal Perth Golfing Society: A Century of Golf in Scotland* [. . .], Munro Press, Perth.

Mitchell, Arthur (1907) *Geographical Collections Relating to Scotland*, Edinburgh University Press, Edinburgh.

Morris, Jean M. (2013) *The Ifs and Putts of British Golf*, Sirmor Publishing, Hove.

Morrison, Michael (2020) 'The Scottish Golfing Boom, 1850–1889', in *Through the Green*, June 2020, 26–30.

Morrison, Michael (2021) 'How Many Golfers? Part II: Women', in *Through the Green*, September 2021, 52–5.

Mortimer, David (2004) *Classic Golf Clangers*, Robson Books, London.

Mumby, Frank Arthur (1922) *The Fall of Mary Stuart: a Narrative in Contemporary Letters*, Houghton Mifflin Company, Boston, MA.

Napier, Mark (1848) *Memorials of Montrose and his Times*, The Maitland Club, Edinburgh.

Newberry, Percy E. (1893) 'Beni Hasan', Part II, in F. L. Griffith (ed.), *Archaeological Survey of Egypt*, Kegan Paul, Trench, Trübner & Co., London.

Nickerson, Elinor (1987) *Golf: A Women's History*, McFarland & Co., Jefferson, NC.

Nijs, Geert and Sara Nijs (2008) *Choule the Non-Royal but Most Ancient Game of Crosse*, Les Editions Geert & Sara Nijs, Saint Bonnet en Bresse.

Nijs, Geert and Sara Nijs (2011) *Games for Kings & Commoners: Colf, Crosse, Golf, Mail*, Editions Choulla et Clava, Saint Bonnet en Bresse.

Nijs, Geert and Sara Nijs (2014) *Games for Kings & Commoners: Colf, Crosse, Golf, Mail*, Part Two, Editions Choulla et Clava, Saint Bonnet en Bresse.

Nijs, Geert and Sara Nijs (2015) *Games for Kings & Commoners: Colf, Crosse, Golf, Mail*, Part Three, Editions Choulla et Clava, Saint Bonnet en Bresse.

O'Callaghan, E. B. (1868) *Laws and Ordinances of New Netherland, 1638–1674*, Weed, Parsons & Company, Albany, NY.

Osterhoudt, Robert G. (2006) *Sport as a Form of Human Fulfillment*, Trafford Publishing, Victoria.

Ouseley, William (1819) *Travels in Various Countries of the East; More Particularly Persia*, Rodwell & Martin, London.

Pagan, John H. (1897) *Annals of Ayr in the Olden Times 1560–1692*, Alex. Fergusson, Ayr.

Pascoe, A. B. (1898) 'Ladies' Golf', in Garden Smith (ed.), *The World of Golf*, Chapter XVIII, A. D. Innes & Company, London.

Paton, Henry (ed.) (1905) *The Register of Marriages for the Parish of Edinburgh 1595–1700*, Scottish Record Society, Edinburgh.

Paul, James Balfour (1875) *The History of the Royal Company of Archers: The Queen's Body-Guard for Scotland*, William Blackwood & Sons, Edinburgh.

Paul, James Balfour (ed.) (1882) *Registrum Magni Sigilli Regum Scotorum: The Register of the Great Seal of Scotland, A.D. 1424–1513*, HMSO, Edinburgh.

Paul, James Balfour (ed.) (1900) *Compota Thesaurariorum Regum Scotorum: Accounts of the Lord High Treasurer of Scotland, Vol. II, A.D. 1500–1504*, HMSO, Edinburgh.

Paul, James Balfour (ed.) (1901) *Compota Thesaurariorum Regum Scotorum: Accounts of the Lord High Treasurer of Scotland, Vol. III, A.D. 1506–1507*, HMSO, Edinburgh.

Paul, James Balfour (ed.) (1902) *Compota Thesaurariorum Regum Scotorum: Accounts of the Lord High Treasurer of Scotland, Vol. IV, A.D. 1507–1513*, HMSO, Edinburgh.

Paul, James Balfour (ed.) (1903) *Compota Thesaurariorum Regum Scotorum: Accounts of the Lord High Treasurer of Scotland, Vol. V, A.D. 1515–1531*, HMSO, Edinburgh.

Penner, Richard H., Lawrence Adams and Stephani K. A. Robson (2013) *Hotel Design Planning and Development*, Routledge, New York.

Pilley, Phil (ed.) (1988) *Golfing Art*, Stanley Paul, London.

Pinner, John (1988) *The History of Golf*, The Apple Press, London.

Pitcairn, Robert (1833) *Ancient Criminal Trials in Scotland*, Bannatyne Club, Edinburgh.

Pitcairn, Robert (1842) *Autobiography and Diary of Mr James Melvill*, The Wodrow Society, Edinburgh.

Pitcarnii, Archibaldi (1727) *Selecta Poemata*, Edinburgh.

Plans, Miriam (1994) *Collectomania: Your Trinkets and Treasures*, Treasure Trove Press, Scottsdale, AZ.

Playfair, Edward H. L. and William H. Gibson (2017) 'India's First Golf Club', in *Through the Green*, March 2017, 44–7.

Porter, Darwin and Danforth Prince (2008), 'Scotland', in *Frommer's Europe*, Tenth Edition, Wiley, Hoboken, NJ.

Powell, J. G. F. (1988) *Cicero Cato Maior de Senectute*, Cambridge University Press, Cambridge.

Pritchard, R. Telfryn (1992) *The History of Alexander's Battles (Historia de prellis – the J^1 Version)*, Pontifical Institute of Mediaeval Studies, Toronto.

Punia, Bijender K. (2008) *Tourism Management: Problems and Prospects*, A. P. H. Publishing, New Delhi.

Rhoads, James Lane (1995) *The Hacker's Golf Guide*, Cloverleaf Golf Publishing Company, San Diego, CA.

Riach, Steve (2018) *The Average Joe's Super Sports Almanac*, Harvest House, Eugene, OR.

Rice, Johnathan (1995) *Curiosities of Golf*, Pavilion Books Ltd, London.

Richardson, Louise (2010) University of St Andrews Golf Graduation Address, 13 July 2010, http://tinyurl.com/pcz42mr (archived 30 September 2015).

Richardson, Norman and Michael Sheret (2014) 'Alexander Brodie Spark 1792–1856', in *Through the Green*, March 2014, 40–9.

Ring, Trudy (ed.) (1995) *International Dictionary of Historic Places*, Routledge, Oxford.

Ritchie, A. I. (1883) *The Churches of Saint Baldred: Auldhame, Whitekirk, Tyninghame, Prestonkirk*, J. Moodie Millar, Edinburgh.

[Robb, George (using the pseudonym 'A Golfer')] (1863) *Historical Gossip About Golf and Golfers*, John Hughes, Edinburgh.

Robbie, J. Cameron (1936) *The Chronicle of the Royal Burgess Golfing Society of Edinburgh 1735–1935*, Morrison & Gibb, Edinburgh.

Robertson, John (1784) *The Universal Scots Almanack for the Year of Our Lord M,DCC,LXXXIV* [. . .], Edinburgh.

Robertson, James K. (c. 1967) *St Andrews Home of Golf*, J. & G. Innes, St Andrews.

Rorke, Martin (2001) *Scottish Overseas Trade 1275/86–1597*, PhD thesis, University of Edinburgh, Edinburgh.

Rosen, Friedrich (1930) *Oriental Memories of a German Diplomatist*, Methuen & Co., London.

Rowe, Julian (1996) *Sport: Making Science Work*, Heinemann, Oxford.

Roy, Neil (1792) 'Topological Descriptions of the Parish of Aberlady', in *Archaeologica Scotia or Transactions of the Society of Antiquaries of Scotland*, Society of the Antiquaries of Scotland, Edinburgh.

Ruskin, Bill and Tom Renfrew (2010) *The American Golfer's Guide to Scotland*, AuthorHouse, Bloomington, IN.

Russell, Jean M. (1988) *Old Manchester Golf Club 1818–1988*, Frank Peters, Kendal.

Salmond, J. B. (1956) *The Story of the R&A*, Macmillan, London.

Scaife, Neil (2009) *Four Hundred Years of the Blackheath Goffer 1608–2008*, Royal Blackheath Golf Club, London.

Scarth, John (2013) 'Golf History for Golf Historians & Collectors', in *Golfika*, 12, Summer 2013, 6–8.

Schwab, Don W. (1985) *Legacy of The Links: Explore Golf's History with Lee Trevino* [VHS video], Paramount Pictures.

Scott, Edward J. L. (1901) 'Early Golf in England', in *The Athenaeum*, 6 April 1901, 434.

Scott, Tom (1972) *The Story of Golf: From its Origins to the Present Day*, Arthur Barker Ltd, London.

Scott, Tom (1975) *The Observer's Book of Golf*, Frederick Warne & Co. Ltd, London.

Seltzer, Leon Z. (2007) *Golf: The Science and the Art*, Tate Publishing, Mustang, OK.

[Sharpe, Charles] (c. 1815) *Extracts from the Household Book of Lady Marie Stewart, Daughter of Esme, Duke of Lenox, and Countess of Mar*, Edinburgh.

Sherman, Adam (2002) *Golf's Book of Firsts*, World Publications Group, North Dighton, MA.

Simson, Thomas (1744) 'Histories of the Separation of the Villous Coat of the Intestines in Diseases', in *Medical Essays and Observations*, Vol. V, Part II, 654–65, Edinburgh.

Simpson, W. G. (1887) *The Art of Golf*, David Douglas, Edinburgh.

Sidorsky, Robert (2008) *Golf 365 Days: A History*, Abrams, New York.

Sinclair, John (1807) *The Code of Health and Longevity or, a Concise View of the Principles Calculated for the Preservation of Health and the Attainment of Long Life*, Arch. Constable & Co., Edinburgh.

Skae, Hilda T. (1912) *Mary Queen of Scots*, T. N. Foulis, London.

Skene, Feliz J. H. (1877) *Liber Pluscardensis, Vol. I, The Historians of Scotland, Vol. VII*, William Paterson, Edinburgh.

Skene, Feliz J. H. (1880) *The Book of Pluscarden, Vol. II, The Historians of Scotland, Vol. VII*, William Paterson, Edinburgh.

Small, John (ed.) (1893) *The Poems of William Dunbar*, William Blackwood & Sons, Edinburgh.

Smeaton, Oliphant (1904) *Edinburgh and its Story*, J. M. Dent & Co., London.

Smeaton, Oliphant (1905) *The Story of Edinburgh*, J. M. Dent & Co., London.

Smith, Charles (1909) *The Aberdeen Golfers: Records & Reminiscences*, published privately, London.

Smith, Garden G. (1898) *Golf*, Frederick A. Stokes Co., New York.

Smith, Garden G. (1912) 'Golf: Its Origin and History', in Harold H. Hilton and Garden G. Smith (eds), *The Royal & Ancient Game of Golf*, Golf Illustrated Ltd, London.

Smith, Gregory G. (1890) *The Days of James III 1488–1513*, David Nutt, London.

Smith, Rob. Howie (1867) *The Golfer's Year Book for 1866*, Smith & Grant, Ayr.

[Smollett, Tobias] (1771) *The Expedition of Humphry Clinker*, Dublin.

Sommers, Robert (1995) *Golf Anecdotes*, Oxford University Press, Oxford.

Starkey, David (2003) *Six Wives: The Queens of Henry VIII*, Chatto & Windus, London.

Steel, Donald and Peter Ryde (eds) (1975) *The Shell International The Encyclopedia of Golf* (1975), Ebury Press and Pelham Books Ltd, London.

Steel, Donald (1980) *The Guinness Book of Golf Facts & Feats*, Guinness Superlatives, London.

Steen, Rob (2014) *Floodlights and Touchlines – A History of Spectator Sport*, Bloomsbury, London.

Stirk, David (1987) *Golf: The History of an Obsession*, Phaidon Press Ltd, Oxford.

Stirk, David (1989) *Carry Your Bag Sir? The Story of Golf's Caddies*, H. F. & G. Witherby, London.

Stirk, David (1998) *Golf History & Tradition 1500–1945*, Excellent Press, Ludlow.

Story, Douglas (1902) 'The Birth of Golf', in *Munsey's Magazine*, Vol. XXVII, No. 3, June 1902, 321–6, Frank A. Munsey, New York.

Stott, A. J. (1957) 'The History of the Game', in Tom Scott (ed.), *Golfing Techniques in Pictures*, Hutton Press, London.

Straus, Alex R. (2006) *Guerrilla Golf*, Watermill Books/Rodale Inc.

Strickland, Agnes (1842) *Lives of the Queens of England, from the Norman Conquest*, Vol. IV, Henry Colburn, London.

Strickland, Agnes (1846) *Lives of the Queens of England, from the Norman Conquest*, Vol. IX, Henry Colburn, London.

Strutt, Joseph (1801) *Glig-Gamena Angel Đeod or The Sports and Pastimes of the People of England*, J. White, London.

Stuart, John (ed.) (1874) *Registrum de Panmure: Records of the Families of Maule, de Valoniis, Brechin, and Brechin-Barclay, United in the Line of the Barons and Earls of Panmure*, Edinburgh.

Taneja, Anil (2009) *World of Sports Outdoor*, Vol. 2, Kalpaz Publications, Delhi.

Tayler, Alistair and Henrietta Tayler (1933) *The Ogilvies of Boyne*, Aberdeen University Press, Aberdeen.

Temmerman, J. (1987) *Golf*, Mappanundi, Knokke.

Temmerman, Jacques (1993) *Golf & Kolf: Seven Centuries of History*, Martial & Snoeck, Belgium.

ter Gouw, Jan (1871) *De Volksvermaken*, Erven F. Bohn, Haarlem.

Thomas, Frank (2011) *From Sticks and Stones: The Evolution of Golf Equipment Rules*, Frankly Publications, Reunion, FL.

Tipping, H. Avary (1929) *English Homes, Period III – Vol. I: Late Tudor and Early Stuart 1558–1649*, Country Life, London.

Turner, Sharon (1826) *The History of the Reign of Henry the Eighth: Comprising the Political History of the Commencement of the English Reformation*, Longman, Rees, Orme, Brown & Green, London.

Twiss, Richard (1775) *Travels Through Portugal and Spain in 1772 and 1773*, G. Robinson, T. Becket & J. Robson, London.

Tyler, Martin (ed.) (1976) *The Sportsman's World of Golf*, Marshall Cavendish, London.

Tytler, W. (1792) 'On the Fashionable Amusements and Entertainments in Edinburgh [. . .]', in *Archaeologia Scotica or Transactions of the Society of Antiquaries of Scotland*, Vol. I, 499–504, Society of Antiquaries of Scotland, Edinburgh.

Tytler, Patrick Fraser (1864) *The History of Scotland from the Accession of Alexander III, to the Union*, Vol. III, William P. Ninno, Edinburgh.

Unger, W. S. (1939) *De Tol van Iersekeroord: Documenten en Rekeningen 1321–1572*, Martinus Nijhoff, 's Gravenhage (The Hague).

van Chandelier, Six J. (1657) *Poësy*, Joost Pluimert, Amsterdam.

Van Dam, Lee H. (2016) *Golfing: a View Through the Golf Hole*, LHVD Books, Sandy, UT.

van den Boom, Rick (2007) 'Steven JH van Hengel', in *Through the Green*, December 2007, 24–5.

van Hengel, S. J. H. (1972) *Early Golf: History and Development*, published privately, Netherlands.

van Hengel, Steven J. H. (1982) *Early Golf*, Drukkerij Tesink, Netherlands.

van Hengel, Steven J. H. (1985) *Early Golf*, Second Edition, Frank P. van Eck Publishers, Vaduz.

van Laer, A. J. F. (1923) *Minutes of the Court of Fort Orange and Beverwyck 1657–1660*, University of the State of New York, New York.

Vans Agnew, Robert (1887) *Correspondence of Sir Patrick Waus*, Ayr and Galloway Archaeological Association, Edinburgh.

Walker, Patrick (ed.) (1835) *Letters to King James the Sixth* [. . .], The Maitland Club, Edinburgh.

Warner George F. (ed.) (1893) *The Library of James VI. 1573–1583 from a Manuscript in the Hand of Peter Young, His Tutor*, Scottish History Society, Edinburgh.

Watson, Jennifer C. (2003) *Scottish Overseas Trade 1597–1645*, PhD thesis, University of Edinburgh.

Weir, Alison (2008) *Mary Queen of Scots and the Murder of Lord Darnley*, Vintage, London.

Wemyss, James (1791) 'Parish of Burntisland', in John Sinclair (ed.), *The Statistical Account of Scotland*, Vol. 2, 423–33, William Creech, Edinburgh.

Wemyss, Alice (ed. John Sibbald Gibson) (2003) *Elcho of the '45*, The Saltire Society, Edinburgh.

Wesson, John (2009) *The Science of Golf*, Oxford University Press, Oxford.

White, Colin (2011) *Projectile Dynamics in Sport: Principles and Applications*, Routledge, Abingdon.

White, John (2014) *The Golf Miscellany*, Third Edition, Carlton Books, London.

Whitelaw, Charles E. (1977) *Scottish Arms Markers*, Arms and Armour Press, London.

Whitney, Casper W. (1895) *A Sporting Pilgrimage, Riding to Hounds, Golf, Rowing, Football. Club and University Athletics. Studies in English Sport, Past and Present*, Harper & Brothers, New York.

Wilcock, John (1903) *The Great Marquess: Life and Times of Archibald, 8th Earl, and 1st (and Only) Marquess of Argyll (1607–1661)*, Oliphant Anderson & Ferrier, London.

Williams, Samuel (1844) *The Boy's Treasury of Sports, Pastimes, and Recreations*, D. Bogue, London.

Williamson, John (2018) *Born on the Links: A Concise History of Golf*, Rowman & Littlefield, Lanham, MD.

Wilson, Daniel (1848) *Memorials of Edinburgh in the Olden Times*, Vol. II, Edinburgh.

Wingfield, Emily (2013) 'The Composition and Revision of Sir Gilbert Hay's Buik of King Alexander the Conquerour', *Nottingham Medieval Studies*, 57, 247–86.

Wiren, Gary (1991) *The PGA Manual of Golf: The Professional's Way to Play Better Golf*, Macmillan, New York.

Wodrow, Robert (1842) *Analecta: or Materials for a History of Remarkable Providences; Mostly Relating to Scotch Ministers and Christians*, The Maitland Club, Edinburgh.

Wodrow, Robert (1845) *Collections upon the Lives of the Reformers and Most Eminent Ministers of the Church of Scotland*, Glasgow.

Wolohojian, Albert Mugrdich (1969) *The Romance of Alexander the Great by Pseudo-Callisthenes*, Columbia University Press, New York.

Wood, Marguerite (ed.) (1931) *Extracts from the Records of the Burgh of Edinburgh 1604 to 1626*, Oliver & Boyd, Edinburgh.

Wood, Marguerite and Helen Armet (ed.) (1954) *Extracts from the Records of the Burgh of Edinburgh 1681 to 1689*, Oliver & Boyd, Edinburgh.

Xing, Wayne and Christoph Meister (2021) 'China's First Golf Links Founded in 1878', in *Through the Green*, June 2021, 42–7.

Young, Douglas (1969) *St Andrews: Town and Gown, Royal and Ancient*, Cassell, London.

Young, Philip (2002) *Golf for the People: Bethpage and the Black*, 1st Books, Bloomington, IN.

Index

Note: n indicates page in the endnotes